Spacing Ireland

MANCHESTER
1824
Manchester University Press

Spacing Ireland

Place, society and culture in a post-boom era

Edited by Caroline Crowley and Denis Linehan

Manchester University Press

Published by Manchester University Press
Altrincham Street, Manchester M1 7JA, UK
www.manchesteruniversitypress.co.uk

British Library Cataloguing-in-Publication Data is available

Library of Congress Cataloging-in-Publication Data is available

ISBN 978 1 7849 9381 8 *paperback*

First published by Manchester University Press in hardback 2013

This edition first published 2016

The publisher has no responsibility for the persistence or accuracy of URLs for any external or third-party internet websites referred to in this book, and does not guarantee that any content on such websites is, or will remain, accurate or appropriate.

Printed by Lightning Source

Contents

Contents

Figures

Tables

Contributors

Caroline Creamer is deputy director of the International Centre for Local and Regional Development (ICLRD) and a research fellow with the National Institute for Regional and Spatial Analysis (NIRSA) at the National University of Ireland, Maynooth. A qualified town planner, her research interests include collaborative and participative decision making, inter-territorial and cross-border development, and spatial planning practice and policy.

Caroline Crowley is a research associate with the Institute for Social Sciences in the 21st Century (ISS21) at University College Cork and co-author of *Irish Agriculture at the Millennium: A Census Atlas* (2008). Currently a rural development consultant, her postdoctoral research with young people from family farms in Ireland was funded by the Irish Research Council for the Humanities and Social Sciences (IRCHSS).

Sally Daly is a researcher whose interests include food sustainability issues and agrarian class relations. She is working on her Ph.D. at the Centre for Transcultural Research and Media Practice, Dublin Institute of Technology. Her research examines social relations along the horticultural supply chain, particularly in relation to retailers, growers and workers.

Patrick J. Duffy is professor emeritus in the Department of Geography, National University of Ireland, Maynooth and is author of *Exploring the History and Heritage of Irish Landscapes* (2007) and *Landscapes of South Ulster: A Parish Atlas of the Diocese of Clogher* (1993). The gift of a 1940 issue of *National Geographic* from his son Michael suggested the idea for his chapter.

Ronan Foley is a lecturer in geography at National University of Ireland, Maynooth. Author of *Healing Waters: Therapeutic Landscapes in Historic and Contemporary Ireland* (2010), he is also interested in the geographical connections between water and health and is currently researching swimming practices and the therapeutic benefits of 'blue space'.

Daithí Kearney is a lecturer in music at Dundalk Institute of Technology. As an ethnomusicologist, geographer and performer, his research is primarily focused on Irish traditional music but extends to include performance studies, community music, music education and the connection between music and place.

Philip Lawton completed his Ph.D. in geography at Trinity College, Dublin in 2009, where he researched the relationship between urban planning and everyday use of public space. He is currently a postdoctoral researcher at the Centre for Urban and Euregional Studies at Maastricht University, where he is examining the role of culture in urban development.

Denis Linehan is a lecturer in human geography in the School of Geography and Archaeology: The Human Environment at University College Cork with a particular focus on the contemporary and historical conditions of urban life. He is co-editor of *Ordnance: War, Architecture and Space* (2013) and *Atlas of Cork City* (second edition 2011).

Sara McDowell is a lecturer in human geography at the University of Ulster. Her research interests lie primarily in the relationship between memory, power and terri-toriality. She is currently working on an ESRC-funded project exploring these issues in South Africa, Israel/Palestine, Sri Lanka, the Basque Country and the former Yugoslavia.

Aisling Murtagh is completing a Ph.D. on food politics and alternative food initiatives in Ireland in the Department of Food Business and Development, University College Cork with funding support from the IRCHSS. She is also a journalist, and focuses her writing on food, health and consumer issues.

Cian O'Callaghan is an urban and cultural geographer. He completed his Ph.D. in University College Cork in 2008. He is currently based at the National University of Ireland, Maynooth, where he is working on a project on ghost estates funded by the IRCHSS. He regularly contributes to the blog irelandafternama.wordpress.com.

Brendan O'Keeffe is a lecturer in geography at Mary Immaculate College, University of Limerick, specialising in political and regional geographies. He has extensive ex-perience as a community development practitioner and has worked with voluntary bodies and partnership organisations in Ireland and internationally.

Bernadette Quinn lectures in the College of Arts and Tourism at the Dublin Institute of Technology. She is a human geographer whose research has been published in such journals as *Gender, Place and Culture*; *Social and Cultural Geography*; *Leisure Studies*; *Urban Studies* and *Annals of Tourism Research*.

Naomi Tyrrell (née Bushin) is a lecturer in human geography at Plymouth University. She is co-author of *Childhood and Migration in Europe* (2011), and co-editor of *Transnational Migration and Childhood* (2012) and *The Changing Faces of Ireland* (2011). Her research interests include family migration, children's geographies and academic mobility.

Preface

The origins of *Spacing Ireland: Place, Society and Culture in a Post-Boom Era* lie in the sharp realisation that following the economic crash in 2008, Irish society had reached a major juncture in its development and that somewhere in the vibrant and critical work produced by geographers lay an opportunity to gather together new research to interpret this transition and make sense of Ireland's place in a more turbulent world.

In taking up this challenge, we thank the collection's contributors for their unique insights and crisp, perceptive essays, which 'map' Ireland in novel ways. These essays, we hope, will engage and interest readers who are searching for new voices to interpret the rise and fall of the Celtic Tiger. Moreover, the advice of our contributors, their cooperation and their geniality throughout the publication process is gratefully acknowledged.

A number of colleagues have enhanced the contributions made by the authors. Our thanks in particular go to the cartographers Michael Murphy and Noel Cashman at University College Cork, for refining and improving the maps in the book. We also extend our thanks to the artist Brian McCarthy for his generous offer to reproduce his paintings from his collection 'Boomtown'. Likewise, for permission to reproduce photography, we are grateful to Derek Speirs, Irene Stevenson at The Irish Times, Liam Griffin at the Griffin Group and Susan Henry at *National Geographic* magazine. For support with some of the costs associated with the graphics in the book, we express our thanks to the College of Arts, Celtic Studies and Social Sciences at University College Cork.

For their helpful advice throughout the book's evolution, we thank all the team and external readers at Manchester University Press who chaperoned the book to completion.

Finally, our heartfelt gratitude to family and friends for their support during the book's development, particularly to our respective partners, Brian and Katharina.

Caroline Crowley and Denis Linehan

Introduction: geographies of the post-boom era

Denis Linehan and Caroline Crowley

A mother and daughter face Dublin in flames as the giant figure of Justice looms out of the darkness; a lone sheep lingers on a mountain track beneath a dilapidated Las Vegas-style sign announcing 'Hibernia'; a group of conspirators raise a giant Irish flag by the quayside, as lights from the office windows of banks twinkle ominously late into the night. These are images from artist Brian McCarthy's compelling collection *Boomtown*, notable for its critical observations on issues of economy, society and nationhood in this unprecedented period of crisis and turbulence in Ireland. McCarthy's vision captures the mood of a society stretched between rage and bewilderment, whose memories of betrayal burn. In his signature image *Boomtown*, McCarthy presents a crowded landscape of slum-like dwellings, cramped together on the hillsides, overlooked by an unfinished Tower of Babel. The allusion is towards the *favelas* of Latin America but this landscape seems also to be a striking observation on the ruinous effects of over-development. The dense landscape seems mired in despair. The tricolour hangs from the balconies of houses. The national flag is a constant motif running though his collection, billowing on emigrants' boats, or rising up from the street in preparation for revolution. In *Delirium* – another telling image – a prosaic Dublin shop-front is transformed into a Head Shop.[1] The window advertises 'Celtic Tiger pills' amidst a faded display of champagne, designer accessories, gold and a toy helicopter. As a comment on the character of the Irish banking sector and the practice of excess, it sums things up more clearly perhaps than the Nyberg Report (Commission of Investigation into the Banking Sector in Ireland, 2011). The artist depicts money blowing up 'Easy

Figure 0.1 Brian McCarthy, *Boomtown*

Street' in front of the shop – like the credit that littered the Irish landscape with abandoned, unfinished houses. McCarthy's use of magical realism constructs a counterfactual landscape that is deliberately antagonistic to the spectacle and narratives of the boom-time (Figure 0.1). His disruptive treatment of the Irish landscape, which has long been the repository of 'Irishness', eviscerates the images and iconography of the Celtic Tiger, a period of economic growth in Ireland that ran from 1995 to 2007.

McCarthy's work reflects the growing dissonance around the national narrative, as well as the groundswell of political dissatisfaction that characterises the contemporary scene in Ireland. Tellingly, while occasionally framing Ireland as South America or Asia, his work suggests that new perspectives, if not new maps, are required to evaluate Irish society; the turbulent qualities of the present call for new ways of seeing. Following the economic crash in 2008, Irish society has been thrown into a tumultuous period of adjustment. The social and economic consequences of the crisis present Irish society with a series of new challenges related to high levels of unemployment, emigration and the social impacts of austerity programmes. However, as the Celtic Tiger was as much an imaginative construct as a material one, Irish society is presented with a double-barrelled betrayal. The collapse of the Celtic Tiger represented not only the decline of a certain economic model but also the disintegration of the powerful national narrative that imagined the State as a perpetual growth machine. The State's self-congratulatory story of its exemplary success, and with it the international community's portrayal of Ireland as a role model for globalisation, has imploded. From underneath its brash surface, the problems of inequity and imbalanced development have become increasingly apparent; anxious questions about the social dividends of the Tiger years and widening inequalities in Irish society shape the content of public debates and discourse (Kirby, 2010).

As difficult and painful as the material consequences of the recession are, the shock of collapse has also thrown up a kind of social trauma. It has created a void in the national narrative: the question of national identity (along with the qualities and meaning of the State) lies in contention. In the resulting vacuum, anxious attempts to fashion a new national narrative in the post-crash era characterise contemporary debates. The collective memory of the crash, together with distrust of the political system and intense scepticism about the powerful role of international markets that displaces a sense of where power actually lies, challenges the contract that citizens make with their state. As Ulrich Beck has noted, faced by a mix of impossible demands from international markets and the EU, a 'fear of losing all sense of security, be it socio-economic or the mental security inherent in the national self-image' characterises the political climate in debtor countries like Ireland, Greece and Portugal (Beck, Bielefeld and Tietze, 2011: 8). Not only does Irish society have to deal with the economic and social crises of unemployment and emigration, but it also faces a crisis of identity. Society has to come to terms with the realisation that the narrative of progress was a fabrication based on a kind of 'casino capitalism', where the Government effectively absconded from its duty to protect the State's economic sovereignty by permitting the banking sector to borrow without limits and the property sector to build new developments and inflate prices regardless of demand. In a way, the recognition forced upon Irish citizens by the crash is the realisation that during the Celtic Tiger period 'we were not who we thought we were'. Not only that but 'the map was not the territory' either. Land, that entity at the core of the Irish psyche, became our downfall. These recognitions are immensely de-stabilising.

The arrival of the International Monetary Fund (IMF) to Ireland, on 18 November 2010, is seared into public memory. This watershed moment can be recalled in Ireland in the same way as older generations of Americans remember the assassination of President John F. Kennedy. On the evening of the announcement, the historian Diarmaid Ferriter reflected the national mood on TV3 when he raised the spectre of the sacrifice of the 1916 Easter Rising, a sentiment repeated in a remarkable editorial of *The Irish Times* the next day – a newspaper that rarely engages in nationalist rhetoric: 'Is this what Irish heroes died for?' went the question. 'It is a milestone', said

Ferriter. 'It is a terrible time. It's a time of great shame and great embarrass-
ment and despondency' (Ferriter, 2010). In the midst of recession, on internet
bulletin boards and radio phone-in talk shows, it is now quite common for
people to talk about Ireland in the language of ruin. Filmed on the streets of
Melbourne, Australia, a young Irish emigrant railed against the impact of the
crash on his hometown in Tipperary: 'there is nothing there: nothing, nothing,
nothing' (*Arrivals*, 2011).

The impact and attempts at resolution of many of these issues were revealed
during the 2011 Irish presidential election. In the debates and manifestos presented by the candidates, questions of identity loomed large. These involved
pleas to community, locality, core values, roots and national pride. That Michael
D. Higgins, a poet, a lover of the Irish language and a politician whose values
predate the excesses of the Celtic Tiger, was elected revealed something of the
distance, or indeed the sanctuary, that Irish society sought from the recent
past. The 2011 Global Economic Forum,[2] held at the sumptuously restored
Farmleigh Estate in Dublin, provided a comparable opportunity for similar
soul-searching narratives. It is revealing that in offering variously retrospec-
tive reappraisals of Irishness and Ireland at this meeting (involving, amongst
others, Bono, Bill Clinton and the Goldman Sachs International chairman,
Peter Sutherland), it was culture, community, locality and creativity that were
grasped as the authentic touchstones of who the Irish are. Somehow, a return
to the heartland seems to offer the antidote to the globalised cosmopolitan
excess when the Irish 'lost their soul', while at the same time offering the elixir
through which Irish pride and the national economy might be restored.

Spacing Ireland: infinite places and singular locations

As part of this regrounding, questions of geography have risen to prominence.
At their heart, these pleas to culture, to core values and to Irishness underlie
the significance of place and the relationships made in global networks. In
this very real sense, the material and imaginative management of Irish space
remains central to contemporary cultural, social and political entanglements.
Embedded in this premise, *Spacing Ireland* invites readers to engage with the
contours of transformation of Irish society through a series of distinct epi-
sodes and sites where change can be confronted. With the term 'spacing', we
refer to the appropriation, settlement, mobilisation and geographical reconfiguration that occurred on a variety of scales and amongst a range of sites and
subjects: the city, the holiday, the home, the road, the health spa, the migrant,
the shopper, the travel writer. Some contributions in the collection acknowledge how the transformations wrought by the boom and its aftermath re-made

place, reframed the qualities of social life, altered the landscape, fractured the national space and expanded social and economic relations of society into an ever-widening global network. Chapters intersect to varying extents with the boom and bust themes to explore the economic and social implications of the recession in terms of processes as diverse as cross-border development, farming knowledges, food movements, and the evolution of traditional Irish music. Observations on the overarching theme of 'change' run through the case studies and topics addressed in this collection, which are also attentive to the relationships between space, place, landscape, identity and society.

In both historical phases – boom and bust – the modernisation of Irish society during the Celtic Tiger and its subsequent demise was a 'spatial drama' involving transformation in the material landscape and the imaginative representation of the island. Fuelled by what the progressive Irish think-thank TASC has characterised as the Dublin Consensus – a mix of neoliberal and entrepreneurial discourses that consistently denied growing inequality and social exclusion – the Tiger years were read as the 'best of times' (Fahey, Russell and Whelan, 2007; Jacobson, Kirby and Ó Broin, 2006). The Celtic Tiger was very successful at generating a coherent image of Ireland in absolute terms – the most globalised, the most successful, and so forth. These sentiments were represented in portrayals of Ireland as a knowledge economy that emphasised the liberating capacity of information and communication technology (ICT), particularly from the constraints of geography. In the archive of the boom-time, there is an interview in *Business Week* with one key figure in the Celtic Tiger story, Mary Harney, the leader of the now defunct right-of-centre political party the Progressive Democrats and then Tánaiste and Minister for Enterprise, Trade and Employment, where she was depicted as a New European. She remembered 'her country in the 1980s as an inward-looking place, locked into age-old doctrines and rivalries' (Baker, 1999). She concluded that to deal with the challenges of globalisation, '[g]eography has to be irrelevant'. With this vision came new depictions of Ireland on the global stage.

On the cover of Harney's 1999 Asia Strategy Group report (Department of Enterprise, Trade and Employment, 1999), Ireland is depicted floating in the South China Sea. In this image of the island liberated from geography, Ireland is shown connected to the global cities of Beijing, Seoul, Shanghai, Singapore and Tokyo. The fantastical map mirrors the notion of the space of flows that became the signature of power and spatial organisation under neo-liberal forms of globalisation (Castells, 1996). This type of geographical spectacle was a sign of the times and reflected new sentiments and perspectives created in Ireland in the face of material transformation of place and economy. The reconfiguration of the Irish geographical imaginary ran concurrent with new experiences of time and space in Europe and the world: the vibrant juxtaposition of near and far reflected in ICT, new modes of working and travel, and the rapid rise in the influx of migrants and international corporations. Spatial transformation occurred so quickly that debates abounded about how the progression 'has also been a process of estrangement. Home has become as unfamiliar as abroad' (O'Toole, 1997: 173).

The geographies of boom and bust mark the landscape. The boom is represented in the spectacles of construction and motorway expansion, the housing bubble, and the significant regeneration and transformation of the built environment and public space. The bust is represented in ghost estates, zombie hotels, half-empty trophy airport terminals, vacated retail units and the cars of emigrants for sale along country roads. These transformations have had innumerable local impacts with both positive and negative legacies. In Cork city, the Docklands became a place where certain visions of a 'New Cork' coalesced. Planners and speculators were inspired to imagine a cosmopolitan post-industrial future: a Docklands of Desire. An addictive cocktail of urban boosterism and commercial speculation coveted the land for waterfront living, new-generation office space, luxury apartments, spa hotels, concert venues and exhibition halls. These visions were moored to the passions of the Celtic Tiger. However, as is the case in so many places around Ireland following the crash, this is a vision that lies in tatters. On YouTube, a low-resolution film of the €1 billion Atlantic Quarter project proposed for the docks is amongst the lasting echoes of the boom.[3] This computer-animated film of 'Cork's passport to the future' begins with a journey into outer space, where the viewer orbits the Earth for five years and then returns through the atmosphere to Europe, then Ireland and finally to Cork in 2013 to witness the arrival of two towers designed by Norman Foster, surrounded by a new quarter of hotels, exhibition centres and even more apartments. A close look at the towers reveals a waterfall plunging from the rooftops. Like the apparitions of the Virgin Mary that periodically appear in the Irish countryside, this vision of cosmopolitan and extra-modern progress was a symptom of the transient grip on reality that typified so many boom-time plans.

In light of the innumerable interventions that characterise the transformation of Ireland over the last two decades, to interrogate questions of 'space' and 'place' offers a wealth of opportunities to understand the nature of major social, cultural and economic change in contemporary Ireland. *Spacing Ireland* recognises how the events of the last twenty years or so reshaped Irish society, unravelled its ethnic and cultural homogeneity, and restructured the links between different parts of Ireland to one another and the relationships that Ireland has with Europe and the rest of the world. Transformations in Ireland came into being through the political and cultural contingencies of place, the nation and the global. These forged new relationships to place, new forms of settlement, and new ways of moving around. As considered in this collection, the chapters reveal the struggles and terrains of modernisation. Place became a site of consumption, performance and circulation – one shaped by concerns about transformation and the political contexts of corruption, environment, planning and quality of life. The profound restructuring of senses of place and cultural location was not unique to Ireland. These are phenomena found in all rapidly modernising societies. Its uniqueness revolved around how trans-formations were interpreted through the plasma of existing histories and identities. Given these conditions, geographical perspectives are well placed to comment on recent times.

In *Spacing Ireland*, the contributors share a common concern for space and, embedded in their special area of interest, each registers the spatial signature of the Celtic Tiger and its aftermath to varying degrees. The diversity of the topics addressed in the collection and the plurality of spaces they represent are an essential part of the book's appeal. Ireland is a turbulent place. It is fruitful to consider the contemporary geographies of the island through the various and multiple forms where change is expressed. Given, as noted by Law and Urry (2004: 390), that 'in the twenty-first century … social relations appear increas-ingly complex, elusive, ephemeral, and unpredictable', a broken line of flight through contemporary Ireland, as represented in the diverse urban and rural contexts considered in the collection, seems an appropriate strategy.

In bringing these discussions to the page, we seek to avoid a sense of ex-ceptionalism and singularity. While the impacts of the recession have been profound, these kinds of impacts are neither unique to Ireland nor to this historical period. Like other countries caught up in the maelstrom of glo-balisation over the years, Irish society was obliged to negotiate a rolling and multi-scalar process of restructuring that re-engineered the social context of everyday life, altered the nature of work, and challenged closely held notions of identity and ontological security. Consequently, we expect that the material addressed in *Spacing Ireland* has some purchase in comparative contexts. Nor have we worked on the premise that one version of Ireland ceased and another took over once the boom stopped. Long-term and deeper structural changes, continuities and legacies reverberate through these times. As such, elements of the collection insist on the significance of rootedness and continuity in the ways that space, economy and society are organised in Ireland. In acknowledg-ing these issues, the collection provides a kind of antidote to the post-crash literature in Ireland and to the superficial views of Ireland often expressed in the commentary pages of the *New York Times* or *Der Spiegel*. Ireland from afar may well look like a laboratory for globalisation and its disasters but it is not simply that, as attention to place always reveals.

As editors, our concern when putting the collection together was to identify authors who could explore the intersections between everyday life and global exchanges through the contexts of the 'stuff' and banalities of contemporary everyday encounters: food, housing, leisure, migration, music, shopping, travel and work. These are the multiple layers of space we now inhabit. In all of these areas, the unstable socio-spatial relations forged in this epoch that framed the rise and fall of the Celtic Tiger have produced more complex relations between the individual, space and society (Sonnabend, 2003). These realities have arisen because of globalisation, because of information technology, and the intensification and increased complexity of social and cultural mobility. In *Spacing Ireland*, we interrogate the social and cultural dynamic of life against the background of these experiences. We argue that these fluid social and cultural geographies provide rich insights, sometime overlooked in systematic reviews that tend to emphasise economistic and prognostic readings of Ireland.

The thematic focus on spatiality moves beyond common-sense notions of geography as fixed, as still, to a version of social and cultural geography that appeals to the infinite connection of places while simultaneously cherishing their singularity (Solnit, 2011). The epoch of conceiving the entire spatial emplacement of Irish social life in the parish, the county or the nation has come to an end. Our conceptualisation of space has shifted from localisation to the space of relations (Massey, 2005). Some of the impacts and experiences of the spatial dramas of contemporary Ireland can be grasped conceptually within new directions in human geography that have animated the interpretative frameworks through which place and society are understood. In particular, the rise of relational geography has unravelled the view of place as a discrete spatial unit by emphasising how people and processes are continuously entangled in powerful undulating spheres of influence and connections (Amin, 2004; Massey, 2005). Deleuze and Guattari (1988: 203) ask us to consider 'a map that ... is always detachable, connectable, reversible, modifiable, and has multiple entryways and exits'.

Place remains a powerful mode of experience and encounter, and its historical legacies will always shape the present. But geographers have also demonstrated that place becomes constituted through multi-directional relationships that can override the boundaries of the nation state (Marston, Jones and Woodward, 2005). The congruence of spatial theory and lived reality remain at our fingertips. Migrants, emigrants and those who stay behind use email, social networking sites, Skype, online chatting platforms and mobile phones to connect across time zones and distant sites. These spatial propositions – theoretical and empirical – that run through the collection, encourage the reader to grasp how the geographies of Ireland are changed or changing.

The book is divided into three parts that work through well-established concepts such as belonging, mobility, space, consumption, culture and place, but in innovative ways that fragment well-worn categorisations and present a rich substrate for novel geographical thinking and analysis.

Part I: Spacing belonging

In Part I, the collection explores the revolving intersections of identity politics with place. In the opening chapter, 'Ghost estates: spaces and spectres of Ireland after NAMA' (National Asset Management Agency), Cian O'Callaghan interprets the now iconic ghost estates of half-finished and empty houses that litter the Irish landscape and have become a symbol of the abandoned excess of the Celtic Tiger. The geography of such estates charts the fevered speculation, uneven development, and unsustainable commuting and consumption patterns of the boom while the stark hauntology of these post-crash spaces confronts its values. This chapter tracks the discovery of the ghost estate and the ways in which it has been implicated in debates about the Irish economic crash, complicating ideas of home and community. The chapter shows how the spatialities of the ghost estate extend beyond bricks and mortar to range into a whole imaginary composed of narratives of loss, rage and, surprisingly, hope.

In Chapter 2, '"Of course I'm not Irish": Young people in migrant worker families in Ireland', Naomi Tyrrell shifts the focus to immigration, a rather novel phenomenon for Irish society experienced during the second half of the boom, following the accession of new EU member states in 2004. She explores the precarity of migrant families and the impact this has on the lives of '1.5 generation' teenagers, particularly in the context of the recent recession. Rather than aligning with the migrant/non-migrant binary, differences within the migrant youth category are highlighted, and rather than concentrating on their national affiliations, the local socio-spatial practices of youth migrants together with reflections on social integration are explored. She discusses how their own reflections on social integration relate to their intentions to remain in Ireland, return to their 'home' country or migrate to a new destination.

Sally Daly picks up on the theme of Ireland's new migrants to query other manifestations of place, experience and identity in the context of horticultural production in Chapter 3, 'Migrants in the fields: making work pay'. Public discourse and policy debates on immigration highlight the role of migrants in filling labour and skill shortages, especially in those jobs that grew increasingly unattractive to Irish workers during the boom. Drawing upon her ethnographic research into horticulture, an increasingly specialised and technologised agricultural sub-sector notorious for its long hours and physically arduous work, Daly reveals how uneven production within horticulture, aligned with changes to state welfare provisions, affects migrant workers and their families. Even with post-Celtic Tiger Ireland's rising unemployment rates, horticulture remains contingent on the availability of migrant labour. But the impermanent nature of horticultural production has direct implications for the reproduction and integrity of transnational families and Daly's work uncovers some of the human cost of locally produced food in contemporary Ireland.

In Chapter 4, 'Raising the emerald curtain: communities and collaboration along the Irish border', Caroline Creamer and Brendan O'Keeffe turn the spotlight on Ireland's own international border where migration is a daily routine. They critique EU, British and Irish policies that have sought to improve cross-border connections and to address long-standing fractures in social networks and natural trading hinterlands in a bid to sustain rural communities. They argue that in spite of the 1998 Belfast Agreement, the Celtic Tiger boom, and the shift in perception of the border from fraught barrier to site for collaborative action, the area continues to be characterised by underlying structural problems including peripherality and high unemployment. Their case studies reveal the disconnect between the short-term nature of funding programmes on which local economic development along the Irish border depends and the lived realities of its communities.

Part II: Mobility, space and consumption

In Part II, the contributors turn their attention to questions of mobility and consumption in urban and rural contexts. Denis Linehan brings these themes together in Chapter 5, 'Reading the Irish motorway: landscape, mobility and politics after the crash', where he presents a reading of the new Irish motorway network as a contested space at the heart of discourses of the boom and its subsequent bust. As the Celtic Tiger's workers and socialites pulsed along them, these arteries challenged notions of progress and heritage, drawing on symbols of mythology to legitimate the social and environmental change they wrought. In the current period of recession and 'peak oil', the Irish motorway network may symbolise little more than a fruitless act of political and economic hubris.

In Chapter 6, 'Lone parents, leisure mobilities and the everyday', Bernadette Quinn regrounds the discussion with a look at the challenges of one marginal societal group and their space in contemporary Ireland. Her chapter is concerned with lifestyle and quality-of-life issues, particularly with the role of free time, leisure and holidaying in the lives of lone parents during the Celtic Tiger and its aftermath. As the majority of lone-parent families in Ireland are headed up by women, the study investigates the spatiality of leisure by exploring how the spaces of the home and local environments variously facilitate and limit lone mothers' mobility and engagement in leisure activities. It shows how women develop new understandings of space through engagement with leisure and establish strategies for countering the weight of constraints routinely faced in the course of their everyday lives.

Everyday urban space is the topic addressed by Philip Lawton's work on urban policy. In Chapter 7, 'Rethinking the liveable city in a post boom-time Ireland', Lawton examines the limitations of recent planning policy and practice in Ireland, which envision urban space as the nexus of unproblematic interaction and the 'good life'. In so doing, he addresses the perceived connections between the pursuit of an imagined social reality on the one hand, and the unlimited urban expansion and redevelopment that was at the core of the property boom on the other. He also imagines a role for NAMA in reorientating the Celtic Tiger view of land use and development away from private gain and towards the public good.

The tensions between private gain and public good also come to our attention in Sara McDowell's contribution. Chapter 8, 'Flocking north: renegotiating the Irish border' shows how the rise and fall of the Celtic Tiger has impacted on the everyday geographies of people living on both sides of the Irish border. This chapter explores the ways in which the Republic of Ireland's changing economic fortunes have influenced how people conceptualise and negotiate a political border that has become increasingly permeable. These have occasioned new patterns of consumption with more and more 'euro shoppers' flocking north to avail of cheaper goods. McDowell reveals how the malleability of the boundary with Northern Ireland has arguably exposed the delicate nature of the island's political geography.

Consumption is at the heart of Aisling Murtagh's Chapter 9, 'Growth amidst decline: Ireland's grassroots food growing movement'. She evaluates the rise of community gardens in Ireland, and more recent adaptations of the 'grow your own' movement, such as a new demand for allotments. While many in society moved in sync with the Celtic Tiger economy, some questioned its sustainability and, at the grassroots level, micro-spaces of an alternative society at odds with the dominant model of economic development emerged, including new spaces for food growing. As boom turned to bust, interest in these growers and their growing spaces appeared to ripple out across society. Murtagh asks if these 'spaces of hope' can go beyond their early populism and mature to something more than just an alternative.

Part III: Culture and place

In Part III, the collection explores diverse cultural practices and some long-standing representations of Ireland. In Chapter 10, 'Ancestors in the field: Irish farming knowledges', Caroline Crowley looks at knowledge in agriculture, a key indigenous industry. Not only does the agricultural sector have a significant role to play in Ireland's economic recovery from recession but success seems to call for a flexible and entrepreneurial approach to innovation among farmers. The chapter considers the limitations imposed on this role by existing farming knowledge cultures/networks and the hegemony of productivism, and suggests the role of knowledge mediators in the re-embedding of knowledge creation and knowledge use in place.

Ronan Foley looks at the rise of the spa during the boom in Chapter 11, 'Health and wellness or conspicuous consumption? The spa in Celtic Tiger Ireland'. Spas are interesting sites in that they can simultaneously comprise contradictory spaces of reflective mindfulness and striking excess. The impact of the Celtic Tiger is reflected in the ways in which health and cultural performances were re-commodified within the modern spa space as luxurious and pampered spaces. While performances of health at the spa have always been a mix of the curative and the social, with the downturn, health-based narratives appear to have been rediscovered.

In Chapter 12, 'Traditional music here tonight: exploring the session space', Daithí Kearney takes the reader on an autobiographical tour of the pub session. Through this novel filter, as well as taking a look at the evolution of traditional music itself during the Celtic Tiger years especially, the chapter also explores concepts of identity and tradition in a changing Ireland. It considers the complex relationship between music and the economy, a link that is central to the geography of Irish traditional music. With a new-found appreciation for the value of 'culture' in healing Ireland's damaged image internationally, the downturn offers a new opportunity for Irish traditional music to develop in response to the political and economic environment.

Patrick Duffy, in Chapter 13, 'Through American eyes: a hundred years of Ireland in *National Geographic* magazine', concludes the collection with a chronicle of feature articles on Ireland since 1915 and its representation as an exotic other on the edge of Europe. From newly independent state in the 1920s, whose past was embedded in American experience through immigration, the contrast between American material living standards and the pre-electric Irish countryside up to the 1950s permeated the *National Geographic*'s (NG) commentary on Ireland. Even during the brash years of the Celtic Tiger, NG's representations of Irish landscape and society frequently reached back to its earlier lyrical imagery of a laid-back, misty isle. The recession, as well as a perceptible reassessment of cultural values at home, will likely facilitate a reprise of NG's more enduring images of a timeless Ireland in the future.

Hubris, Crisis, Regeneration – like characters from some epic poem who roam the land in search of absolution, debates on these grand themes and their daily expression in the twists and turns of their cousin Austerity occupy the current Irish imagination. All have their own geographies mediated by an increasingly turbulent politics and culture that shift across time and space. One day, the EU has our fate in its hands, the next day, the outcome of a general election far away multiplies our concerns. As Captain Boyle laments in Seán O'Casey's 1924 play, *Juno and the Paycock*, it seems 'th' whole world's in a terrible state o' chassis'. In holding such things to account, and linking their impact to the ordinariness of everyday life, we have aimed in this collection to supply new lines of thought and to open up effective ways of interpreting the ongoing transformation of people, place and landscape. Nobody doubts the grave challenges facing contemporary Irish society, not just in terms of economic recovery but also finding the politics needed to create a just society and a country that has the integrity to know who it is and what it means. Perhaps fragments of the answers – shards of hope – are to be found in *Spacing Ireland*.

Notes

1   Head shops, selling drug paraphernalia and 'legal highs', began to open up around the country after the collapse of the Celtic Tiger.
2   A follow-up to the inaugural forum in 2009 and the subsequent establishment of the Global Irish Network that calls on the experiences and imaginations of the Irish diaspora as well as those of people at home and abroad with an interest in Irish affairs and the future of its economy (see www.globalirishforum.ie/).
3   See www.youtube.com/watch?v=ZyK6r5YpiKo.

References

Amin, A. (2004) 'Regions unbound: towards a new politics of place', *Geografiska Annaler: Series B, Human Geography* 86, 1: 33–44.

Arrivals (2011) RTÉ One, 21 November, 21:30.

Baker, S. (1999) 'Mary Harney/Ireland: high-tech Hibernia', *Businessweek Online*, www.businessweek.com/1999/99_45/b3654024.htm, accessed 12 July 2000.

Beck, U., Bielfeld, U. and Tietze, N. (2011) 'More justice through more Europe'. Translated from German by N. Kinsky. Vienna: Eurozine, www.eurozine.com/articles/2011–12–29-beck-en.html, accessed 4 December 2011.

Castells, M. (1996) *The Rise of Network Society.* London: John Wiley.

Commission of Investigation into the Banking Sector in Ireland (2011) *Misjudging risk: causes of the systemic banking crisis in Ireland*. Dublin: The Stationery Office.

Deleuze, G. and Guattari, F. (1988) *A Thousand Plateaus: Capitalism and Schizophrenia*. Translated from French by B. Massumi. London: The Athlone Press.

Department of Enterprise, Trade and Employment (1999) *A strategy for long-term development of foreign earnings in Asia*. Dublin: The Stationery Office, www.djei.ie/publications/commerce/2002/arep.pdf, accessed 15 December 2011.

Fahey, T., Russell, H. and Whelan, C. T. (eds) (2007) *Best of Times? The Social Impact of the Celtic Tiger*. Dublin: Institute of Public Administration.

Ferriter, D. (2010) Interview. *Tonight with Vincent Browne*. TV3, 17 November, 23:05.

Jacobson, D., Kirby, P. and Ó Broin, D. (2006) *Taming the Tiger: Social Exclusion in a Globalised Ireland*. Dublin: New Island.

Kirby, P. (2010) *The Celtic Tiger in Collapse: Explaining the Weaknesses of the Irish Model*. Second edition. Basingstoke: Palgrave Macmillan.

Law, J. and Urry, J. (2004) 'Enacting the social', *Economy and Society* 33, 3: 390–410.

Marston, S., Jones, J. P. and Woodward, K. (2005) 'Human geographies without scale', *Transactions of the Institute of British Geographers* 30, 4: 416–32.

Massey, D. (2005) *For Space*. London: Sage.

O'Toole, F. (1997) *Ex-Isle of Erin: Images of a Global Ireland*. Dublin: New Island.

Solnit, R. (2011) *Infinite City: A San Francisco Atlas*. Berkeley, CA: University of California Press.

Sonnabend, R. (ed.) (2003) *Serve City – Interactive Urbanism*. Berlin: JOVIS Verlag GmbH.

Part I

Spacing belonging

I

Ghost estates: spaces and spectres of Ireland after NAMA

Cian O'Callaghan

We spotted it from the road before we saw the signs. The building site faced the oncoming traffic showing a hill of scraped dirt, husks of houses and forgotten foundations. We were driving around County Cork, looking at points on a map, finding the route and keeping our eyes open for the billboards, signs and other markings of what were then beginning to be called ghost estates. As we approached the entrance of the estate, billboards advertising the development in illustrious terms stood next to mounting piles of debris left over from construction. The estate of about fifty houses was like a dreamscape; surprisingly calm, and a little eerie. We disturbed the solitude of the pigeons and crows that had taken up residence in the dwellings, and their squawking, flapping and cawing echoed through the estate as we got out of the car. Of the fifty houses, ten were still under construction. These were cordoned off behind steel railings on one side of the estate and were little more than foundations. All building activity had ceased. Of those houses completed, only four were occupied; three at the front of the estate facing onto the road and one solitary dwelling at the bottom of the estate with the building site on one side and a row of thirty empty houses on the other. There were none of the signs of life that we had seen in other estates that day – no children playing, no parents pushing strollers, no residents going to and from their houses, nor what we took to be developers eyeing us suspiciously as they drove by slowly in 4x4s – but instead what Edensor (2005) calls the sense of ghostly calm that emanates from derelict places.

Figure 1.1 An unfinished estate in the south-west in 2012, abandoned
mid-construction

The inevitable collapse of the Irish property market in late 2008 has left
its mark in the form of empty houses, abandoned retail parks, and half-built
estates; fragments of Celtic Tiger developments that now stand as unfinished
or unoccupied shells (Figure 1.1). Kitchin, Gleeson, Keaveney *et al.* (2010) estimated that there were more than 338,031 vacant units around the country
in 2009 (120,248 properties in excess of demand). A Department of the
Environment, Heritage and Local Government survey in May 2010 recorded
2,846 unfinished estates in the country, 777 of which met the criteria of a ghost
estate – an estate of ten or more houses where 50 per cent are either vacant or
under construction. Ghost estates are a particularly austere material symbol of
the spectacular collapse of the Celtic Tiger, a metaphor for the glut of excess
characteristic of the era and of impending social dissolution. The remnants
of construction sites stand frozen in time, often with cranes, diggers, porta-
cabins and other artefacts abandoned behind steel fences that cordon them
off from any nearby occupied dwellings. Perhaps the starkest examples are in
rural areas, where small populations and overdevelopment have resulted in
high levels of vacancy and transformed landscapes. Ghost estates have become
symbolic spaces in the national narrative capturing the transition from boom
to bust, unprecedented growth to almost unfathomable collapse, prosperity to
negative equity.

This abrupt collapse of the property sector has had cataclysmic spatial and social effects. The interrelated activities of bankers, builders and buyers that kept one another aloft through the consistent movement of capital suddenly and cumulatively ceased to function, resulting in an almost apocalyptic freeze-frame of the state of development at that time. What had been parts in constant motion have settled, at least momentarily, into a landscape of crisis and dereliction that simultaneously underlines the lie of the Celtic Tiger's myth of eternal growth and offers an archaeological cross-section through which to explore and understand this period and the factors that contributed to the crisis. This chapter provides a short synopsis of the ghost estate issue, detailing the factors that contributed to the phenomenon, the way in which the estates have been invoked as symbolic spaces within the national narrative of collapse, and the State's response in the form of the National Assets Management Agency.

The Irish property bubble

The presence of ghost estates in the Irish landscape exemplifies the problems associated with the Celtic Tiger property boom. Put simply, too many houses were built. From 1996 to 2005, 553,267 houses were built in Ireland and by 2007, Ireland was producing more than twice as many units per head of population than any other European country with the exception of Spain (Kitchin *et al.*, 2010). This was coupled with dramatic increases in both house prices (rising as much as 429 per cent in certain parts of the country between 1991 and 2007) and land prices (leaping from an average of €10,000 per hectare in 1998 to €58,400 per hectare in 2006) (Savills HOK, 2007). Mortgage debt in Ireland trebled between 2002 and 2007, rising from €47.2 billion to over €139.8 billion, while the size of the average residential mortgage nearly doubled over the same period (CSO, 2008). The collapse of the property market in late 2008 saw a similarly dramatic reversal of these trends. By 2011, house prices had dropped sharply back to 2005 levels, land values had plummeted, construction output had fallen catastrophically, and the availability of mortgage capital had evaporated (see Kitchin *et al.*, 2010). Ghost estates offer one, albeit highly visible, articulation of these trends and to understand their origin requires an understanding of the factors contributing to the Irish housing bubble.

From the early 1990s, Ireland experienced a significant transformation of its demographic profile, coupling natural population growth with a reversal in migration trends. In 2004, the population exceeded four million for the first time since 1871 (Kitchin and Bartley, 2007: 1) and between 1991 and 2006, it increased by over 20 per cent from 3.53 million to 4.24 million (CSO, 2006). This population growth occurred in parallel with increased household fragmentation. The resultant need for new housing was shaped geographically by a series of urban renewal objectives that sought to regenerate dilapidated urban areas. The 1986 Urban Renewal Act put in place a number of tax incentives that were integral in kick-starting the Irish property market by allowing developers to claim back tax on income over a ten-year period; projects included several flagship urban redevelopments, initially in Dublin and later in other cities (MacLaran and McGuirk, 2001; Moore, 2008; O'Callaghan and Linehan, 2007). From 1998, the Pilot Rural Renewal Scheme for the Upper Shannon Region – a predominantly rural area encompassing counties Leitrim and Longford and parts of counties Cavan, Roscommon and Sligo (Department of Finance, 1999) – provided tax reliefs for the construction of rural dwellings. Over time, these schemes led to a dramatic increase in the housing stock in the region, with one in three houses constructed between 2002 and 2009 (Kitchin *et al.*, 2010). The growth in the property sector was further supported through the proliferation of pro-growth and entrepreneurial discourses amongst local authorities who, in the absence of devolved fiscal functions and more sustainable residential property taxes, were financed from the accrual of development levies. Furthermore, the balanced spatial development advocated by the National Spatial Strategy (NSS) (Department of the Environment, Heritage and Local Government, 2002) was consistently undermined by local politicians, many of whom had a vested interest in the property market and excessively zoned land for development (O'Toole, 2009). Within this taxation and political system, there was a predilection for development.

Added to these factors was the involvement of the domestic banking sector in a lending war driven by escalating profits, personal bonuses, and a seemingly never-ending supply of property investors, speculators and buyers. Embroiled in the increased mobility of capital through global (particularly European) financial markets (Harvey, 2010), Irish banks, taking advantage of favourable lending rates, underpinned their loans by borrowing from international banks and private equity funds. This influx of capital was made available for mortgages, flooding the market and offering borrowers easier access to less rigorously regulated forms of credit, such as 100 per cent mortgages over longer time periods for home buyers and deferred interest payments and interest-only mortgages for investors (Honohan, 2010). It is difficult to overestimate how profound a transformation this represented in the credit markets. For previous generations, and even until the later years of the boom, 100 per cent mortgages were nonexistent. Potential home buyers needed to have large deposits and were rigorously stress-tested before being approved. However, by the end of the boom, banks were desperately trying to offload mortgage capital, in some cases cold-calling customers to offer them loans.

Readily accessible credit was combined with strong discourses of home ownership and a burgeoning interest in buy-to-let and buy-to-flip speculation. Ireland has a high rate of home ownership, with almost three-quarters of private dwellings in the State being owner-occupied in 2006 (Kitchin *et al.*, 2010). While the rental sector is well-established as a short-term housing option, a market for renting as a long-term option has not been developed or encouraged. During the boom period, these trends were coupled with a simultaneous retreat from social housing provision. The proportion of social housing stock maintained by local authorities has fallen considerably as a result of tenant purchase schemes that allow local authority tenants to buy their homes, the rolling-out of affordable housing schemes offering certain buyers subsidised mortgages, and the progressive disinvestment by local authorities in social housing.

The extent to which the discourse of property speculation was normalised during the boom period was extraordinary. A sketch from the RTÉ television series *The Savage Eye* satirised attitudes at the time in a dinner party scene depicting guests talking about how many houses they own. When one guest sheepishly admits to owning 'only one house', the others look at him with disdain before excluding him from the rest of the conversation. The property market was ubiquitous. Soaring house prices were almost uniformly met with enthusiasm as more and more people became involved in the market as owners and investors. First-time buyers felt pressurised to get onto the property ladder for fear of being left behind in a constantly escalating market while renting was derided as 'dead money'. Despite the evidence of the inevitability of boom/bust cycles in property markets, there was a perception that house prices would continue to rise and that owning property was equivalent to having savings in the bank earning interest. One of the visible, and yet underplayed, articulations of this trajectory was the increasing size of property sections and supplements in newspapers, along with a growing number of television programmes about buying houses. These created tangible commodity fetishism around property, carving up the market into desirable items exhibiting allure both as material goods and investment assets. Newspapers began to accrue large profits from these sections – essentially advertising revenue – and consequently became increasingly entangled in the perpetuation of myths around the housing market, mostly failing to provide commentary counterbalancing the feverishly positive discourses (McGarr, 2007).

This property fetishism was encouraged surreptitiously by the government through lax planning regulation and policies designed to encourage growth, but also advocated vocally by politicians, most notably by Fianna Fáil, Ireland's largest political party that held uninterrupted power from 1997 to 2011. Their well-publicised tent at the Galway Races, which functioned as a vehicle for supporters of the party (including many property developers) to make large donations, offers an example of the casually paraded close relationships between politicians and developers. These visible ties were coupled with less perceptible and more obviously corrupt relationships demonstrated through the revelations of the Mahon Tribunal into planning corruption (see O'Toole, 2009). Moreover, critics of the property sector were vilified publicly by politicians and the press. The most oft-cited example occurred in 2007 when then Taoiseach (Prime Minister) Bertie Ahern (leader of the Fianna Fáil party), indirectly responding to an article by economist Morgan Kelly that predicted the economic crash, wondered why people who engage in 'cribbing and moaning … don't commit suicide' (Ahern, 2007). The point that needs to be emphasised here is how pervasive the Celtic Tiger property boom was. Discourses of home-ownership, accumulation and speculation were everywhere, perfectly encapsulating an example of what Walter Benjamin calls a 'collective dream' (see Gilloch, 1999: 105–6), so unreal yet seemingly real, only revealing its strangeness on our waking.

Ghost estates as iconic spaces

While the associations elicited by the metaphor 'crash' may suggest the sudden, the abrupt and the violent, the nation's awakening from the collective dream of the Celtic Tiger was rather more subtle and protracted. The term ghost estate was coined in 2006 when it was first used in an article by economist David McWilliams. He wrote:

> All over Ireland, 'ghost estates' are enveloping many of our towns. Driving back from the West, these spooky ghost estates emerged out of the mist announcing places like Termonbarry, Frenchpark and Edgeworthstown. Anywhere there is a tax-driven scheme, there are ghost estates. You don't have to be a child or believe in Halloween to find that scary … In the years ahead, these ghost villages, like our famine villages, may stand testament to a great tragedy which, although predicted by concerned observers, was never fully appreciated until the morning the crops failed. (McWilliams, 2006)

Despite McWilliams' prescient warning in 2006, the fact that construction output still rose marginally between 2006 and 2007, before dropping substantially in 2008 (Kitchin *et al.*, 2010), highlights just how out of sync supply and demand in the market had become. People had effectively become desensitised to seeing a constant stream of construction. The building site had become part of a national landscape aesthetic, a reassuring sight at the periphery of people's vision signifying the continued growth and well-being of the Celtic Tiger economy. While for some, like McWilliams, their omnipresence was worrying, for many others new housing developments were simply business as usual.

However, as the effects of the global credit crunch and Ireland's entangled property market began to be felt more strongly – as the chronic hole in the banks' capital became apparent, as unemployment soared in the construction industry, as empty estates were exposed by inactivity – ghost estates took on an iconic quality expressive of the spectacular collapse of the Celtic Tiger. By 2011, Ireland had entered a period in which the traces of recent economic prosperity, cultural cosmopolitanism and, particularly, property investment were now overlaid by the trauma of unemployment, negative equity and the death of a dream. The geography of ghost estates charts the fevered speculation, uneven development, and commuting and consumption patterns that emerged during the boom especially in the commuter belts around the main cities (Figure 1.2).

There are ghost estates in every county in Ireland. Many are located concentrically along the main commuter zones around major urban areas. Due to escalating house prices and the entrenched culture of owner-occupancy, the development of estates was pushed further and further out from urban centres, resulting in people commuting increasingly longer distances to work (Gleeson, Kitchin, Bartley *et al.*, 2008; Linehan, 2007). Some counties, such as Cork, have a large number of ghost estates due to their size and population. However, if we standardise by population, it is the counties covered by the Rural Renewal Scheme of the Upper Shannon Region that emerge with the highest number (Figure 1.3). Thus, while the (over)construction of housing estates was ubiquitous throughout Ireland, it was significantly exacerbated by tax-incentive schemes rolled out by the government. Rather than regulating the property sector or leaving things up to the market, these tax-incentive schemes actually skewed the spatial distribution of housing. It is perhaps significant that while the Celtic Tiger is primarily represented as an urban phenomenon, the crash has been visually documented by ghost estates in rural areas. Although ghost estates are by no means a strictly rural manifestation, their incidence in urban areas tends to be in the form of higher-density apartment developments, which do not have the same aesthetic appeal for journalists compared with their more iconic rural counterparts. While rural ghost estates are often construed as more problematic due to the high vacancy levels they represent in areas with little prospect of economic or demographic growth, in reality over-development and housing vacancy permeates both urban and rural contexts and, thus, should be viewed as relational components of the same system.

The Celtic Tiger property sector comprised a variety of actors ranging from development companies with international reach (and the resources to go with it) to local entrepreneurs seeking to capitalise on the seemingly insatiable

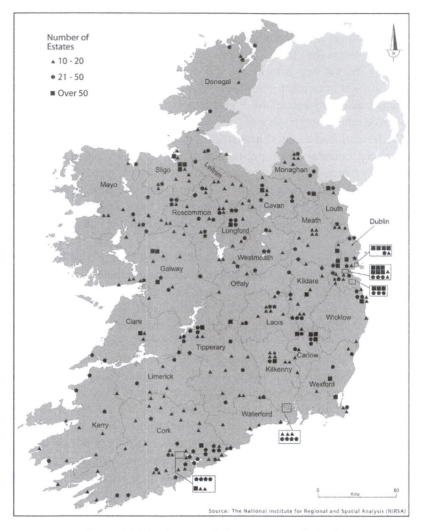

Figure 1.2 Distribution of ghost estates in Ireland

demand for housing by developing a small parcel of land. The significant variation in the typology of ghost estates is contingent upon multiple factors – the price of land, the resources and competence of the developer, the regulatory regimes of different local authorities, the location of estates in relation to their respective urban centres, the availability of tax incentives, and so forth – that influenced the logic underpinning their construction. Ghost estates, therefore, mark the landscape in a way that underscores the patterns of development that occurred in Ireland during the latter part of the Celtic Tiger period. As such,

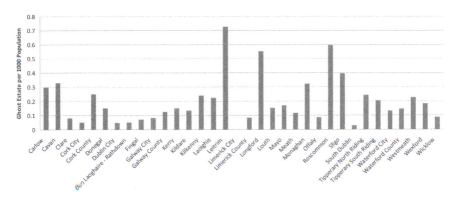

Figure 1.3 Number of ghost estates per county normalised by population, 2009

they have a spectral presence that brings the past to bear upon the present by enabling us to view the spatial and social conditions of the previous era in a new light. The ghost estate encapsulates what Wylie (2007: 172) calls 'the very conjuration and unsettling of presence, place, the present, and the past'. Materially and metaphorically, visually and psychologically, personally and communally, they represent the intense transformations and aspirations of the Celtic Tiger period and the sobering anxieties and uncertainty of the current period. They are literally places haunted by the Celtic Tiger.

Boym (2002) suggests that in critical periods of transition, national myths are replaced with new ones and iconic sites become implicated as symbolic spaces in this process. Within this context, it is unsurprising that under-occupied or unfinished estates have become a symbol of the untrammelled greed, political ineptitude and squandered potential that the Celtic Tiger represents within the national narrative that has emerged post-crash. Memory – 'a process of continually remaking and remembering the past in the present rather than a process of discovering objective historical "facts"' (Till, 2005: 11) – plays a pivotal role in times of transition and the Celtic Tiger is currently being re-membered through the ghost estate.

Ghost estates have been mobilised discursively in both politics and the media to portray this national revising. O'Hearn (1998: xi) suggests that during the Celtic Tiger period, people emerged from a sense of 'public guilt at being Irish' and into a feel-good wave, and thus accepted the discourses of the 'economic miracle' in an unproblematic manner that overlooked the unsustainable nature of the changes, demonstrated most immediately by 'rising poverty, inequality and social marginalisation', but also over time by a destructive property boom that produced the current housing and debt crisis. The economic crash undermined the set of discourses that sustained the Celtic Tiger project, exposing what was labelled a coherent economic strategy to be rather a set of short-term and emergent plans, deals and actions that were rationalised after the fact.

The series of bank recapitalisations that followed the crash, despite involving billions of taxpayers' money, were discussed in a way that effectively excluded the majority of the population from understanding the extent of the crisis. If the deficit in the banks remained abstract and esoteric, visualised through stacks of numbers, deficits and credit defaults, ghost estates provided a physical and symbolic dramatisation of the issues; row upon row of empty new houses, half-built houses, unfinished estates, plans come undone, dreams never to be realised. However, as is evident from the length of time between McWilliams first coining the term and its widespread usage in the media, empty houses signified nothing without the understanding that the property sector had crashed. As Edensor (2005) suggests, dereliction is usually associated with older manufacturing sites that have ceased to be functional once industry has left the area. Ghost estates, conversely, are derelict before they even have a chance to be new. As a result of the property and banking crises, these estates went from being half-built in the sense that they were not *yet* completed to being half-built in the sense that they would *never* be completed.

The major turning point in this realisation was the establishment by the State of the National Asset Management Agency (NAMA). NAMA was set up in September 2009 to deal with toxic property debt held by the banks. The 'Draft NAMA business plan' (National Asset Management Agency, 2009) details that a loan book of €77 billion plus €9 billion in rolled-up interest was to be transferred to NAMA from five Irish banks (Allied Irish Banks plc, Anglo Irish Bank Corporation Limited,[1] Bank of Ireland, Educational Building Society Ltd and Irish Nationwide Building Society). Following court cases, €74 billion was the final total transferred. In return, the banks received government-backed bonds to be used to borrow from the European Central Bank, the underlying logic being that economic recovery will be enabled by removing impaired assets and injecting liquidity into the Irish banking system. NAMA draws upon similar programmes elsewhere, such as the Resolution Trust Corporation in the USA. As a response to the property and banking crises, NAMA is a conservative strategy that ignores spatial and social concerns, and aims to re-inflate the property market and reinstate the same unsustainable system that caused the crash. This is indicative of both the increased neoliberalisation (Brenner and Theodore, 2002; Harvey, 2005) of the nation state and, more specifically in the Irish case, of the short-termist and reactionary modus operandi of Irish politics that then unfolds into a de facto longer-term response and seeks to protect as much as possible the interests of the developer and financial class.

While these types of neoliberal policies have continued unabated, re-sulting ultimately in the State accepting an €85 billion European Union (EU)/International Monetary Fund (IMF) bailout in November 2010, and the collapse of the Fianna Fáil/Green Party coalition government the following February, the perception that the property sector should be re-inflated has come to be viewed very critically by large sections of the Irish population. In terms of their place within iconic national narratives that revised the Celtic Tiger period, ghost estates have played a key role in this transition in terms of visualising the destructive economic policies and practices of the era.

Ghost estates as lived spaces

As Ireland's economic crisis revealed itself more fully, ghost estates became an international news story, with journalists flocking to get a first-hand look. While the international media latched onto a particular type of estate through which to report on the phenomenon, the reality is more nuanced in terms of the typology, geography and issues affecting these estates. In November 2010, a team of French journalists asked to be shown around a few estates in the Dublin region. As we pulled the car into an estate, children were playing while neighbours chatted to each other, and when our car got stuck on the ice one resident succeeded in freeing us. This vision of a functioning community was not what the crew had in mind and they promptly decided that it was not ghostly enough. They settled for the next estate we visited, although what they were really looking for was an almost desolate estate like the one described in the introduction.

Depending on their location, stage of development, occupancy and a range of other factors, the issues currently affecting different estates and their future prospects are highly divergent. Nevertheless, many ghost estates do exhibit traits – such as issues relating to health and safety, poor aesthetics and under-developed physical and community infrastructures – that are troubling for their residents. In 2007, the government published the *Building Homes, Sustaining Communities* document, which puts in place an overarching vision for how the Irish housing sector should develop over the next ten years. It defines sustain-able communities as: 'places where people want to live and work, now and in the future. They meet the diverse needs of existing and future residents, are sensitive to their environment, and contribute to a high quality of life. They are safe and inclusive, well planned, built and run, and offer equality of opportu-nity and good services for all' (Department of the Environment, Heritage and Local Government, 2007: 1). The mere existence of ghost estates marks a clear failing on the part of the State to provide for such sustainable communities and their prevalence suggests a fundamental disconnect between housing policy and housing provision in Ireland. At best, this policy is an example of too little too late.

Recognising the particular health and safety threats posed by unfinished estates (of which ghost estates form a particular subset), the Department of the Environment, Heritage and Local Government in February 2011 made a safety fund of €5 million available to address the most problematic estates. Due to legal machinations relating to outstanding planning permissions and the ongoing acquisition of loans by NAMA, it is unlikely that many estates will be able to access this fund in the short term. Nevertheless, it offers a first step in terms of the political recognition that these are highly problematic spaces for the people living in them.

In addition to the physical problems associated with ghost estates, they are also likely to form acute spaces of emotional and psychological upheaval. Post-Celtic Tiger Ireland is a society grappling with the fallout of intense collapse, not only of the economy but of the series of narratives and identities that under-pinned the whole era. This is reflected in the everyday lives of citizens, many of whom have lost jobs or are in precarious economic positions, struggling with heavy mortgages, angry that the opportunities afforded to them have been lost for their children. As spaces at the forefront of the national re-imagining, ghost estates and their residents are susceptible to this emotional upheaval perhaps more than most. This observation is twofold. Firstly, since ghost estates are pri-marily those built during the later stages of the Celtic Tiger, their residents are likely to have bought at the height of the boom and are consequently in severe negative equity. Coupled with this are the physical problems presented by the estates themselves: health and safety concerns, dilapidation and the shortfall of infrastructural provisions. Thus, residents are faced with very real problems that will need to be addressed in the short to medium-term. Secondly, because ghost estates have been mobilised as symbolic spaces of the crash, they will also be the places most immediately and unavoidably confronted with the in-adequacies of the Celtic Tiger myth. In this sense, the search for a new national narrative will be folded into the very fabric of everyday life on these estates.

Thus, on top of the series of issues outlined above, residents of these estates will need to reconcile themselves with the prospect of living in homes that continue to lose their value, among few neighbours, in places that remain unfinished, starkly contrasting with the fading billboards that still advertise the developments' promised lifestyles in glowing rhetoric. They will need to commute to their workplaces, raise their children, attend school meetings, and socialise and organise within and through these places. Thus, what happens at the local scale on ghost estates will be affected by the key transitions happening on the national (and international) level.

Conclusions

Ghost estates are spaces of complex material and ethereal contradictions; new *and* derelict, home-place *and* uncanny (literally unhomely), and signify various manifestations of presence and absence (Wylie, 2009). They are significant in terms of how they have been drawn upon and understood as symbolic spaces that encapsulate the crash of the Celtic Tiger period of economic growth. Moreover, ghost estates are key spaces within the emerging economic geographies of Ireland, inextricably linked into banking debt, unemployment and the crisis in the public finances. These estates will undoubtedly be at the forefront of the recalibration of the nation post-crash. However, more than being interesting laboratories in which new social and economic geographies will emerge, they are first and foremost ordinary places of everyday life. Ghost estates are iconic places and problematic places, but also places in which residents must continue to live their lives, raise families, form communities and address the physical and emotional deficits encapsulated in them, ultimately with the hope of building something better from these incomplete spaces.

Notes

1   In 2011, Anglo Irish Bank Corporation Limited was merged with Irish Nationwide Building Society and renamed Irish Bank Resolution Corporation Limited.

References

Ahern, B. (2007) 'I don't know how people who engage in that don't commit suicide', online video, www.youtube.com/watch?v=hfjGSfuSQpA, accessed 17 October 2011.

Boym, S. (2002) *The Future of Nostalgia*. New York: Basic Books.

Brenner, N. and Theodore, N. (eds) (2002) *Spaces of Neoliberalism: Urban Restructuring in North America and Western Europe*. London: Blackwell Publishing.

Central Statistics Office (CSO) (2006) *Quarterly National Household Survey Quarter 4 2005,* www.cso.ie/releasespublications/documents/labour_market/current/qnhsssiaq42005.pdf, accessed 20 October 2011.

Central Statistics Office (CSO) (2008) *Construction and Housing in Ireland*, www.eirestat.cso.ie/releasespublications/documents/construction/current/constructhousing.pdf, accessed 20 October 2011.

Department of the Environment, Heritage and Local Government (2002) *National Spatial Strategy for Ireland 2002–2020: People, Places and Potential*. Dublin: The Stationery Office.

Department of the Environment, Heritage and Local Government (2007) *Delivering Homes, Sustaining Communities: Statement on Housing Policy.* Dublin: Department of the Environment, Heritage and Local Government.

Department of Finance (1999) *Rural Renewal Scheme: Tax Reliefs for Owner-occupied and Rented Residential Accommodation,* www.revenue.ie/en/tax/it/leaflets/it65. pdf, accessed 3 April 2011.

Edensor, T. (2005) *Industrial Ruins: Space, Aesthetics and Materiality.* Oxford: Berg.

Gilloch, G. (1999) *Myth and Metropolis: Walter Benjamin and the City.* Cambridge: Polity Press.

Gleeson, J., Kitchin, R., Bartley, B., Driscoll, J., Foley, R., Fotheringham, S. and Lloyd, C. (2008) *The Atlas of the Island of Ireland.* Naas, Kildare: All-Island Research Observatory and the International Centre for Local and Regional Development.

Harvey, D. (2005) *A Brief History of Neoliberalism.* Oxford: Oxford University Press.

Harvey, D. (2010) *The Enigma of Capital and the Crises of Capitalism.* London: Profile Books.

Honohan, P. (2010) *The Irish Banking Crisis: Regulatory and Financial Stability Policy 2003–2008.* Dublin: Irish Central Bank.

Kitchin, R. and Bartley, B. (2007) 'Ireland in the twenty-first century', in B. Bartley and R. Kitchin (eds), *Understanding Contemporary Ireland.* Dublin: Pluto Press, pp. 1–26.

Kitchin, R., Gleeson, J., Keaveney, K. and O'Callaghan, C. (2010) *A Haunted Landscape: Housing and Ghost Estates in Post-Celtic Tiger Ireland.* NIRSA Working Paper, No. 59. Maynooth, Kildare: National Institute for Regional and Spatial Analysis (NIRSA), National University of Ireland, Maynooth. www.nuim.ie/nirsa/research/documents/WP59-A-Haunted-Landscape.pdf, accessed 10 July 2011.

Linehan, D. (2007) 'For the way we live today: consumption, lifestyle and place', in B. Bartley and R. Kitchin (eds), *Understanding Contemporary Ireland.* Dublin: Pluto Press, pp. 289–300.

MacLaran, A., and McGuirk, P. (2001) 'Changing approaches to planning in an "entrepreneurial city": the case of Dublin', *European Planning Studies* 9, 4: 437–57.

McGarr, S. (2007) 'Sold! The Irish Times property supplement'. *Tuppenceworth,* 7 March, www.tuppenceworth.ie/blog/2007/03/07/sold-the-irish-times-property-supplement/, accessed 17 October 2011.

McWilliams, D., 2006. *A Warning from Deserted Ghost Estates.* 1 October, www. davidmcwilliams.ie/2006/10/01/a-warning-from-deserted-ghost-estates, accessed 3 September 2011.

Moore, N. (2008) *Dublin Docklands Reinvented: The Post-Industrial Regeneration of a European City Quarter.* Dublin: Four Courts Press.

National Asset Management Agency (2009) *Draft NAMA Business Plan,* www.nama. ie/publications/?wpfb_file_year=2009, accessed 13 March 2011.

O' Callaghan, C. and Linehan, D. (2007) 'Identity, politics and conflict in docklands redevelopment in Cork, Ireland: European Capital of Culture 2005', *Cities* 24, 4: 311–23.

O' Hearn, D. (1998) *Inside the Celtic Tiger: The Irish Economy and the Asian Model.* London: Pluto Press.

O'Toole, F. (2009) *Ship of Fools: How Stupidity and Corruption Sank the Celtic Tiger.* London: Faber and Faber.

Savills HOK (2007) 'Values approach €60,000 hectare', *Irish Agricultural Land Research* (online, no longer available).

Till, K. (2005) *The New Berlin: Memory, Politics, Place.* Minneapolis, MN: University of Minnesota Press.

Wylie, J. (2007) 'The spectral geographies of W. G. Sebald', *Cultural Geographies* 14, 2: 171–88.

Wylie, J. (2009) 'Landscape, absence and the geographies of love', *Transactions of the Institute of British Geographers* 34: 275–89.

2

'Of course I'm not Irish': young people in migrant worker families in Ireland

Naomi Tyrrell

The volume of research on (and with) migrant children and young people has been increasing in recent years but this often focuses on migrants who are deemed to be particularly vulnerable (see White, Ní Laoire, Tyrrell *et al.*, 2011), such as those seeking asylum, and tends to portray a narrow definition of who migrant children and young people are. At the same time, the popular concept of transnationalism and the study of migrants' lives across borders have been enhancing migration research by incorporating migrants' experiences, feelings and narratives into our understandings of what it means to migrate. This chapter brings these two bodies of research together by focusing on the experiences of children and young people in migrant worker families in Europe, i.e. children and young people who have migrated to Ireland because one or both of their parents have migrated for employment. These children's and young people's experiences often are overlooked because of the narrow definitions related to child migration and the assumption that European migrants are young, single and mobile, rather than family migrants. While many migrant workers from Central and Eastern Europe (CEE) in Ireland can be categorised as non-family migrants, one of the largest migrant groups in Ireland is 'couples with children' (Ní Laoire, Bushin, Carpena-Méndez *et al.*, 2009), including large numbers of CEE families. Both types of migrant workers are considered in Chapter 3 by Sally Daly.

The number of migrant families who moved to Ireland from EU countries in CEE between 2004 and 2008 was unprecedented and underestimated. Many children and young people from CEE moved to Ireland with, or to join, one or more migrant worker parent. These young people are the '1.5 genera-tion' – those who are born in a migrant-sending country but experience their childhood and adolescence elsewhere. The experiences of young people who migrate at this age are interesting to consider because often they are at an age when they are developing social networks beyond their families and socialis-ing with peers. Friendship and socialisation are important aspects of young people's lives (Cotterell, 1996) and it is useful to explore the ways in which migration affects and influences young people's social networks.[1]

Studies have pointed to the important roles that children and young people in migrant families play in connecting their families to local communities and to building and retaining transnational ties (de Block and Buckingham, 2007, Ní Laoire, Carpena-Mendez, Tyrrell et al., 2011; Orellana, Thorne, Chee et al. 2001; Skrbis, Baldassar and Poynting, 2007). However, the social integration of young migrants and their families in Ireland has received attention in political circles and in the popular press due to a number of 'moral panics' concern-ing children's education and socialisation (Ní Laoire et al., 2009) and, more recently, the economic recession. In times of economic uncertainty, immigra-tion often is perceived as a threat and of concern to society. Recent research by Spencer, Ruhs, Anderson and Rogaly (2007) in a UK context suggests that migrant workers who migrate with children are more likely to intend to remain living in their host country, specifically because they are more likely to feel part of communities and because their children are settled in schools. Although children in migrant worker families may be children when they migrate, they do not remain so – they age and develop their own independent thoughts and plans. Therefore, young people in migrant worker families are an interesting group to explore. In the context of the economic recession, it is fruitful to consider their everyday lives in Ireland, the ways in which they are living tran-snational lives and their plans for the future. This is the focus of this chapter. Firstly, however, the next section provides some context for these young peo-ple's migrations by outlining several key features of contemporary migration to Ireland during the Celtic Tiger years and beyond.

EU migrant worker families in Ireland

Ireland has undergone rapid economic and population change since the mid-1990s. The Celtic Tiger period, approximately from 1995 to 2007, transformed Ireland's global profile. During these prosperous years, emigration from Ireland reduced and rates of immigration increased, enhanced by Irish return migrants who seized the chance to return to their homeland. In 2002, just under 6 per cent of the total population usually resident in Ireland had non-

Irish nationality (Ruhs, 2006). By 2006, that proportion had grown to over 10 per cent (CSO, 2008) of a total population that had itself risen by 8 per cent since 2002 (CSO, 2007). Thus, the increase in the share of the population with non-Irish nationality was primarily due to migration.

In relation to children and young people, Taguma, Kim, Wurzburg *et al.* (2009) estimate that approximately 10 per cent of children in primary schools and 8 per cent of children in secondary schools in Ireland are from immigrant backgrounds. Ní Laoire *et al.* (2009) have used the detailed information from the population census of 2006 to highlight several relevant points concerning immigrant children in Ireland. For example, just over 7 per cent of all children living in Ireland do not have Irish nationality; the most common nationality of immigrant children living in Ireland is British (22,157 children), followed by EU15-25 (13,828 children) and African (9,788) (Ní Laoire *et al.*, 2009).

The scale and speed of recent immigration flows to Ireland have been re-marked upon because the sheer numbers exceeded all expectations (Barrett, 2009). This includes the migrations of those who are the focus of this chapter – young people in CEE migrant worker families. Migrant workers and their families comprised the largest in-migrant group in Ireland during the latter stages of the economic boom, but the majority of research into their experiences of migration and integration has focused on the adults in these families rather than the young people. The fluid and mobile nature of EU migrant workers makes it difficult to calculate accurate numbers but almost 14,000 children from new EU countries were living in Ireland at the time of the population census in 2006 (Ní Laoire *et al.*, 2009). Nationals from these countries migrated to Ireland between 2002 and 2006, with more than 44 per cent migrating to Ireland since 2005. This rise in in-migration of European migrant workers from countries such as Poland, Lithuania and Latvia, occurred as a result of the Irish Government's decision not to place restrictions on new European migrant workers (a decision replicated by the UK and Sweden). Between 2004 and 2007 inclusive, net inward migration to Ireland totalled more than 225,000, which was equivalent to over 5 per cent of the resident population (Barrett and Bergin, 2009).

Research from countries with a longer history of immigration, such as the UK and the USA, has explored issues of immigrants' experiences of their new residential locations and the question of social segregation (e.g. Ellis, 2001; Finney and Simpson, 2009; Peach, 1996). Often, this research is working within what can be called an immigrant incorporation or social inclusion perspective and some studies on immigrant social inclusion have begun to emerge in the Irish context (see Fanning, 2011). In Ireland, immigrants' residential locations tend to reflect affordable housing options hence, in general, immigrants are found in areas with a supply of private rented housing close to places of employment. These tend to be urban and suburban areas but it is important to note that one in seven non-Irish nationals (excluding UK nationals) were living in rural areas at the time of the 2006 Census (CSO, 2008). This pattern of settlement likely reflects both the policy of dispersing asylum seekers across Ireland and the employment sectors of migrant workers.

Economic decline and rising unemployment in Ireland since 2008 have resulted in a decrease in immigration and an increase in emigration. The highest number of out-migrants between 2008 and 2009 were nationals of new EU accession states (CSO, 2009) as unemployment affected this group disproportionately, with an almost 20 per cent annual employment loss in 2009 compared with just 7 per cent for the Irish-born population (Smyth, 2011). However, between 2009 and 2010 the highest numbers of out-migrants were Irish nationals (CSO, 2010) reflecting the worsening recession. As yet, despite the census household type 'couples with children' being common among non-Irish nationals in 2006 (Ní Laoire et al., 2009), substantial evidence of large numbers of migrant families out-migrating is lacking. Some likely reasons for this are: young people in EU migrant worker families who moved in 2004 or 2005 are now at important stages of their education therefore families may decide to remain until children leave school; many EU migrant worker families satisfy the habitual residence condition that entitles them to have access to state benefits, such as child welfare allowance and unemployment benefit; research has shown that Ireland is perceived as offering a good quality of life for children (Gilligan, Curry, McGrath et al., 2010; Ní Laoire et al., 2009); and this author's research with migrant mothers in Cork suggests that many of them want to build family lives in Ireland (some had recently married Irish spouses) and do not envisage returning to their home countries to raise their children.

Not surprisingly, the number of migrant workers moving to Ireland from new EU countries has dropped significantly but there is still an inflow of such migrants, albeit on a much smaller scale; and there is still a sizeable European immigrant population according to national embassies in Dublin (Smyth, 2011). Evidently, Ireland remains an attractive country for some groups of immigrants because of 'the way of life and the positive treatment they get from people and State bodies' according to Gregory Jagielski at the consular section of the Polish embassy (quoted in Smyth, 2011). Early results from the 2011 Census reveal that net migration to Ireland between the censuses of 2006 and 2011 continued and was higher than predicted, with 100,000 more people living in the country than had been forecasted (CSO, 2011).

The small body of research on immigrant children and young people in Ireland often considers ideas related to transnationalism, either implicitly or explicitly, by focusing on children's experiences of living across borders (see Bushin and White, 2010; Charles, 2009; Darmody, Tyrrell and Song, 2011;

Devine, 2011; Gilligan *et al.*, 2010; Ní Laoire *et al.*, 2009; Ní Laoire *et al.*, 2011). However, research focused on young migrants from CEE is less common than that on what are considered to be more vulnerable groups. The remainder of this chapter is based on research with young people, aged from twelve to seventeen years, who were born in CEE and migrated to urban and suburban locations in Cork and Dublin from locations in Central and Eastern Europe, either with, or to join, at least one migrant worker parent.[2] A variety of qualitative participatory methods were drawn upon, including interviews, photovoice (a method that draws out participants' narratives of their photographs) and drawing.

Tales of the unexpected? Migrant young people's plans for the future

The number of youths younger than eighteen years who moved to Ireland in migrant worker families or to join migrant worker parent(s) was unexpected and unplanned for, specifically in relation to education (Bryan, 2009; Devine, 2011). In some ways, young people who migrated to Ireland from countries that joined the EU in 2004 are a fairly privileged group in comparison to other groups of migrant young people. This is because they have free movement within the EU and their family migrations to Ireland were unrestricted. Their ability to move freely between countries was not lost on the young people themselves when considering their plans for the future.

Adult migrants from CEE often experienced de-skilling or under-skilling in Ireland, gaining places in the labour market that were below their qualifications and skills level. Often, this has been presented as being worthwhile for migrants because of wage differentials between their home country and Ireland, even when working in jobs that they would not have considered doing at home. However, for the migrant young people and parents in this research, although economic considerations motivated many of their moves, migration was not considered to be a short-term measure. It was often part of a longer-term family plan in which financial gains were important but not the only factor. For example, the advantages of learning English were recognised by both young people and their parents, and some also spoke of Ireland offering a safer family environment than their home countries, with less crime and fewer drugs. Although these points could be debated and, to an extent, depend on the location in Ireland to which families moved, it is interesting that perceptions of Ireland followed these lines. While economic factors may push migrants out of their home countries, when they have more than one destination open to them, factors beyond economics are also considered.

Despite migration to Ireland being presented as a medium or long-term family plan by many of the participants in the research, it is fair to say that young migrants' economic prospects look far from stable if they plan to remain in their new country context. Although many of them entered the Irish education system when they first arrived, those who arrived at age eleven, shortly after unrestricted movement was enabled in 2004, are now of school-leaving age and ready to embark on their next life-stage. Ruhs and Quinn (2009) note that the economic recession in Ireland has affected non-Irish nationals to a greater extent than their Irish counterparts – their unemployment was 14.7 per cent in the first quarter of 2009 compared to 9.4 per cent for Irish nationals. This relates to migrants' tendency to work in sectors that have suffered most from the decline of the Celtic Tiger economy such as construction, retail and hospitality, and it may increase the likelihood of them out-migrating (Somerville and Sumption, 2009). Unlike many of the migrations of their parents, however, it may not be financial gains and disparity in wage levels that prompt young migrants' future migrations, but rather the opening up of possible opportunities for adventure, learning and fun. They are at a different stage of their lives, without the responsibilities of children, and only beginning to embark on further education that will enable their chosen career paths. Out-migration from Ireland may be the next step in their migratory futures, embodying the new European young migrant generation – open to considering multiple migratory pathways, unrestricted by the shackles of the past.

Sally, aged fourteen and from Poland, is one example of a young migrant who was in the midst of considering many of the options available to her: 'I would like to study here and maybe stay here or go back to Poland or travel like my sister. Maybe I want to be a pianist or an artist. Maybe I would like to be a teacher as well'. In Sally's drawing depicting her future (Figure 2.1), she featured herself as the 1960s cartoon character 'Atom Ant'. Atom Ant has superpowers: super strength and the ability to fly.[3] She depicts some of her possible future occupations – a chef or a teacher – but it is pertinent to her experience as a migrant that 'in character' she portrays herself as robust and invulnerable. Migration to Ireland was not unproblematic for Sally. She lived with her mother and her sister in Ireland while her father worked away (sometimes in another part of Ireland or sometimes overseas) for an Irish company and felt that she was only just getting to know her father again as he had recently returned to working closer to their home in County Cork. In Poland, she was used to socialising with her friends at weekends and making visits to their houses. This was not common when she arrived in Ireland and primarily she had made friends with other Polish young people or young people with other migrant backgrounds. However, migration-related optimism for the future, cohering to the original aims of the European project that included

Figure 2.1 Sally's drawing of herself in the future

the free movement of people in a Europe without borders, is too simplistic in assessing some young migrants' plans. Many of them were engaged in the process of weighing up the perceived potential advantages and disadvantages of staying in or leaving Ireland.

It is important to note that the young people were actively considering their futures even before the beginning of 2009 and the growing realisation of the scale of Ireland's economic woes. This may be a reflection of their recent mobile experiences. In some ways, the transitory aspects of their lives had not ended with their in-migration; rather, it had continued in the vein of considering migration as a process rather than a singular event (Halfacree and Boyle, 1993). In many cases, the young people interviewed had experienced a series of residential relocations since entering Ireland. Migrant workers in Ireland often inhabited rental properties, either by choice or because of lack of funds. Migrant families tended to share accommodation, with more than one family occupying one dwelling, at least for a short time subsequent to their arrival (see Box 1). This meant that some of the young people did not feel settled in a particular community, having changed residential location, and sometimes schools as well.

A mobile lifestyle involving several adjustment moves seemed to impact upon young people's feelings of rootedness, with them commenting that they did not know many local people, preferring to socialise in friendship groups based on shared nationality (e.g. Polish with Polish as described in Box 1) or shared migrant status (e.g. Hungarian with Lithuanian) (see Ní Laoire *et al.*, 2011). Often, young people's feelings and experiences of not being integrated in their local communities in Ireland were reflected in their plans for the future. In the short and sometimes medium term, some of them wanted to stay in Ireland, but they envisaged their long-term futures as being elsewhere. Their future migration intentions were not concretised but the pull of friends and family, as well as decisions about where to study and work, are important to consider when trying to gain an understanding of their future plans.

Box 1

Mauva, age seventeen

Mauva stayed in Poland, moving to live with her grandmother in a different town, while her mother and sister migrated to Ireland. Her parents are separated and her father lives in Poland. She moved to Ireland after one year of living with her grandmother because 'we argued all the time' and she wanted to improve her English. She, along with her mother and sister, lived with another migrant family for a few weeks before moving to their own single-occupancy rented accommodation. They have moved their domestic pets from Poland to Ireland – a sign of stability perhaps. When she first moved to Ireland, she 'hated this place' for three months but considers that to be in the past. She feels that her relationships with her mother and sister have improved since she moved to Ireland – she is more reliant on them because her social networks have been downsized. She has started a relationship with a Polish young man who she met on the internet and he has now moved to Ireland to live with her family. She thinks that out-migrating from Ireland would be difficult because of the friendships she has made and as 'it is another part of my life'.

One aspect of stability that all of the migrant young people discussed was their national identity. They often felt that their lives were in a state of flux, precarious because of their mobile situations, and it was their sense of belonging to a national collective that enabled them to maintain and develop their sense of self, their identity, while encountering change. For example, rather than considering that they were able to develop hybridised identity, such as Lithuanian-Irish or Polish-Irish, young people from CEE countries were keen to emphasise their singular national identity, as Samantha, age fourteen, pointed out in a comment in her photobook: 'Of course I'm not Irish. I'm Lithuanian and proud of it ☺'.

In some ways, these young people's lack of identification with Ireland, beyond it being the country in which they were currently living, differs from the perspectives and portrayals of other migrant young people, such as African-Irish or returning-Irish (see Ní Laoire et al., 2011). We might have considered the fact that they are intra-EU migrants as influencing their senses of identity and feeling of attachment to their home countries and Ireland. However, the research participants did not express a shared sense of 'European-ness', or of having a shared sense of belonging with Irish young people. Reay and Lucey (2000) consider that localities shape the people we are but also the people we are not, and it was both the social and educational experiences of the young people that emphasised their difference from Irish young people. For example, they felt uncomfortable with the labels that had been ascribed to them in their school situations and in wider society, such as 'newcomer' and 'non-national'; thus, many of them brought their national identity to the foreground, as exemplified by Samantha.

According to Bash and Zezlina-Phillips (2006), young people negotiate their identity not only in terms of where they are now, but also of where they have come from and of where they want to be. Ireland was viewed by many as being a transnational stepping stone, as offering opportunities for learning that could be utilised. Interestingly, however, young people were often critical of the Irish education system and did not think it was of a high standard in comparison to the education system in their home countries. Standards of discipline and learning were commented on by some young people as being lower than they were used to. Some young people thought that this was an advantage as they did not have to work so hard to achieve good results; others were aware of the perceived importance of gaining an education in Ireland and Irish qualifications, through the medium of English, and had decided that this would give them an edge in a competitive global labour market (see case study of Antoni in Box 2).

Philip was one participant who commented on the ease of the subjects he learned at school in Ireland in comparison to his home country, Poland. When asked to draw a picture and describe his plans for the future, he produced the drawing shown in Figure 2.2. He commented that he had seen many Irish people in his neighbourhood who were 'drunk' and that they 'hung out' in the local park which he frequented with his friends. He did not feel that he would become an alcoholic if he stayed in Ireland but he did speculate on the situation of people on the margins of Irish society. His parents, particularly his mother, were keen to remain living in Ireland but they had retained a property in their home city in Poland in case his father had to return to work there. Philip and

Box 2

Antoni, age fifteen

Antoni had moved to Ireland along with his younger brother nine months before this interview. He had not been out of Poland before. He moved to live with his father, leaving his seventeen-year-old sister behind in Poland, living with their grandmother, because she did not want to migrate. They have visited each other since he migrated but he does not think that they really miss each other. His father works very long hours so when they are not in school, Antoni and his brother make their own entertainment. They have Polish friends, who they meet at school in their English language classes, and these are the people they socialise with at weekends. They visit each other's houses and go to the local park. Antoni keeps in touch with his friends in Poland using internet technologies. He is unsure where he wants to live in the future but he is pleased that he has learnt good English since moving to Ireland as he thinks this is beneficial for his future employment options.

Figure 2.2 Philip's drawing of himself in the future

his family were very aware of the precarious nature of their existence in Ireland, dependent on his father being able to keep his job. As conjecture over the state of the Irish economy and what the future held for Ireland grew, families such as Philip's were keenly aware that they needed to have a plan for the future, one that would provide for their financial needs.

Conclusions

Similarities can be drawn between the CEE young migrants who moved to Ireland in the first decade of the 2000s, some of whom are likely to out-migrate predominantly because of the economic situation and associated unemployment, and those Irish young people currently emigrating to Australia, the USA, the UK and other European countries in increasing numbers (CSO, 2010). Free movement within the EU, and the possibility of applying for visa and work permits in other western nations, enables these young people to decide their futures in the context of possible migration and frequent mobility. Having experienced migration once, adjusting to a new country and culture and living transnationally, the prospect of migrating again was not off-putting for some of the CEE young people who participated in this study. Based on qualitative analysis, it may be best to conceptualise their out-migration from Ireland not as return-migration (i.e. to the location of origin), as is frequently speculated, but as onward migration to new destinations. Quantitatively, it is too soon to tell how many of these young people have emigrated or how many are planning to. However, for those who do, although their senses of stability seem to be found in their national identity, their experiences of intra-EU migration and transnationalism are likely to have enabled them to develop cross-cultural competencies that they can draw upon in their new migratory situations.

Notes

1 For discussion of these young migrants' subjective identities see Ní Laoire, Carpena-Méndez, Tyrrell et al. (2011), Chapter 4.
2 Conducted as part of the Migrant Children Project at University College Cork funded by a European Marie Curie Excellence grant.
3 www.internationalhero.co.uk/a/atomant.htm, accessed 1 February 2011.

References

Barrett, A. (2009) EU Enlargement and Ireland's Labour Market. IZA Discussion Paper No. 4260. Bonn: Institute for the Study of Labour (IZA).

Barrett, A., and Bergin, A. (2009) 'Estimating the impact of immigration in Ireland', *Nordic Journal of Political Economy* 35, 2: 1–15.

Bash, L. and Zezlina-Phillips, E. (2006) 'Identity, boundary and schooling: perspectives on the experiences and perceptions of refugee children', *Intercultural Education* 17, 1: 113–28.

Bryan, A. (2009) 'The intersectionality of nationalism and multiculturalism in the Irish curriculum: teaching against racism?', *Race, Ethnicity and Education* 12, 3: 297–317.

Bushin, N. and White, A. (2010) 'Migration politics in Ireland: exploring the impacts on young people's geographies', *Area 42*, 2: 170–80.

Central Statistics Office (CSO) (2007) *Census 2006: Volume 1 – Population Classified by Area*. Dublin: Stationery Office.

Central Statistics Office (CSO) (2008) *Census 2006: Non-Irish Nationals Living in Ireland*. Dublin: Stationery Office.

Central Statistics Office (CSO) (2009) *Population and Migration Estimates – April 2009*. Cork and Dublin: Central Statistics Office.

Central Statistics Office (CSO) (2010) *Population and Migration Estimates – April 2010*. Cork and Dublin: Central Statistics Office.

Central Statistics Office (CSO) (2011) *Census Commentary 1 & 2 – June 2011*. Cork and Dublin: Central Statistics Office.

Charles, K. (2009) *Separated Children Living in Ireland: a Report by the Ombudsman for Children's Office*. Dublin: Ombudsman for Children's Office.

Cotterell, J. (1996) *Social Networks and Social Influences in Adolescence*. London: Routledge.

Darmody, M., Tyrrell, N. and Song, S. (2011) *The Changing Faces of Ireland: Exploring the Lives of Immigrant Children and Young People*. Rotterdam: Sense.

de Block, L. and Buckingham, D. (2007) *Global Children, Global Media: Migration, Media and Childhood*. Basingstoke: Palgrave Macmillan.

Devine, D. (2011) *Making a Difference? Immigration and Schooling in Ireland*. Manchester: Manchester University Press.

Ellis, M. (2001) 'What future for whites? Population projections and racial imaginaries in the US', *International Journal of Population Geography* 7: 213–29.

Fanning, B. (2011) *Immigration and Social Cohesion in the Republic of Ireland*. Manchester: Manchester University Press.

Finney, N. and Simpson, L. (2009) *Sleepwalking to Segregation? Challenging Myths about Race and Immigration*. Bristol: Policy Press.

Gilligan, R., Curry, P., McGrath, J., Murphy, D., Ní Raghallaigh, M. and Rogers, M. (2010) *In the Front Line of Integration: Young People Managing Migration to Ireland*. Dublin: Trinity College Dublin.

Halfacree, K. and Boyle, P. (1993) 'The challenge facing migration research: the case for a biographical approach', *Progress in Human Geography* 17: 333–48.

Ní Laoire, C., Bushin, N., Carpena-Méndez, F. and White, A. (2009) *Tell Me About Yourself: Migrant Children's Experiences of Moving to and Living in Ireland*. Cork: University College Cork.

Ní Laoire, C., Carpena-Méndez, F., Tyrrell, N. and White, A. (2011) *Childhood and Migration in Europe: Portraits of Mobility, Identity and Belonging in Contemporary Ireland*. Farnham: Ashgate.

Orellana, M., Thorne, B., Chee, A., and Law, E. (2001) 'Transnational childhoods: the participation of children in processes of family migration', *Social Problems* 48, 4: 572–91.

Peach, C. (1996) 'Does Britain have ghettos?', *Transactions of the Institute of British Geographers* 22, 1: 216–35.

Reay, D. and Lucey, H. (2000) '"I don't really like it here but I don't want to be anywhere else" – children and inner city council estates', *Antipode* 32, 4: 410–28.

Ruhs, M. (2006) 'Recent trends in immigration to Ireland', in *Managing Migration in Ireland: A Social and Economic Analysis. A Report by the International Organization for Migration for the National Economic and Social Council of Ireland, No. 116*. Dublin: National Economic and Social Council, pp. 9–22.

Ruhs, M. and Quinn, E. (2009) *Migration Information Source. Ireland: From Rapid Immigration to Recession*, www.migrationinformation.org/Profiles/display.cfmID=740, accessed 2 June 2010.

Skrbis, Z., Baldassar, L. and Poynting, S. (2007) 'Introduction – negotiating belonging: migration and generations', *Journal of Intercultural Studies* 28, 5: 261–9.

Smyth, J. (2011) 'Over 500 destitute EU nationals sent home', *Irish Times*, 5 March, www.irishtimes.com/newspaper/ireland/2011/0305/1224291372271.html, accessed 16 September 2011.

Somerville, W. and Sumption, M. (2009) *Immigration in the UK: The Recession and Beyond*. London: Equality and Human Rights Commission.

Spencer, S., Ruhs, M., Anderson, B. and Rogaly, B. (2007) *Migrants' Lives Beyond the Workplace: The Experiences of Central and Eastern Europeans in the UK*. York: Joseph Rowntree Foundation.

Taguma, M., Kim, M., Wurzburg, G. and Kelly, F. (2009) *OECD Reviews of Migrant Education: Ireland*. Paris: OECD.

White, A., Ní Laoire, C., Tyrrell, N. and Carpena-Méndez, F. (2011) 'Children's roles in transnational migration', *Journal of Ethnic and Migration Studies* 37, 8: 1159–70.

3

Migrants in the fields: making work pay

Sally Daly

This happens. You know, one Saturday night we decided to make a small party; it had been agreed that we would be free the next day. Then, at eleven o'clock [p.m], he was there at the window, telling us that he needed us to work at seven a.m. [Sunday] for an order that had just been faxed through. What could we do?
(Andrzej and Evelina, interview in farm accommodation, November 2009)

This chapter draws from ethnographic fieldwork to consider recent changes in the profile of horticultural labour in Ireland and attempts to situate the behaviour and actions of growers and workers in relation to local and global economic processes.[1] It explores how uneven production within horticulture, aligned with changes to state welfare provisions following accession of the EU-12, has impacted on migrant workers and their families. The migrant workforce has made it possible for Irish growers to invest in specific cropping choices in order to maintain production in a highly competitive market. Even with post-Celtic Tiger Ireland's rising unemployment rates, rescaling and adaptations within the horticultural sector remain contingent on the availability of migrant labour. The alternative to the migrant labour force is not a return to domestic labour but rather reduced production or even exit from the market (Bord Bia, 2007). However, the impermanent nature of horticultural production has direct implications for the reproduction of transnational family units and their ability to maintain family integrity. The migrant family stories shared here begin to reveal a human cost to locally produced food.

During the first decade of the new millennium, the discussion on the future of agriculture and food production was bifurcated between promoting the export potential of Irish food and shifting production to more localised (and thus supposedly sustainable) food systems. Consumable horticulture is implicated in the latter because, with the exception of mushrooms, it is largely targeted at the domestic market. But horticulture has emerged as a precariously positioned production sector because individual producers operate without subsidies unlike other areas of agriculture supported under the Common Agricultural Policy (CAP).[2] In addition, power relations within food chains have become reorganised with multinational retail corporations exerting increasing control over both food supply sources and activities of food processors and traders (Lang and Heasman, 2004; Tovey, 2007). These factors render the agricultural sector in general, and horticulture in particular, highly vulnerable to market fluctuations and producers must continuously strive to reduce their costs.

Changes in production to meet consumer demand: the role of migrant labour

In parallel with changes such as centralised distribution along with concentration within the food retail market, production within the horticulture sector has seen significant consolidation. During the first decade of the twenty-first century, the number of growers in field crop, protected vegetable crop and soft fruit production declined while overall production areas and value of output increased (DAFF and Bord Bia, 2008; 2009) following long-term trends evident since the 1980s (e.g. Bord Glas, 2001a; 2001b; 2001c). Between 1999 and 2008, the number of field vegetable growers declined by 44 per cent (DAFF and Bord Bia, 2009) and soft fruit growers dropped by 66 per cent (DAFF and Bord Bia, 2008). At the same time, although horticulture represents a marginal proportion of the agricultural sector in terms of farm-gate value and scale of production, it has a disproportionately larger labour force highlighting its labour intensity (Bord Bia, 2007). Therefore, while the number of growers is in decline, the type of crops increasing in production area and that represent higher value output, including broccoli, cabbage, lettuce, scallions and strawberries, all require manual harvesting and thus a reliable workforce. Wells' (1996) work on profiling the strawberry industry in California provides a relevant comparative analysis for the Irish sector. She identified an investment in manually harvested crops and away from mechanisation and capital-intensive production as a strategy implemented by growers. In that case, it was the labour-intensive nature of speciality crops that buffered growers from external shocks because it lessened the cost-price squeeze of high capital investments in machinery. She noted that specific cropping choices were partly motivated by the availability of cheap and plentiful labour (i.e. undocumented labour), relative to the high costs of fixed capital, as well as the high per acre income. Evidence from Irish growers suggests that the turn to specific cropping choices has also been contingent upon the availability of a migrant labour force, as borne out by the following account:

> It must have been the late '90s when, suddenly, you had a rush of East Europeans and … that changed everything. What that meant, like, was that you could actually go after producing products that took a lot of labour. You could physically get people to work, like; you could not get an Irish person to work picking, there is no way. (Tim, a former field crop vegetable grower, November 2010)

Even with highly mechanised crop production, there are a number of activities that require a labour force, including the work done in co-located pack-houses on farms to process output, and this has also underpinned the demand for horticultural labour. During the Celtic Tiger years, consumers sought out pre-packaged horticultural products. The shift towards such convenience foods reflected new consumption practices associated with changing labour trends and rising disposable income (Boucher-Hayes and Campbell, 2009; Warde and Martens, 2000). Accordingly, the number of on-farm pack-houses and cold storage units increased in Ireland, particularly for protected crops and soft fruit production (DAFF and Bord Bia, 2008), and between 1999 and 2009 nearly all field vegetable growers shifted from producing a basic commodity to turning out shelf-ready product (DAFF and Bord Bia, 2009).

In the case of horticultural intensification in the UK, Geddes and Scott (2010) suggest that the availability of a migrant workforce has acted as a de facto industry subsidy to keep food prices low and to avoid excessive reliance on imports. While the benefits to consumers are obvious, this has negative implications for workers. In an analysis of African immigrant employment in Spanish agriculture, Hoggart and Mendoza (1999) emphasise the uncertainty of farm work due to the lack of permanent contracts accompanied by low wages and poor working conditions.

A brief profile of the horticultural labour force

As Geddes and Scott (2010) have observed, data capture for an industry with a large need for a temporary and mobile workforce is an inherently difficult task. In 2002, an estimated 10,800 full-time equivalents[3] (FTEs) were employed in both food and amenity horticultural production; the most recent available estimate is more than 6,100 FTEs in 2007 (Bord Bia, 2007). According to Bord Glas (2002), the shift to employing non-EU workers in the Irish horticultural sector began in the 1999/2000 period, the first full year of production and supply into a centralised distribution system. They noted that by 2000/2001, 17 per cent of work permits issued by the Department of Enterprise Trade and Employment (DETE) were for the agricultural/horticultural/fisheries sector with the mushroom and field vegetable sub-sectors obtaining the highest numbers. Subsequently, the expansion of the EU in 2004 and 2007 to include the twelve new member states (NMS) provided Irish growers with access to a considerable migrant workforce. Since 2004, a large number of accession country workers have taken up employment as hired farm workers on growing sites in Ireland to the extent that by 2006, 84 per cent of the horticultural workforce was identified as non-Irish (Bord Bia, 2007).

Why choose Ireland?

Key drivers of post-accession migratory flows include labour market disequilibria, employment opportunities and wage differentials (World Bank, 2008) as well as the existing welfare gap, with real and material differences in the standards of living and levels of social security between the EU-15 and NMS. Even with the economic downturn in Ireland, and improved conditions in some Central and Eastern European economies, Krings, Bobek, Moriarty *et al.* (2009) suggest that continued participation in the Irish labour market reflects the comparably worse situation in the home countries. However, it is important to recognise that the decision to migrate is not exclusively an economic one. East–West migration may be informed by participation in social networks and may thus be made in a collectivist context, especially that of a family (Oyserman, Coon and Kemmelmeier, 2002). It may also be informed by exposure to social, ethnic and gender conflicts (Godzimirski, 2005).

The uneven nature of production and making work pay

In the past, short periods of production could be met by Irish people willing to work for the season, as one former processed-strawberry grower described in July 2010: 'We'd have buses coming from Waterford or Hacketstown, or Tumon or Wexford Town. It was all summer, kind of, casual labour, you know: children from school holidays, from primary and secondary school, and their parents and families, whole families used to come and pick.' But the nature of contemporary production practices militate against such a casual labour force. Furthermore, the quality requirements of supermarkets have influenced work-place regimes aimed at intensifying workers' efforts at harvesting and ensuring that only those products that meet quality requirements are packaged (Rogaly, 2008). Irish worker expectations have also changed. During the Celtic Tiger years, recruitment drives targeted horticultural labour from outside Ireland as 'it was during this time that our young and educated workforce became more selective in terms of seeking white-collar employment in the information and communication sector rather than unskilled manual work' (Bord Glas, 2002: 6). Although, as Bradley (1988) has suggested, farm labour has never carried a high social status in Ireland. Therefore, even with rising unemployment nationally, the low pay and insecure nature of horticultural employment that characterises it as part of the secondary labour market also renders it unattractive to the Irish workforce and dependent on migrant labour. In addition, evidence from supporting welfare beneficiaries into short-term, seasonal work (Bord Glas, 1988; 1994) highlights the challenge of aligning work that tends to be erratic in nature with benefit payments. This has a direct impact on the ability of seasonal horticultural labourers to manage a coherent year-round work strategy. As Geddes and Scott (2010: 212) suggest, 'the episodic nature of low-paid work can make it difficult for domestic workers to make work pay, and it will probably always be easier to move in and out of the secondary labour markets than move in and out of the benefit system.'

State intervention in the horticultural labour market

Labour demand volatility is a well-established trait of the horticultural sector. Intensification in horticultural production combined with the transition to centralised distribution in the late 1990s increased demand for horticultural workers. Consequently, the State moved to support the horticultural labour market with the 2001 introduction of a contract labour programme called the Seasonal Horticultural Workers Scheme (SHWS)[4] building on the more general work permit system initiated in 1999. Such temporary labour programmes within agriculture are part of an established response to the fluctuating demands of the sector and other examples include the Seasonal Agricultural Workers Scheme (SAWS) in the UK (Rogaly, 2008) and the Bracero program in the USA (see Wells, 1996). A key labour market policy came into force when the EU enlarged with the accession of ten NMS in 2004, followed by the qualified accession of Romania and Bulgaria in 2007; Ireland was one of only three countries in the EU (along with Sweden and the United Kingdom) to give citizens of the acceded countries full access to its labour market (Barrett, 2009).

What has emerged, as seen with horticultural labour markets elsewhere, is the need for a consistent supply of workers to occupy temporary and insecure positions on farms. Segmented labour market theory (Piore, 1979) shows how firms can offset the costs of an uncertain market, an issue highly pertinent to the unpredictable vagaries of food supply and demand, by passing the uncertainty onto groups of workers. Thus, while a core group of staff is needed onsite on a relatively permanent basis, a segment of the labour force is employed as and when needed. Therefore, in contrast to higher paid and more secure jobs in the primary labour market where employees also enjoy recourse to benefits when laid off such as redundancy payments, the secondary labour market is characterised by Piore as 'a means of evasion, a sector of the labour market that is not subject to restrictions or lay-off and discharge to which the unstable portion of demand can be transferred' (1979: 79).

Corresponding with the evasive nature of secondary labour markets identified by Piore, there is evidence in Ireland of informal farm-level arrangements overriding formal labour market regulations within agriculture. Official policy states that Romanian and Bulgarian nationals can only take up insurable employment (that in turn enables access to welfare benefits) in Ireland if they hold a valid work permit or if, prior to 1 January 2007 when both countries acceded to the EU, they were working in the State on a work permit valid for at least twelve months (Free Legal Aid Centre, 2010). However, in 2007, while some 14,300 Romanians registered for work eligibility in Ireland,[5] only 119 work permits were actually issued to Romanian nationals.[6] Thus, there is an inconsistency between those registering for work eligibility and those taking up official work permit positions that offer the potential to access the welfare system eventually should the need arise. Anecdotal evidence suggests that while Romanians have been employed across many industry sectors, legitimately paying into the social insurance and tax systems, because they do not have work permits, and thus are not officially sanctioned to work, they are prohibited from accessing state support. The precarious nature of migrant workers' social welfare protection was actually exacerbated with the accession of the EU-10 in 2004 when the State imposed restrictions on access to welfare entitlements in the form of the Habitual Residence Condition (HRC). Such restrictions have a direct impact on the horticultural workforce whose employment, and therefore residency, can be erratic in nature. Although the mobility of workers across the EU is facilitated by the regulations on social security (Regulations 1408/71 and 574/72), in practice, the ease with which individuals can migrate between positions in secondary labour markets across different countries as well as in and out of welfare systems is likely to be problematic. The next section assesses the challenging realities of being such migrant labourers in the Irish horticultural sector through the stories of two transnational family groups.

Family strategies

Seasonal rhythms within horticulture have long called for a temporary workforce (Geddes and Scott, 2010; Mitchell, 1996; Wells, 1996). What has changed within the context of horticultural production in Ireland is the scale of the industry and innovations in growing techniques that extend seasons with resultant implications for labour requirements. Catalina, a forty-three year-old Romanian Roma woman, has interacted with specific labour market policies for over a decade to support her family and to meet essential healthcare needs for herself and her children. In 2000, she entered into insurable employment through the asylum system, which at the time granted asylum applicants access to the labour market (Loyal, 2002). Catalina was recruited into her first position by her landlady in Cork to work on a local farm with a three-month labour demand during the harvest. Her husband, Gregorz, joined her from Romania and thus they initiated a ten-year episodic relationship with a grower, which allowed them to plan a strategy, albeit precariously, around work on his farm from January to March. They successfully used their family network to source other positions, as well as getting job referrals to other sites through employers, migrating back to Romania during periods of unemployment. Their 2007 return-trip to Ireland coincided with Romania's accession to the EU, when they were joined by Cosmina and Kostal, their daughter and son, respectively. Cosmina and Kostal both successfully registered for work eligibility and were inserted into this precarious labour pattern. The family's migratory employment pattern entailed periods of work interspersed with unemployment for which they had no recourse to benefits. Amongst the Romanian cohort, something of the peripatetic life of workers in Mitchell's (1996) California is called to mind. He writes of itinerant workers journeying between different geographical regions, always prompted by news of another job, another short-term possibility, and considering themselves as 'permanent "floaters"' who had abandoned the idea of steady work (1996: 51).[7] Cosmina described the different types of short-term, seasonal work she has been involved with over the years:

> Yes, in 2007, 2008, 2009, I worked all the time, fruit picking and packing. [Open-field] flower picking, [Christmas] wreath making, in one place. I was also cutting the branches [of the Christmas trees] and, after that, I cut the foliage and we made the wreaths from a machine for the doors. Also, packing flowers, making bouquets. I started the next season again

before Easter, the flowers again, packing. They were paying by the hour.
(Catalina and Cosmina, interview in rented house, May 2010)

The duality of the family's position in making social insurance contributions and paying into the tax system while not being afforded any of the associated benefits is particularly exposed at times of illness. Kostal became ill in 2010, leaving him without work and with the added problem of requiring medical attention, thus exposing the limitations of their family's position within the labour market. Catalina secured work on a farm as a cleaner so that she could afford to pay for her son to have an operation in Ireland although he had to return to Romania to recover as he had no recourse to benefit support during this period of unemployment in Ireland. Catalina herself was diagnosed with cancer in Cork in 2002; accordingly, her work strategy has involved trying to secure work close to where she first received treatment for cancer. Ultimately though, maintaining access to a standard of healthcare in terms of cancer treatment has become secondary in relation to her part in the reproduction of the wider family. Although she and her husband have made claims for unemployment benefit following harvests, they have not been successful. These accounts show how family members have used the locations of both Ireland and Romania to make a coherent living and working strategy possible for themselves.

By contrast, with full access to the labour market following Poland's accession to Europe in 2004, Andrzej and Evelina, both in their late twenties, signed up to the SHWS through their university in Krakow. Both had undertaken degrees in food science, although neither of them came from an agricultural background. They had not planned on making a long-term move to Ireland but instead pursued a temporary strategy of saving money with a view to returning to Poland with more secure prospects. As their work strategy has evolved, it resonates with Piore's concept of 'target earners' (1979: 95–8), where their aim has been to earn a certain amount of money while abroad, staying and working longer to meet their targets. This strategy has coincided with the development of the cropping pattern on site and their period of employment has extended each year as the grower has used innovative technology to prolong the seasonal reach of the crop. In the last two years, they have worked onsite for between eight and nine months. Andrzej explains how they benefit from longer periods on the farm, which is directly related to the problem of securing temporary employment in Poland in between periods on the farm:

> It's good staying longer because we don't have a job in … Actually, I had a job in Poland but not so good. And when you come here, it's much different when you stay here [over successive years]. Three months, four, five, it's much better when you stay here longer because you can

make more money … When you go back to Poland, for example, in November, it's very difficult to find another job in Poland because it's last of, end of year, we can't find another job … And we decided to start to build a house so we need more money. (Andrzej and Evelina, interview in farm accommodation, October 2009)

Six years on from their initial encounter with the Irish horticultural labour market, Andrzej and Evelina have graduated to supervisory positions on the site, taking on an increased level of responsibility. However, their hours of work are long, they frequently work without a day off during the season and the length of the working season on the farm remains hard to predict. Thus, even as they have become inserted into more long-term positions, Evelina and Andrzej's ability to plan is still very much informed by the demands of the specific crop, which are in turn affected by the vagaries of weather patterns and biological processes. For example, an abundant harvest in September 2009 was attributed by the grower to the late planting of his second crop due to production pressure earlier in the year. The weather remained mild late into 2009, encouraging further growth of the crop. In 2010, the grower revised his planting schedule to avoid an oversupply in September and growth was further curtailed by the early frost. Thus in 2009, Andrzej and Evelina's working season finished in December, while in 2010, it ended in late October, highlighting the uneven nature of production within a single site over a two-year period.

In addition, while they have worked within Ireland for a six-year period, extending the working year up to eight and nine months over the last two years, their intention to start a family in 2011 has been impacted by the social security rules that govern access to maternity benefit. Due to the seasonal nature of the work and their strategy of living in Poland over the 'off peak' season, during which time Evelina does not work, they do not qualify for maternity benefit in Ireland. To qualify for contributory payments in Ireland (e.g. maternity benefit), a worker must have accrued a specific amount of social insurance payments in the relevant tax year, that is two years prior to the year of application (DSFA, 2010: 13). Thus, the uneven nature of production within their primary worksite has directly impacted on their ability to plan for the future, even down to their family planning.

Conclusions

The horticultural sector in Ireland is precariously positioned vis-à-vis the broader export-focused and heavily subsidised agricultural market. Growers are under pressure to compete in a globalised marketplace with supermarkets sourcing cheaper produce through international buying chains. Since the late 1990s, the horticultural industry has had access to a deregulated trans-European labour force. This labour force operates with a level of mobility and transiency within a precarious employment sector driven by the uneven and impermanent nature of production.

As Anderson suggests, subjectivities are not bound to the present but are concerned with the future, 'with potential, with where one is going, as well as where one is' (2009: 420). How this relates to the temporal nature of immigration or labour market controls is important in understanding the positioning of both sets of workers evidenced here. Attention to the temporal dimension of migration has specific resonance with the horticultural labour market. By taking matters of time into consideration (period in a job, length of time between periods of work, hours of work and the seasonal reach of specific crops), the insecure labour conditions of precarious workers are highlighted. Indeed, Waite suggests that 'the exploitation of the precarious worker may occur primarily through the medium of time' (2009: 414).

A more detailed consideration of workers' experiences on sites of production can paint a picture of place-based experiences of labour. As Rogaly (2009) notes, it helps to uncover how agency is manifest on sites of production, even where that agency might be informally negotiated and outside the context of collective bargaining. What the research in this chapter reveals is how precarity is inherent within the Irish horticultural labour market, even with extensions in seasons facilitated by innovative technology and notwithstanding growers' efforts to maintain year-round production.

Importantly too, evidence suggests that the horticultural labour force constitutes a new secondary segment of the Irish labour market. The short-term nature of much of the work, exacerbated by the poor contractual arrangements and the problematic nature of accessing work-related benefits, may all act as disincentives for those workers who find an improved work offer elsewhere. However, the existence of workers with restricted labour market access within the secondary labour market, who thus may more readily accept poor terms and conditions, reinforces the segmentation of the labour market (Martin, 1993). As seen in this research, where both sets of workers operated without contracts, informal farm-level arrangements can override formal labour market regulations and these arrangements tend to favour growers as the stronger party in the employee–employer relationship.

The seasonality of horticultural work may provide an opportunity for migrant workers to remain embedded in their own material reality. Labrianidis and Sykas (2009) have shown how Albanian migrant workers in Greece successfully exploit seasonal work there to enable material gain in the home country. Problems arise, though, where the episodic nature of the work can make it difficult for workers to make work pay and to develop a coherent strategy both across the secondary labour market and in relation to benefit payments. What is evident with both transnational family groups considered in this chapter is the problematic nature of horticultural work in providing a stable income throughout the year and the extent to which it limits their ability to manage a coherent, year-round work strategy.

Where formerly the State intervened to support the horticultural labour force, evidence from this research suggests that the uneven development of production within horticulture persists and innovations in production have not resolved the negative impact on the labour force. The extent to which the cost of social reproduction is currently borne by migrants on these farms points to the issue of the hidden cost for the workforce. And so the local draws upon the global recursively and in a hidden process.

Notes

1   During ethnographic fieldwork, sixteen grower and twenty worker interviews were conducted. There was sustained engagement with three families over a twenty-four month period, of which two inform this discussion. Relationships developed with families were preceded by periods of participant observation involving work on two horticultural sites. All names and crop references have been changed to ensure anonymity.

2   The Common Agricultural Policy has provided direct price supports to horticulture via producer organisations. These have been successful within mushroom production but have had significantly limited uptake within the broader horticultural sector (Department of Agriculture, Fisheries and Food, 2010).

3   1 FTE = one employee working full-time. It allows the calculation of comparable statistics in a sector where people work varying hours per week.

4   The Seasonal Horticulture Workers Scheme was established to run from 2001 to 2009 and targeted students from Eastern and Central Europe (Bord Bia, 2007).

5   Personal Public Service Numbers – Allocation By Nationality – All Countries 2007, www.welfare.ie/EN/Topics/PPSN/Pages/ppsn_all_month07.aspx, accessed 14 May 2011.

6   Statistical Tables and Company Listings for the Employment Permits Section, www.djei.ie/labour/workpermits/statistics.htm, accessed 12 August 2011.

7   Holmes (1998) writing about the Irish 'tattie-hookers', migratory potato pickers in Scotland in the early twentieth century, also has points of comparison with this contemporary workforce.

References

Anderson, B. (2009) 'What's in a name? Immigration controls and subjectivities: the case of au pairs and domestic worker visa holders in the UK', *Subjectivity* 29: 407–24.

Barrett, A. (2009) *EU Enlargement and Ireland's Labour Market.* IZA Discussion Paper No. 4260. Bonn: Institute for the Study of Labour (IZA).

Bord Bia (2007) *Labour Review of Horticulture in Ireland.* Dublin: Bord Bia.

Bord Glas (1988) *Horticultural Newsletter,* 1 (7). Dublin: Bord Glas.

Bord Glas (1994) *Horticultural Newsletter,* 8 (3). Dublin: Bord Glas.

Bord Glas (2001a) *Market Intelligence. Sector Profile. Fruit.* Dublin: Bord Glas.

Bord Glas (2001b) *Market Intelligence. Sector Profile. Potatoes.* Dublin: Bord Glas.

Bord Glas (2001c) *Market Intelligence. Sector Profile. Protected Crops.* Dublin: Bord Glas.

Bord Glas (2002) *Horticultural Labour Force Review.* Dublin: Bord Glas.

Boucher-Hayes, P. and Campbell, S. (2009) *Basket Case: What's Happening to Ireland's Food?* Dublin: Gill and Macmillan.

Bradley, D. (1988) *Farm Labourers: Irish Struggle 1900–1976.* Belfast: Athol Books.

Department of Agriculture, Fisheries and Food (DAFF) (2010) *Ireland's Horticulture Sector: Background Paper – Food Harvest 2020.* Dublin: Department of Agriculture, Fisheries and Food.

Department of Agriculture, Fisheries and Food (DAFF) and Bord Bia (2008) *Soft Fruit and Protected Crop Census.* Dublin: Department of Agriculture, Fisheries and Food and Bord Bia.

Department of Agriculture, Fisheries and Food (DAFF) and Bord Bia (2009) *National Field Vegetable Census.* Dublin: Department of Agriculture, Fisheries and Food and Bord Bia.

Department of Social and Family Affairs (DSFA) (2010) *Your Social Security Rights in Ireland: a Guide for EU Citizens.* Dublin: Department of Social and Family Affairs, www.welfare.ie/EN/Policy/EU/Pages/SocialSecurityRightsIreland.aspx, accessed 16 July 2011.

Free Legal Aid Centre (2010) *Guide to the Habitual Residence Condition.* Dublin: Free Legal Aid Centre (FLAC), www.flac.ie/download/pdf/habitual_residence_condition_guide_final.pdf, accessed 23 August 2011.

Geddes, A. and Scott, S. (2010) 'UK food businesses' reliance on low-wage migrant labour: a case of choice or constraint?', in M. Ruhs and B. Anderson (eds), *Who Needs Migrant Workers? Labour Shortages, Immigration and Public Policy.* Oxford: Oxford University Press, pp. 193–218.

Godzimirski, J. M. (2005) *Tackling Welfare Gaps. The East European Transition and New Patterns of Migration to Norway.* Oslo: Norwegian Institute of International Affairs (NUPI).

Hoggart, K. and Mendoza, C. (1999) 'African immigrant workers in Spanish agriculture', *Sociologia Ruralis* 39: 538–62.

Holmes, H. (1998) 'Improving the housing conditions for the Irish migratory potato workers in Scotland: the work of the Bishops' (Gresham) Committee', *Rural History* 9, 1: 57–74.

Krings, T., Bobek, A., Moriarty, E., Salamonska, J. and Wickham, J. (2009) 'Migration and recession: Polish migrants in post-Celtic Tiger Ireland', *Sociological Research Online*, www.socresonline.org.uk/14/2/9.html, accessed 14 July 2011.

Labrianidis, L. and Sykas, T. (2009) 'Geographical proximity and immigrant labour in agriculture: Albanian immigrants in the Greek countryside', *Sociologia Ruralis* 49, 4: 394–414.

Lang, T. and Heasman, M. (2004) *Food Wars: The Global Battle for Mouths, Minds and Market.* London: Earthscan.

Loyal, S. (2002) 'Nation, capitalism and the right to work of asylum seekers in Ireland', in M. Corcoran and M. Peillon (eds), *Ireland Unbound.* Dublin: Institute of Public Administration, pp. 186–99.

Martin, P. L. (1993) 'The missing bridge. How immigrant networks keep Americans out of dirty jobs', *Population and Environment* 14: 539–65.

Mitchell, D. (1996) *The Lie of the Land: Migrant Workers and the California Landscape.* Minneapolis, MN: University of Minnesota Press.

Oyserman, D., Coon, H. and Kemmelmeier, M. (2002) 'Rethinking individualism and collectivism: evaluation of theoretical assumptions and meta-analyses', *Psychological Bulletin* 128: 3–72.

Piore, M. (1979) *Birds of Passage: Migrant Labour and Industrial Societies.* Cambridge: Cambridge University Press.

Rogaly, B. (2008) 'Intensification of workplace regimes in British agriculture: the role of migrant workers', *Population, Space and Place* 14: 497–510.

Rogaly, B. (2009) 'Spaces of work and everyday life: labour geographies and the agency of unorganised temporary migrant workers', *Geography Compass* 3, 6: 1975–87.

Tovey, H. (2007) 'Food and rural sustainable development', in S. O'Sullivan (ed.), *Contemporary Ireland – a Sociological Map.* Dublin: University College Dublin Press, pp. 283–98.

Waite, L., 2009. 'A place and space for a critical geography of precarity?', *Geography Compass* 3, 1: 412–33.

Warde, A. and Martens, L. (2000) *Eating Out: Social Differentiation, Consumption and Pleasure. Cambridge*: Cambridge University Press.

Wells, M. (1996) *Strawberry Fields: Political Class and Work in California Agriculture.* Ithaca, NY: Cornell University Press.

World Bank (2008) *EU October 2008. In focus: an Update on Labor Migration from Poland.* Washington, DC: World Bank, http://siteresources.worldbank.org/ECAEXT/Resources/258598-1225385788249/infocuslaboroct08.pdf, accessed 9 June 2011.

4

Raising the emerald curtain: communities and collaboration along the Irish border

Caroline Creamer and Brendan O'Keeffe

Up until the early 1990s, areas adjacent to the border between the Republic of Ireland and Northern Ireland were synonymous with ethno-nationalist tensions and socio-economic decline. The descent of the 'emerald curtain',[1] with the partition of the island of Ireland in 1921, divided communities politically and economically but had a limited impact on social and cultural interactions. From the late 1960s, however, political agitation following the Civil Rights Movement, the subsequent deployment of British troops, emerging paramilitarism, and direct rule from Westminster, would collectively lead to thirty years of violence, generally referred to as the Troubles. During this period of conflict, the emerald curtain became increasingly impenetrable as communities along the border became disconnected, marginalised and peripheral from both Dublin and Belfast.

By 2011, almost fifteen years after the adoption of the 1998 Belfast (Good Friday) Agreement that addressed relationships between both sides of the island among others, local communities are strong advocates of cross-border cooperation. This has been facilitated greatly by the adoption of dedicated EU policies and the emergence of targeted funding programmes, which acknowledge the Irish border region as a distinct area with special needs. Inter-community collaboration at the micro-level advanced considerably during the period of the Celtic Tiger, thus helping to drive the peace process forward and slowly raise the remnants of the emerald curtain. Such collaboration is serving to redress decades of internal isolationist socio-economic, political and physical development policies by promoting social progress, ecological conservation and innovations in economic development, and improving access to local services.

The opening up of the Irish border and the progress of collaborative initiatives along it, parallels a process of deepening integration throughout the European Union (EU). This is associated with nations putting the legacy of world wars and territorial disputes behind them, and striving for peace. The prevalence of peace throughout Europe helped to realise the greatest levels of prosperity ever in the continent's history. In addition, the endorsement of regional development and social, economic and, more recently, territorial cohesion – as part of the wider European project – assumed greater importance. Together, these advances motivated stakeholders across the island of Ireland to pursue a peace process that promotes cross-border engagement, which is increasingly tied to a territorialised social and economic agenda.

This chapter notes how the Irish border has transitioned from a physical, economic and political barrier to a focus for collaborative action, most notably across small-scale settlements (or micro-regional contexts). It considers how, by engaging in cross-border collaboration, communities have contributed to opening up the border and, in turn, availed of the opportunities that arose through the peace process, leverage of funds and the emergence of collaborative and place-based approaches to rural development and spatial planning. The chapter concludes by assessing how the current economic crash and the actual and pending redirection of funding will have consequences for the sustainability of cross-border partnerships and spatial planning in the Irish border context.

A physical, social and economic divide

Borders represent increasingly dynamic aspects of the political, economic and social landscape (Beck, 2008). In Western Europe generally, their role is changing from that of being a divider of societies to becoming a focal point for inter-jurisdictional, inter-governmental and inter-community collaboration. Yet, borders are, first and foremost, physical barriers that represent the political division of spaces (Newman, 2006; Paasi, 2002). In addition, borders can represent and permeate divisions between people and can define sociocultural, socio-economic, and ethno-nationalist identities (Anderson, 2008; van Houtum and Strüver, 2002). The border separating Northern Ireland from the Republic of Ireland has long been a contested space (Coakley and O'Dowd, 2004; 2007); not to the same extent politically as was once the case,[2] but rather 'physically and mentally as many citizens perceive the border as being inconsistent with local economic, community and social linkages and

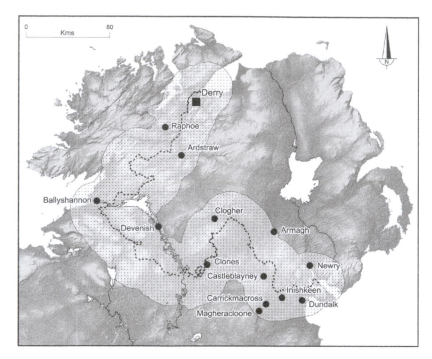

Figure 4.1 The Irish border corridor

patterns' (Creamer, Blair, O'Keeffe *et al.*, 2008: 3). Partition, as laid out in the Government of Ireland Act 1920, has had varying impacts across border towns and villages (Murtagh, 1999; 2002); the construction of the emerald curtain becoming 'a tale of unintended and unforeseen consequences' (Harvey, Kelly, McGearty and Murray, 2005: 12).

In parallel to the Troubles, the 1980s were for the most part a time of economic and demographic crisis for communities across the island of Ireland; particularly so for those located in the rural west/north-west of the island (Varley, Boylan and Cuddy, 1991) and along the Irish border corridor[3] (see Figure 4.1). In these peripheral communities, this crisis was to translate into a reduction in the number of farms, an increase in part-time/off-farm employment, the hollowing out of towns, and generally, a brain-drain from rural communities. The Celtic Tiger boom from the late 1990s – largely confined to south of the border – only went a very small way to addressing these and other challenges facing the border region.

Despite the boom, the Irish border region continued to over-rely on agriculture, and later construction, as the main source of local employment, and remained at a relative disadvantage in terms of attracting external investment.

The persistence of these challenges is attributed to infrastructural deficits and the legacy of disconnected governance, legislative, policy-making and planning systems across both jurisdictions on the island. Yet, the peripherality that was to feed into this cycle of economic decline was a major factor in bringing local communities together to advocate for greater connectivity.

Planning for the borderlands

Cross-border partnerships emerged in the context of post-productivist approaches to rural development from the late 1980s onwards, characterised by a declining emphasis on financial supports for agriculture, and a parallel prominence being placed on the growth of a broader rural economy (ESPON, 2007; Maillat, 1997; O'Keeffe and Douglas, 2009). Initial EU rural programmes tended to focus on compensating for the disadvantages and inequalities of the countryside, with the result that rural areas were regarded as a liability (Creamer, Blair, Keaveney *et al.*, 2009). Recognising the difficulties with such an approach, a shift in the focus of development policy and practice would subsequently acknowledge that such areas can assist in the achievement of balanced regional development through the potential they offer in terms of social, cultural, economic and environmental capital. In this context, the processes of rural restructuring raised questions about future policy direction and opportunities for integrated action, development patterns and the viability of small and dispersed rural settlements (Creamer *et al.*, 2009). More recently, the EU's cohesion policy – with its initial focus on social and economic development since extended to a territorially based approach to sustainable development – is placing an increasing emphasis on the delivery of positive change through integrated, place-based strategies (Barca, 2009; European Union, 2010).

Corresponding to these changes in policy and perspective, the EU gradually established a range of funding programmes to support their implementation. These, together with exchequer and other monies, enabled national policies to adapt to reflect the changing European agenda and, increasingly, local cum regional realities. In the case of cross-border and transnational cooperation, the International Fund for Ireland[4] (IFI) and the Programme for Peace and Reconciliation (or PEACE programme), both dedicated to Northern Ireland and the southern border counties, aimed to stimulate socio-economic revival and growth. More recently, the EU-wide community initiative, INTERREG, has emphasised collaboration on larger-scale, multi-partner projects. Two decades and more later, these funds continue to facilitate the border's dilution and the redress of problems that transcend administrative, jurisdictional and political boundaries (Lennox, 2008). They, together with political agreements such as the Anglo-Irish Agreement of 1985, are credited with attitudinal change (Tannam, 2006), and have proven to be the catalyst for stakeholders coming together around common interests and identities – often tied to place (Jessop, 2003).

Yet, the achievement of balanced development in contested spaces and the focus of the processes required to achieve this, namely spatial governance and planning, 'cannot be divorced from a deeper appreciation of two cultural identities in conflict' (Neill and Ellis, 2008: 88). This takes time to achieve and in areas of conflict it requires a peace process that, in the context of the island of Ireland, provides the conditions for 'more imaginative policy experimentation' to redress the political-economic problems of both jurisdictions (Bradley, 1995: 146). In terms of collaborative spatial planning, this was initially advanced with the publication of the *European Spatial Development Perspective* (European Commission, 1999). This EU-wide emphasis on territorial and vision planning, rather than sectoral and trend planning, would be articulated in two loosely connected spatial strategies for the island of Ireland; namely the Regional Development Strategy (RDS) for Northern Ireland published in 2001 and the National Spatial Strategy (NSS) for the Republic of Ireland published in 2002 (Department for Regional Development, 2001; Department of the Taoiseach, 2002). Over the years, these frameworks have gained significance and now lie at the core of all regional and local development policies, supported in their early days by the publication of a number of common chapters and, more recently, a non-statutory collaborative framework[5] to buttress the emerging strategic cross-border collaborative agenda.

The application of integrated approaches to inter-jurisdictional spatial planning, together with the growing emphasis at all territorial scales to adopt place-based approaches to integrated, cross-sectoral actions, has facilitated a move away from back-to-back planning across the Irish border corridor – whereby authorities in both jurisdictions operated without reference to one another. Addressing the peripherality and marginalisation that resulted from decades of such an approach has also been aided by the evolution of the peace process and growing inter-governmental dialogue on – and advocacy of – the merits of cross-border cooperation. The establishment of a number of cross-border bodies under the 1998 Belfast (Good Friday) Agreement such as InterTradeIreland, Tourism Ireland, Waterways Ireland and most significantly, the North South Ministerial Council, has ensured an influence on policy. This, in concert with the Celtic Tiger economic boom, access to EU funding, and a growing favourable investment environment, enabled the southern government's part-funding of large-scale infrastructural projects along the Irish border during the 2000s: namely, the extension of Derry City Airport and the N2–A5 dual carriageway linking (London)Derry and Dublin via Monaghan. Heightened economic investment in both jurisdictions would also accelerate the formation of an all-island energy market in 2007, and the publication of a number of reports articulating the competitive advantages of an all-island economy (British Irish Intergovernmental Conference, 2006; InterTradeIreland, 2006).

Perplexingly, in contrast to the strategic all-island investments being made, the Celtic Tiger only chugged slowly towards the southern border counties, the 'unspoken belief' being that it was 'still stuck behind a slow-moving tractor somewhere out on the R280' (Dillon, 2001). The slow pace is evidenced by the region's sub-standard roads, low-skilled employment base and poor telecommunications system.

Raising the emerald curtain – and keeping it raised

Ireland's border corridor, while being marginal to the early, largely central-ised, approaches to regional and economic development (Maillat, 1997; Molle, 2007) and wider planning issues, provides a window on the application of more contemporary theories and policy. The institutional arrangements and spatial delineation of cross-border activities along the Irish border corridor from the late 1980s to the mid-2000s have tended to be more localised and smaller in scale (Harvey, 2008) than those adopted in frontier regions on the European mainland. For example, collaborative approaches at the level of the micro-region in Spain have been led by municipal authorities. These *man-comunidades* enable municipalities to pool resources and expertise, and jointly deliver services in areas such as enterprise creation, waste management and environmental conservation across municipal, provincial and, in some cases, regional borders (O'Keeffe, 2011). Public authorities have also taken the lead in promoting transnational inter-regional collaboration, as evidenced by the Trinational Eurodistrict Basel (TEB). The objective of the TEB is to promote sustainable development within the functional territory by coordinating cross-border spatial planning across local, regional and national borders, namely those of France, Switzerland and Germany (Driscoll, Vigier and Leith, 2010). In contrast, cross-border collaboration on the island of Ireland has been initiated and driven from the bottom-up with, as noted by Lennox (2008), the number and scope of stakeholders involved in cross-border development tending to increase expo-nentially with the growth of political and economic opportunities.

In order to better understand and highlight the extent and specifics of col-laboration on the island of Ireland, and specifically within the border corridor, the International Centre for Local and Regional Development (ICLRD)[6] un-dertook in-depth studies of cross-border settlements (Creamer *et al.*, 2008).

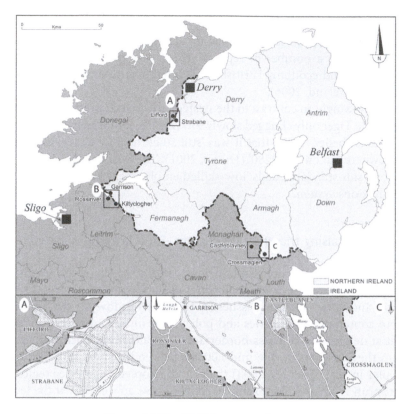

Figure 4.2 The ICLRD case study areas

The research objectives were to determine whether there was an existing cross-border relationship within each settlement cluster (see Figure 4.2), ascertain the driving forces behind that relationship, and determine if these border towns and villages could construct a new collaborative future based on current and potential endogenous growth sectors.

Politically, there had never been a better time for cross-border collaborations; economically, the tide was changing for the worst. Table 4.1 provides a synthesis of the main features of three of these case study clusters. In the case of Lifford-Strabane, the adoption of the twin towns as a flagship project by the IFI was enough to spur a group of local business people from both sides of the border into action. To promote the economic development and regeneration of the area, the Strabane Lifford Development Commission (SLDC) was established in 1993 and, at the advice of local MP and MEP John Hume, this body was constituted as a European Economic Interest Group (EEIG).[7]

Table 4.1 Characteristics of cross-border areas

	Lifford-Strabane	Kiltyclogher-Garrison-Rossinver	Castleblayney-Crossmaglen
Counties	Donegal, Tyrone	Leitrim, Fermanagh	Monaghan, Armagh
Population 2001/2002	13,456 (Strabane) 1,448 (Lifford)	254 (Kiltyclogher) 357 (Garrison) 380 (Rossinver)	1,822 (Castleblayney) 1,459 (Crossmaglen)
Distance between settlements	<1km	10km	12.5km
Historic connections	Informal social and economic linkages; in competition for inward investment – manufacturing hubs; shared work-force and strong family ties.	Social linkages based on existing community links; Kiltyclogher once economic centre for this cross-border area.	Informal cooperation, which continued during the Troubles; emphasis on cultural and social linkages.
Current cross-border activity	Social and economic regeneration; environmental improvements.	Social and eco-nomic regeneration; cultural celebrations; tourism.	Social and economic regeneration; tourism.
Timeframe of current cooperation	Commenced in early 1990s.	Commenced in mid-1980s but not formalised until 2001.	Commenced in mid-1980s but not formalised until 2003.
Examples of initiatives	Strabane Lifford Development Commission; HEART Project; Strabane-Donegal Tourism consortia.	KiltyCashel Project; Rossinver-Belleek Partnership; Green Box Tourism Project.	Castleblayney-South Armagh Partnership; regeneration of South Armagh.
Stakeholders	Private sector through EEIG with local government support.	Community driven; more recently, local government involvement.	Local government driven with growing support from community and other cross-border agencies.
Funding sources	IFI; private sector; PEACE; INTERREG.	IFI; Groundwork NI; INTERREG; PEACE.	IFI; PEACE; INTERREG; local councils.

In a little over a decade, the SLDC had generated funding of more than €25 million for both 'hard' and 'soft' projects in enterprise development and supports, community art projects and physical regeneration schemes. As well as being able to bring together business people and communities from both jurisdictions in the social, economic and cultural regeneration of this cross-border community, the non-political nature of the SLDC has also ensured the support of the respective local councils.

The remaining two cases demonstrate that while attempts were made to maintain cross-border linkages during the Troubles, these were largely informal in nature and failed to stem economic decline and out-migration. They also demonstrate the precariousness of formal partnerships in the current funding structures. The case of Kiltyclogher-Garrison-Rossinver is representative of the many cross-border initiatives that have been led by civil society. Recognising that by working together they could achieve far more for their respective communities than they could by working alone, the KiltyCashel Project was established in 2001. The project has engaged in a range of socio-economic revitalisation programmes including the provision of courses on starting small businesses, establishing a jobs club, and building bridges between the lost generation. However, the partnership was wound up with the cessation of its core funding (under PEACE) in 2009, despite this cross-border community still facing significant social and economic challenges. The KiltyCashel story highlights the critical importance of funding to cross-border collaboration that is small-scale and community-led – a prerequisite at odds with the current shift amongst funding bodies towards large-scale, agency-led projects. Furthermore, it highlights how through endogenous collaborative efforts all aspects of community life can become closely intertwined, although the termination of agency funding means that Kiltyclogher and Garrison are now facing severe challenges in promoting and sustaining economic and social capital.

In a final example, the border towns of Castleblayney and Crossmaglen have continued to lag behind nearby urban centres. This is despite their geographical proximity to the Dublin-Belfast Corridor and the Newry-Dundalk Twin-City Region. In response, and building on existing informal relations, Castleblayney Town Council and Newry and Mourne District Council came together in 2003 to establish the Castleblayney and South Armagh Partnership (CASA). Strategic areas in which CASA is involved include tourism, angling, arts and crafts, business and enterprise, and community development. CASA has greatly enhanced confidence within this cross-border cluster by adopting a multi-agency approach and inviting representatives from a wide range of local agencies, social partners and civil society actors to sit on its management committee. However, with its official funding having come to an end in mid-2008, the partnership is striving to continue its lobbying function on an informal basis.

The experiences from the three case study areas underscore the importance of local collaborative governance in the effective delivery of projects, a strong bottom-up orientation and an emphasis that valorises local assets and resources. They demonstrate the relevance of a territorialised social and economic agenda and the potential of the micro-region[8] as a spatial unit in strategic planning and project development, a theme that finds echoes in the examples of cross-border mobility and consumption patterns discussed by Sara McDowell in Chapter 8.

Inter-jurisdictional and inter-community cooperation along the border remains largely aimed at overcoming the legacies of territorial and political division and redressing the wider economic and social divisions that have caused and accentuated conflict. As such, cooperation tends to be both proactive and reactive, with the majority (because of the emphasis on redressing decades of back-to-back planning) falling into the latter category. With experience, and through the processes of cooperation and collaboration, stakeholders have become border-effective, in principle eliminating the significance of the border. But challenges remain.

Challenges for cross-border partnerships post-Celtic Tiger

Because the manifestation of the Celtic Tiger tended to be sector-specific in the context of the border corridor – rather than being associated with any long-term, strategic, integrated economic or social investment – the localised nature of cross-border projects has largely positioned them below the radar. They tend to suffer from the lack of a 'wow' factor that is often associated with large-scale, strategic initiatives announced by national government. The projects – and more significantly, the funding programmes – can often be at odds with the fast-changing EU policy agenda and with the lack of flexibility built into the funding programmes and associated bureaucratic requirements, meaning that communities cannot adapt or react as fast as they may like.

Consequently, cross-border collaborations are increasingly challenged by the new political and funding environments that emphasise macro-level or regional statistics over local realities. As cumulative figures in 2006/07 showed buoyancy in the Irish economy, funders prematurely perceived that community-level projects were either no longer needed or should become financially self-sustaining, not having envisaged the impending dramatic demise of the Celtic Tiger. While significant levels of funding have been expended on cross-border cooperation between the late 1980s and mid-2000s,[9] the situation for community groups has been complicated by perceived disjointed funding mechanisms, excessively technocratic structures and shifting objectives, and their short-term operations (McCall and O'Dowd, 2008). These operating circumstances can be attributed to the temporary nature and changing focus of funding programmes, and to a transformative EU policy agenda. This has led to a clear disconnect between approaches from the national to the local.

Although partnerships may seek to be sustainable and semi-autonomous, they are in reality dependent on public funding (and thus inevitably funding-driven). This was not a major liability in the past. However, the current economic climate and the loss of government financial supports associated with the collapse of the Celtic Tiger economy threaten the viability of many initiatives, as evidenced by the loss of funding to the KiltyCashel and CASA projects.

Finally, despite cross-border partnerships and their associated activities operating in a defined territory, they have tended to function in parallel and with little reference to the formal planning system in either jurisdiction. This is difficult to explain given that the benefits of such collaborations are most visible at the local level. With an increasing emphasis on place-based approaches to addressing 'disparities, promoting territorial assets ... stimulating local development, and deepening coordination between EU, national and sectoral policies' (European Union, 2010: 20), such disconnects must, like back-to-back planning, be consigned to history.

Conclusions

Political, sectarian and inter-ethnic conflict between the 1920s and 1990s has left a scar on the island of Ireland and, in particular, on communities along the Irish border. The various collaborative initiatives described in this chapter have all contributed – directly and indirectly – to the healing of that scar. Bearing in mind the scale and rurality of most settlements along the border corridor, scale and function have a huge bearing on the thematic focus of cross-border collaboration, and the range of stakeholders who become involved. In parallel, the policy agenda increasingly emphasises the spatial with the sectoral, and advocates both horizontal and vertical coordination between agencies and among local, regional and national-level decision makers. This is significant from a policy perspective, as it is generally considered that development in peripheral and disadvantaged areas should be strategically sequenced; that is, cross-boundary issues should be addressed on a collective basis through, for example, closer policy alignment and joint development plans. Recognising that cooperation can be mutually beneficial, future development should not only be aligned to complementary cross-border settlement policies, where zonings are determined by an identified physical, social and economic need and a clear evidence base, but also tied to jointly recognised – and, where feasible, jointly funded – infrastructure investment programmes.

One of the most effective ways of doing this is through cross-border collaborative engagement that is well-resourced, and recognises and addresses the unremitting and long-standing fractures in social networks and natural trading hinterlands. Putting in place a coherent, medium-term strategy on the future, sustainable, social, economic, cultural and environmental development of border communities is a first step – the beginnings of which are in place through the Barca Report (Barca, 2009), EU 2020 (European Commission, 2010) and the EU Territorial Agenda (European Commission, 2011). With clear objectives and end goals, this cross-border collaborative strategy must continue to support both micro and macro-level initiatives – thus ensuring the viability of the border corridor's towns and villages and the region as a whole, particularly in the aftermath of the Celtic Tiger.

Notes

1   The application of the term emerald curtain to the Irish border is attributed to James Chichester Clark, Prime Minister of Northern Ireland from 1969–71.
2   Northern Ireland still faces considerable political challenges as highlighted during the lengthy negotiations that eventually led to the 2010 Hillsborough Agreement (the focus of which was policing and parades).
3   The most intense area of cross-border activity – and the most challenging milieu (Anderson, 2006) – can be identified as that space represented by the 15km corridor either side of the border itself (Gleeson, 2007). Anderson (2006) defines the border region as an area of 19km either side of the territorial boundary, the distance at which the impact of the border tapers off.
4   Established by the British and Irish governments in 1986.
5   A consultation document entitled *Spatial strategies on the island of Ireland: framework for collaboration* was jointly published in February 2011 by the Department of Environment, Heritage and Local Government (Republic of Ireland) and the Department for Regional Development (Northern Ireland).
6   See www.iclrd.org for further information.
7   The EEIG in effect is the marriage of two bodies: the Lifford Commission and the Strabane Commission. The purpose of an EEIG is to pool the resources of the grouping to support and develop its members' activities and thereby give rise to better outcomes than could be accomplished by an individual group (see Council of the European Communities, 1985).
8   Micro-regions are localised territorial groupings that can span administrative boundaries.

9   Across Northern Ireland and the six border counties, the IFI invested €2.5 billion in over 5,000 projects between 1986 and 2007 (McCarter, 2008), while the PEACE Programme has invested over €1.4 billion in projects between 1995 and 2006, http://europa.eu/legislation_summaries/regional_policy/provisions_and_instruments/g24201_en.htm, accessed 16 June 2011.

References

Anderson, J. (2006) 'Spatial behaviour and political identities in border communities: some research questions.' Presented at the European Urban and Regional Studies (EURS) Conference, Boundaries and Connections in a Changing Europe, 21–24 September, Roskilde, Denmark, www.geography.dur.ac.uk/conferences/Urban_Conference/Programme/pdf_files/James%20Anderson.pdf, accessed 7 December 2010.

Anderson, J. (2008) 'Partition, consociation, border-crossing: some lessons from the national conflict in Ireland/Northern Ireland', *Nations and Nationalism* 14, 1: 85–104.

Barca, F. (2009) *An Agenda for a Reformed Cohesion Policy: a Place-based Approach to Meeting European Union Challenges and Expectations.* Luxembourg: Office for Official Publications of the European Communities.

Beck, J. (2008) 'Lessons from an institute for cross-border cooperation on the Franco-German Border', *The Journal of Cross Border Studies* 3, 38–49.

Bradley, J. (1995) 'Symposium on the economic implications of peace in Ireland', *Journal of the Statistical and Social Inquiry Society of Ireland* 27, 2: 145–70.

British Irish Intergovernmental Conference (2006) *Comprehensive study on the All-island Economy.* Belfast: British Irish Intergovernmental Conference.

Coakley, J. and O'Dowd, L. (2004) 'Studying border change in Ireland: a briefing. Discussion paper (DO1-iii).' Presented at Mapping Frontiers, Plotting Pathways: Routes to North–South Cooperation in a Divided Island, 9 December, Armagh, Northern Ireland.

Coakley, J. and O'Dowd, L. (2007) 'The "new" Irish border: changing political, economic and social dimensions', in J. Coakley and L. O'Dowd (eds), *Crossing the Border: New Relationships between Northern Ireland and the Republic of Ireland.* Dublin: Irish Academic Press.

Council of the European Communities (1985) Council Regulation (EEC) 2137/85 of 25 July 1985 on the European Economic Interest Grouping (EEIG). Luxembourg: Office for Official Publications of the European Communities.

Creamer, C., Blair, N., O'Keeffe, B., Van Egeraat, C. and Driscoll, J. (2008) *Fostering Mutual Benefits in Cross-border Areas – the Challenges and Opportunities in Connecting Irish Border Towns and Villages.* Armagh: International Centre for Local and Regional Development.

Creamer, C., Blair, N., Keaveney, K., O'Keeffe, B. and Driscoll, J. (2009) *Rural Restructuring: Local Sustainable Solutions to the Rural Challenge.* Armagh:

International Centre for Local and Regional Development.

Department for Regional Development (2001) *Shaping Our Future – Regional Development Strategy for Northern Ireland, 2025*. Belfast: Corporate Document Services.

Department of the Taoiseach (2002) *National Spatial Strategy for Ireland 2002–2020: People, Places and Potential*. Dublin: The Stationery Office.

Dillon, W. (2001) 'Where the tiger never roared'. *Irish Independent*, 28 July, www.independent.ie/unsorted/features/where-the-tiger-never-roared-340270.html, accessed 25 January 2011.

Driscoll, J., Vigier, F. and Leith, K. (2010) *The Basel Metropolitan Area: Three Borders – One Metropolitan Area*. Armagh: International Centre for Local and Regional Development.

ESPON (European Spatial Planning Observation Network) (2007) *Scenarios on the Territorial Future of Europe*. ESPON Project 3.2. Luxembourg: ESPON.

European Commission (1999) *European Spatial Development Perspective: Towards Balanced and Sustainable Development of the Territory of the European Union*. Luxembourg: Office for Official Publications of the European Communities.

European Commission (2010) *EUROPE 2020: A Strategy for Smart, Sustainable and Inclusive Growth*. Luxembourg: Office for Official Publications of the European Communities.

European Commission (2011) 'Territorial agenda of the European Union 2020: towards an inclusive, smart and sustainable Europe of diverse regions.' Agreed at the Informal Ministerial Meeting of Ministers responsible for Spatial Planning and Territorial Development, 19 May, Gödöllő, Hungary.

European Union (2010) *Delivering Smart, Sustainable and Inclusive Growth: the Fifth Report on Economic, Social and Territorial Cohesion*. Brussels: European Commission.

Gleeson, J. (2007) 'Socio-economic profile of the border.' Presented at the Audit of Community Development, 26 February, Cross Border Centre for Community Development, Dundalk Institute of Technology, Louth.

Harvey, B. (2008) *Audit of Community Development in the Cross-border Region*. Dundalk: Cross Border Centre for Community Development, Dundalk Institute of Technology, Louth.

Harvey, B., Kelly, A., McGearty, S. and Murray, S. (2005) *The Emerald Curtain: the Social Impact of the Irish Border*. Carrickmacross: Triskele.

InterTradeIreland (2006) *Spatial Strategies on the Island of Ireland: Development of a Framework for Collaborative Action*. Armagh: International Centre for Local and Regional Development.

Jessop, R. D. (2003) 'The political economy of scale and the construction of cross-border micro-regions', in F. Söderbaum and T. Shaw (eds), *Theories of New Regionalism*. Basingstoke: Palgrave Macmillan, pp. 179–96.

Lennox, V. (2008) 'Canada–US cross-border regions: engines of integration at an impasse – the case of Cascadia', *e-International Relations*, 2 September, www.e-ir.info/?p=1070, accessed 27 January 2011.

Maillat, D. (1997) 'Innovative milieux and new generations of regional policies', in D. McCafferty and J. Walsh (eds), *Competitiveness, Innovation and Regional Development in Ireland*. Dublin: The Regional Studies Association, pp. 9–24.

McCall, C. and O'Dowd, L. (2008) 'Hanging flower baskets, blowing in the wind? Third sector groups, cross-border partnerships and the EU Peace Programmes in Ireland', *Nationalism and Ethnic Politics* 14, 1: 29–54.

McCarter, W. (2008) 'Economics of peace making: the case of The International Fund for Ireland', *Asia Europe Journal* 6, 1: 93–9.

Molle, W. (2007) *European Cohesion Policy*. London: Routledge.

Murtagh, B. (1999) *Community and Conflict in Rural Ulster*. Coleraine: University of Ulster.

Murtagh, B. (2002) *The Politics of Territory: Policy and Segregation in Northern Ireland*. Basingstoke: Palgrave.

Neill, W. J. V. and Ellis, G. (2008) 'Spatial planning in contested territory: the search for a place vision after the "troubles"', in C. Coulter and M. Murray (eds), *Northern Ireland after the Troubles: A Society in Transition*. Manchester: Manchester University Press, pp. 88–109.

Newman, D. (2006) 'The lines that continue to separate us: borders in our "borderless" world', *Progress in Human Geography* 30, 2: 143–61.

O'Keeffe, B. (2011) *Collaborative Communities: Cooperation among Rural Municipalities – Insights from Spain*. Armagh: International Centre for Local and Regional Development.

O'Keeffe, B. and Douglas, D. J. A. (2009) 'Rural development in Newfoundland and Labrador and Ireland: governance and its prospects and potentials', in G. Baldacchino, R. Greenwood and L. Felt (eds), *Remote Control – Governance Lessons for and from Small, Insular and Remote Regions*. St John's, Newfoundland: ISER Books, pp. 237–58.

Paasi, A. (2002) 'Regional transformation in the European context: notes on regions, boundaries and identity', *Space & Polity* 6, 2: 197–201.

Tannam, E. (2006) 'Cross-border cooperation between Northern Ireland and the Republic of Ireland: neo-functionalism revisited', *British Journal of Politics and International Relations* 8: 256–76.

Van Houtum, H. and Strüver, A. (2002) 'Borders, strangers, doors and bridges', *Space & Polity* 6, 2: 141–6.

Varley, T., Boylan, T. A. and Cuddy, M. P. (eds) (1991) *Rural Crisis: Perspectives on Irish Rural Development*. Galway: Centre for Development Studies, University College Galway.

Part II

Mobility, space and consumption

5

Reading the Irish motorway: landscape, mobility and politics after the crash

Denis Linehan

During the boom, Ireland went on the move. The country became a commuter state. In this time, the Red Cow Roundabout became as famous as the Rock of Cashel. The stage on which this motion ultimately played out was the new motorway network. This billion-euro infrastructure ripples with ideology, power and culture – and is one of the defining landscapes of the new Ireland. Like the rapid expansion of housing, the Irish motorway network absorbed vast amounts of capital, including EU funding and national taxes, not to mention the massive volume of private debt raised to buy new cars. Debt, sweat, concrete and asphalt re-spaced Ireland. The motorway changed real and perceived notions of distance and travel. It influenced where people could live, from where they could commute, how far they could move for pleasure, for family visits, for business. However, the construction of the motorway, with its promises of speed and connectivity, ran concurrently with the experience and spaces of congestion. Stories circulated of people leaving home before dawn to escape gridlock and then sleeping in company car parks before their offices opened or of parents buying extra copies of school textbooks to assist children with homework via mobile phone while stuck in traffic on the drive home.

Philosophers and architectural critics have often depicted motorways as non-places and a source of modern anomie. As an essential element of the architecture of super-modernity, motorways are said to exemplify the rise of what Augé (1995: 77) defines as non-place, a 'space which cannot be defined as relational, or historical, or concerned with identity' and hence denuded of memory and emotion. But the Irish motorway evades this description. The

Irish motorway is a contested space, revealed as a site of numerous expressions of anxieties about change. It vibrates with life, politics and culture. It is a major source of debate. Its origins and construction are embedded in the discourses of the Celtic Tiger's rise and fall. Its presence as a focus of protest and resistance speaks directly to the dramatic landscapes of social change that have defined the last decade. Consequently, rather than a non-place, the motorway has a very strong cultural location. Its imposition on the Irish landscape represents not one, but many competing visions of nationhood and the State.

The Irish road has a rich and complex cultural geography, linked to the past, and emblazoned with the problem and dynamics of contemporary living. This is reflected in its built environment and in the practices, stories and discourse that bring it into being. By retrieving these contexts, this chapter will focus upon the shifting meanings and reception of the motorway in the boom time and after. In particular, it will reflect on the ways various rationalities about the motorway intersected with Irish identity and more broadly with the troubled fields of modernisation and politics. Floating on a concrete and steel foundation, the motorway is a more fluid space than might be anticipated, one that provides a dynamic insight into how Ireland was re-spaced. The map of this transformation can be reconstructed from the vast social text of road stories. These were distributed on social networking sites, online bulletin boards, radio talk shows, official reports, letters to newspapers and government websites. Taken as both evidence and interpretation, these texts can be regarded as representations of competing rationalities about the motorway and national development. They suggest that the motorway became both a symbol of success and failure. For the State, the motorway system was the path to the new Ireland – an elixir of growth and an expression of confidence. The motorway promised to restructure the time–space geographies of the country and generate valuable political capital from grateful commuters and villages released from the maladies of congestion and the experience of slowness. Official representations of the motorway were characterised by their virtue, value and contribution to national development. Space, place and landscape were key modes through which these visions of improvement were produced, materially and imaginatively. Yet, many contested this narrative of national renewal and were unconvinced by the technocratic narratives of the Celtic Tiger. From the Glen of the Downs in County Wicklow, to the ruined medieval frontier fortress in Carrickmines, south County Dublin, and most intensively at Tara in County Meath, motorway development met stiff opposition. In fact, it seemed that every new kilometre of motorway ruptured an older sense of place and challenged the generally accepted understanding of national identity. Gathered around the motorway, a dynamic social movement made up of preservationist and all manner of historical, nationalist, New Age and ecological groups combined to criticise the costs that the new motorway would have for the environment and cultural heritage.

In a curious contrast to the de-regulation of the State, which character-ised the politics of the boom (notably the financial sector), the road became increasingly regulated. The last decade saw changes to drink-driving laws, new rules on regular car-safety tests and the deployment of speed cameras. In spite of the success these regulations can claim in reducing deaths from traffic accidents, the new policies went against some established patterns of social and spatial behaviour. As limits for alcohol consumption and driving lowered, some rural dwellers complained that they could not socialise, that it contributed to the isolation of the elderly and that it forced the closure of public houses. Like other forms of regulation that impacted on environmental behaviour – notably planning laws on one-off housing or traditional turf-cutting – state intervention in the road was often regarded as an assault on rural ways of life. Moreover, the intersection of motorway development with open borders and globalisation also threw up symptomatic events and spaces in this period. In 2007, land set aside for a new roundabout at the intersection between Ballymun and the M50 in Dublin became home to fifty-four Roma adults and children. They set up shelter in conditions generally only found in developing world slums (Figure 5.1). In a controversy characterised by overt racism, they were eventually deported. Meanwhile, during 2011, in a practice that had echoes of the Whiteboys (the eighteenth-century Irish rural resist-ance movement), several police mobile safety cameras were burned out across the country in protest at billion-euro bank bailouts that forced the State into stinging austerity measures. Far from being a non-place, however one looks at it, the motorway has all the ingredients of a contested space.

Progress in motion

In 2011, forty years after most western European countries completed their mo-torway network, the development of the Irish network halted on the insistence of the International Monetary Fund (IMF), whose recipe for austerity included radical cuts to capital investment. Between 2000 and 2010, and at a cost of €18 billion (three times the original estimate), over 1,000km were added to the network. The ballooning costs were attributed to massive and unregulated profit-taking from land speculation along new routes. In spite of major social concerns about urban traffic congestion and national debates regarding the in-efficient railway service during its development, notably to the West of Ireland, the motorway was enrolled into a state-building project. The motorway reflect-ed the very particular strategies of the Irish State that sought to hold ideas of

Figure 5.1 Roma camp beside M50 roundabout, Dublin 2007

nation and global together in a context shaped by neo-liberalism, rapid social transformation and political patronage. As represented by the National Roads Authority (NRA), the motorway project was enmeshed in the engineering of spatial virtue – a mission that not only aimed to provide new infrastructure but also encompassed a progressive vision of Ireland's past and future. As a setting for the representation of rapid modernisation, the motorway network mirrored the promotion of internet broadband connectivity in its aims to rebrand Ireland as non-peripheral and global. The work of the NRA is in fact open to a range of questions regarding investment, planning irregularities, cost over-runs, toll contracts and buy-outs. But, by creating both a physical and a symbolic framework, which supported the national modernisation project, its Transport 21 initiative – whose logo 'Progress in Motion' had all the hallmarks of a modernist enterprise – manufactured a fiction that supported its mission of transformation, while evading many of the controversies that accompanied motorway construction.

Grand infrastructural projects the world over can have an intoxicating effect on politicians and engineers alike. During the boom, aerial photographs of bypasses and stretches of new motorway adorned the annual reports of Irish County Councils like priceless works of art, projecting barely disguised fantasies of what Dimendberg (1995) describes as 'spatial reverie'. A look at the content of political speeches made about motorways represents this narrative very clearly. The motorway opens up; connects and decongests; boosts the economy; reduces journey times and supports regional connectivity; improves access for tourism; makes driving safer; solves regional imbalance; advances regional well-being; adds to job creation; makes Ireland more competitive; improves quality of life; and returns villages and town once overwhelmed by traffic to the citizen. 'Projects like this are not just about tarmac, diggers or concrete. We are not building roads to admire them – we are building them because they make it possible to protect and grow job opportunities and to protect and grow community life in all parts of our country' (Cullen 2006a). Over and over again, it was made clear that the objective of Transport 21 'is nothing less than a transformation' (Cullen, 2006b). The rituals of road openings provided a rich vein of social text about this process of modernisation. These were often depicted as historic days by the local media. For instance, the spade used by Martin Cullen, then Minister for Transport, to turn the first sod on the new Carlow Bypass in 2006 is now in the collection of Carlow County Museum. Road openings offer insight into a whole area of political theatre. Openings of major motorways were reserved for ministers while bypasses – unless in the bailiwick of a minister – were left to local county councillors and members of the Chamber of Commerce who jostled on the public dais for credit before the camera. At these moments, we enter into the presence of the infrastructure of optimism. In *The Irish Times* online photographic archive,[1] we find a record of the Minister for the Environment and Local Government, Noel Dempsey, leaping into the air with joy, hopping over the crash barrier and riding the new highway in a classic car, while children with balloons wave with glee as he whisks by (Figure 5.2).

Several qualities about Ireland's new motorway bridges – notably the Cathaleen's Falls Bridge over the River Erne, the Boyne Bridge and the River Suir Bridge – also betray this sentiment exceptionally well, especially to the degree they were carefully designed for spectatorship. The bridges were fully enveloped in the tropes of the technological sublime (Nye, 1996). When describing the River Suir Bridge, Waterford City Council maintained that 'this landmark structure reflecting modern "high tech" engineering and graceful and simple aesthetics will become a symbol for the southeast, of which the region can be proud' (Waterford City Council, 2010). The attention paid to illuminating these structures at night, to create giant sculptural presences in the nocturnal landscape, underlines their role not just as infrastructure, but also as symbolic architecture. At the Boyne Bridge, the design success is reliant on the architectural lighting on the pylons, cables and deck, which is positioned to highlight the state-of-the-art technology used on the structure. The lighting

Figure 5.2 Noel Dempsey at the opening of the M50–Southern Cross route, 2001

contributes to the reception and performance of the architecture, which is intended to uplift the car-bound spectator.

Road art and mythic landscapes

The intersection between the motorway and these discourses of national progress is revealed by the art provided along new roads under the Per Cent for Art Scheme – a fund that sets aside a percentage of the total cost of infrastructure, usually for sculpture. An estimated 700 pieces of sculpture funded from this scheme now adorn the side of Irish roads (Lane 2010). When justifying the scale of investment in public art, the then Minister for Arts, Sports and Tourism, John O'Donoghue,[2] drew upon place and culture heavily. He suggested that the scheme 'holds enormous opportunities to shape the spaces we inhabit' and that 'it can contribute to the distinctiveness of the local area and can offer a different reading or interpretation of history or the environment' (Department of Arts, Sports and Tourism, 2004: 5). This art was intended to 'create a dialogue with a people, a time and a place' (Department of Arts, Sports and Tourism, 2004: 16). On the N21 Castleisland bypass in County Kerry, the brief to artists was to provide roadside artwork which 'reflects and draws on the landscape, geography, social and cultural traditions of the area' (Kerry County Council, 2010: 2). Much of the sculpture provided along the new motorways in Ireland follows this prosaic ambition.

This art anticipates criticism about the atomised qualities of auto-mobility where the argument is that the experience of driving works against place in general by restricting the gaze of the driver and enveloping him or her in a high-speed steel capsule (Sheller and Urry, 2000). The art attempts to construct the road as an authentic place by linking the modern infrastructure to the past. The nature of the sculpture is telling. It is usually figurative and typically draws upon Celtic and early Christian legends. Hence, there is a network throughout Ireland of a veritable mythic bestiary rendered in steel and bronze, including bulls, cows, deer, elk, horses as well as unicorns, trees, Celtic Gods and heroes. There are a few abstract pieces such as *The Race of the Black Pig* on the M7 near the Kildare town bypass. Created by the American artist Dan Browne, its linear, successive form seems to celebrate the possibility of speed. One reading might suggest that its abstract quality points towards a contemporary, ahistorical space, escaping the orbit of place and tradition. But, in fact, that is not the case. Organised in three segments, the piece consists of thirty-nine poles, which are intended to rework the traditional reed cross of St Brigid. The artist has observed: 'In working on this proposal I meditated on what the passing motorist might consider in relating to the land outside their windows. I remind them with imagery of the long and significant history to the present life of the Curragh, racing, the oak leaf, St Brigid's cross, the circle, the square, the wings' (Sheridan, 2011). On the M6 motorway, between Kilbeggan and Athlone, the artist Anne Meldon raised a bronze figure of a woman to represent Gráinne Óg, whose roots in the area are asserted in local lore. The curves designed into Gráinne's dress are meant to echo the esker landscape on which the town of Moate was founded. On the M1, *An Tarbh Donn* (The Brown Bull), a three-metre form rendered in steel mesh, adorns the Dundalk bypass. Created by Micheál McKeown, the sculpture is intended to represent the ghost of the brown bull of Cooley, a legendary beast from the Gaelic legend *An Táin* (The Raid). Just as striking is a piece entitled *Saints and Scholars* on the N52 Tullamore bypass in the constituency of the boom-time finale Taoiseach, Brian Cowen. The series is made up of four prominent, 8m-high, steel figures representing the monastic traditions in the area – oblique portraits perhaps of some members of Cowen's cabinet, or then again, perhaps not.

It is remarkable that in choosing what to depict on the twenty-first century motorway, so many county councils drew from the myths created largely during the Celtic Twilight in the late nineteenth century. If all these road sculptures were assembled together in one place – let us call it the Celtic motorway menagerie – it would reveal that in the period of the most rapid social transformation in the last hundred years in Ireland, local politicians reached into antiquity and unleashed a cornucopia of national symbology to decorate motorway space. Irishness, they decided, was culturally located in a mythic landscape. As such, these sculptures fall under those aspects of governance that address the management of memory as the basis for common identity – one of the key cultural techniques of the modern state. Given the criticism the motorway programme faced from preservationists regarding the destruction of national heritage, the sculptures can be regarded as a self-justifying proclamation of local pride and national identity. But these tailored articulations of the past also had a much broader function in the boom-time discourse on modernisation that surrounded the motorway. Susan Sontag has noted that heroic national figures are chosen for one purpose only – ideological mobilisation (Sontag, 1970). Other examples of this fusion of memory politics with the progressive discourse of growth include the legal re-assertion of the Irish language in the 2003 Official Languages Act and the state funeral in 2001 of the disinterred remains of Irish War of Independence hero, Kevin Barry. In the mindset of the Celtic Tiger, these cultural performances were seamlessly integrated with high-tech, smart-economy discourses to link modernisation with Irishness. Comparable appeals towards tradition and modernity found their way into the design of motorway toll buildings. Atkins (2009: no page number) describes their structure on the M1 motorway toll plaza as 'a presence that provided a modern symbol for Ireland's future tolled roads. The concept was to create a sense of place … the design references the prehistoric past of the region as, approaching the complex, monolithic limestone-filled gabion walls rise from the landscape, increasing in scale with proximity to the plaza'. The toll plaza, in other words, attempts to echo an ancient monument. Such narratives and architectures that applaud the co-existence of innovation and tradition saturated the discourse of the motorway. In its wider use, this strategy was deployed to interpret rapid transformation for the public, while forming an international brand for the Celtic Tiger. The discourse mined three major areas of importance: new technology, tourism and localism, each intended to address, respectively, foreign direct investment (FDI), external earnings and electoral support. In framing modernity in this way, many aspects of the boom-time built environment frequently deployed a consensualising message about environmental and social change.

Tar on Tara

Embedded in this motorway narrative was a strategic attempt to create a consensus about how to govern national and regional space, and shape landscape and place. While condemnation for the disturbance of the past and the destruction of heritage has provided some of the most vociferous criticisms of motorway development, there is no doubt that the NRA emphasised the distinction between the ancient and the modern as a way to both legitimate and represent progress. Noting its principled decision to ensure that the results from archaeological excavations would be disseminated to the public, the NRA argued that these 'activities also make a valuable contribution to promoting a greater awareness of the past among local communities through which national road schemes pass' (National Roads Authority, 2009). Remarkably, rather than threatening heritage, the motorway was to be a font of new knowledge about Ireland. Comparable strategies regarding motorways and historical nation-building can be traced back to schemes devised under National Socialism in inter-war Germany, where the new autobahn was peppered with faux historical bridges, or routed through heritage landscapes to interpret nationalist vistas (Rollins, 1995). Critics of motorway development, however, arguably had already seen the fallacy of these discourses. Certainly, they did not accept this watered-down historicism, or the seamless arguments that these developments could occur in harmony with heritage (Bhreathnach and Fenwick, 2004; Ronayne, 2008).

Tara was particularly important in intensifying but also usurping these debates. The Neolithic site is significant in Europe, with an archaeology that predates the Egyptian pyramids. Current thinking suggests that the Hills of Tara, the Skryne Valley and the Gabhra Valley constitute a unified archaeological and cultural landscape but plans are for the M3 to be routed between Tara and Skryne. Once under threat, Tara rapidly emerged as elemental to the cultural heartland of Ireland. Tara, after all, was the name given the estate of the O'Hara family in *Gone With the Wind* (1939), a means, as observed by the novelist Colm Tóibín, 'to conjure up the old country by naming their estate after its most sacred place' (Tóibín, 2005). As the father in the film, Gerald O'Hara, beseeched: 'Do you mean to tell me, Katie Scarlett O'Hara, that Tara, that land, doesn't mean anything to you? Why, land is the only thing in the world worth workin' for, worth fightin' for, worth dyin' for, because it's the only thing that lasts.' While Seamus Heaney's (1990: 77) poetic phrase 'hope and history rhyme' was adopted as the tagline for Celtic Tiger modernity – for instance, it informed the design principle of the Irish exhibition building at the Hanover EXPO in 2000 – he called the M3 'ruthless'. 'If ever there was a place that deserved to be preserved in the name of the dead generations from pre-historic times up to historic times up to completely recently, it was Tara' (*Tar at Tara*, 2008).

It is, however, beyond this identity politics and rather the processes through which the motorway has become a key site for privitisation that ultimately undermines its claim to national progress. If the road was once a public good, the roll-out of Public Private Partnership (PPP) schemes has steadily undone this assumption. While public art and Irish language signage on the motorway may have attempted to establish the Irishness of the motorway, the development of the infrastructure occurred through a network of global financial connections, as international firms won many of the construction tenders. One of the major equity partners that funded the tunnel beneath the River Shannon at Limerick was Meridiam Infrastructure Finance, a company with a global portfolio in PPP infrastructure. The M3 was built by the giant Spanish firm, Ferrovial. The electronic toll system on the M50 is operated by a consortium comprising two French companies, Sanef and CS. Consequently, most of the tolls now collected on Irish motorways leave Ireland to boost the share price of international firms whose Irish road assets complement their very specific global portfolio in peripheral, modernising and largely neo-liberal states such as Singapore and Chile.

Following the 2008 crash, the Irish State now compensates several of these companies for revenues lost from decreased road travel, a scenario that could persist until 2052, when the last of the current motorway PPP contracts expire. For instance, goods vehicles completed 12 per cent fewer journeys in 2010 than in 2009 and 28 per cent fewer than in 2000 (Central Statistics Office, 2010). Rather than flowing on the motorway and generating tolls, the cars of the unemployed are parked up on suburban driveways and small town streets. The driving miles of emigrants left with them. Hundreds of construction vehicles have been sold at auction and exported. But, it is also the case that the population simply avoids tolls. On a daily basis, toll avoidance represents not only the realities of the recession, but also the resistance of local people to support the privatisation of the public highway. The fallacy of motorway discourse and planning that accompanies tolling is sharply exposed at the new bridge over the River Suir in Waterford. As noted above, the bridge was designed with its iconic potential in mind. But, in recent times it has become regarded as a vainglorious piece of infrastructure, avoided by local drivers to circumvent the tolls. As a result, the bridge offers little relief to traffic congestion in Waterford City. Like the Celtic Tiger itself, the bridge has broken its promise. Despite the NRA's 2007 predictions that 12,000 fewer vehicles per day would pass through Waterford city centre once the new bridge opened, the flow of traffic across the older existing river crossing – the Edmund Rice Bridge – decreased by just 2,000 vehicles (*Kilkenny People*, 2011).

Where transport planners expected families to find about €70 a month to cross a bridge is another example of the voodoo economics that underpinned the perverse forms of political arithmetic now recognised as elemental to the reckless management of the Irish economy during the boom. Consequently, rather than becoming a symbol of the south-east, the bridge has become a tarnished trophy for the excess and waste of the Celtic Tiger. At the same time, the political promise the motorway made to develop the regional economy of the south-east has not materialised. Between 2008 and 2011, just as the infrastructure came on-stream, the number of people registered as unemployed in Waterford rose by over 100 per cent. Job losses included the closure of the famed Waterford Crystal plant and the global tele-services provider TalkTalk. These economic problems illustrate that in the world of instant communication and rapid technological innovation, where businesses can operate in the cloud rather than on concrete, the assumptions about the powerful role the motorway plays in shaping economic development needs revision. In the context of the supranational processes now shaping the sustainability of employment, the flow of FDI, and the competitiveness of business, traditional regional planning instruments like upgrading road infrastructure become less impactful. These issues are made all the more critical when, in the future, peak oil may make motorway travel increasingly costly and problematic.

Signs of the times

Marshall Berman once observed that: 'All forms of modernist art and thought have a dual character: they are at once expressions of and protests against the process of modernization' (Berman, 1983: 235). This observation could also be used to consider the built environment of the motorway. As it mirrored the struggles and terrains of modernisation and the geographies of boom and bust, the road became both a symbol of modernisation and its discontent. The motorway came into being through the political and cultural contingencies of place, the nation and the global. It became a site of consumption, circulation and performance. Driving, in addition to its condition as labour and as chore, never escaped its moral context, one shaped by concerns about transformation and the political contexts of corruption, environment, planning, heritage and risk. Official discourses of the motorway attempted to hold these diverse narratives together. But they cannot be held together really.

The re-election of the Fianna Fáil-Green Party-Progressive Democrat coalition government in 2007 illustrated amongst other things how successful the State was in manufacturing a coherent narrative about Irish identity and its place in new era of globalisation. Ireland, quite simply, was the darling of globalisation – a statement that now appears almost hallucinogenic. The crash meant that this fiction also collapsed. In November 2010, with the IMF at the door and just weeks after he had waltzed on his new motorway at Tullamore, the front page of the *Irish Daily Star* ran a photo of Taoiseach Brian Cowen surrounded by a depleted cabinet with the headline: 'Useless Gobshites' (*Irish Daily Star*, 2010: 1). The then Transport Minister, Noel Dempsey, woke up on the morning after the IMF announcement to see the word TRATIORS [*sic*] sprayed in red across the front of his constituency office. He did not contest the next election. The contradictions that blended past, present and future together into this teleology of growth and that were held together during the boom, also collapsed with the crash. In an economic environment defined by recession, it is somehow telling that several roadside sculptures have recently been stolen, presumably for their scrap metal value. At the beginning of 2011, the mythical goddess Danu was stolen on the N72 near Rathmore, Co Kerry. In the same month, Gráinne Óg, described above, also disappeared. The sculpture weighed one tonne. Oddly, its loss was not reported for a week. A local government official in Athlone called the theft 'a diabolical crime. It's an attack on the State and on the public' (Harney 2011: 4). That, or even our mythic heroes have abandoned us; either way, this is a sign of the times. For the motorway and the narratives revealed through the landscape and spaces with which it intersects, its place in the contemporary cultural geography of the Ireland remains open to critique and protest.

Notes

1   www.irishtimes.com/photosales/.
2   Who subsequently fell from grace when his rather princely attitude to limousine hire and first-class air travel paid from the public purse was exposed in the months preceding the arrival of the IMF in Ireland.

References

Atkins (2009) *M1 Motorway Toll Plaza, Administration and Operations Building*, www.atkinsireland.ie/architecture/architecture-project–12.html, accessed 1 June 2011.

Augé, M. (1995) *Non-places. Introduction to an Anthropology of Super Modernity*. New York: Verso.

Berman, M. (1983) *All that is Solid Melts into Air: the Experience of Modernity*. London: Verso.

Bhreathnach, E. and Fenwick, J. (2004) 'The M3 motorway: driving a stake through the heart of Tara', *History Ireland* 12, 2: 5–6.

Central Statistics Office (CSO) (2010) *Road Freight Traffic Survey*. Dublin: The Stationery Office.

Cullen, M. (2006a) Speech by Mr Martin Cullen, Minister for Transport, at the sod-turning of the Carlow bypass, 11 May, www.transport21.ie/MEDIA/Speeches/Speech_by_Martin_Cullen_TD_Minister_for_Transport_At_the_sod_turning_ for_Carlow_Bypass.html, accessed 20 July 2011.

Cullen, M. (2006b) Speech by Mr Martin Cullen, Minister for Transport, at the sod-turning of the N8 Cashel–Mitchelstown road project, 22 May, www.transport21.ie/MEDIA/Speeches/Sod-turning_of_the_N8_Cashel-Mitchelstown_Road_Project.html, accessed 5 July 2011.

Department of Arts, Sports and Tourism (2004) *Public Art: Percent for Art Scheme. General National Guidelines – 2004.* Dublin: Department of Arts, Sports and Tourism.

Dimendberg, E. (1995) 'The will to motorization: cinema, highways, and modernity', *October* 73: 91–137.

Gone with the Wind (1939) directed by Victor Fleming. USA: Selznick International in association with Metro-Goldwyn Mayer.

Harney, D. (2011) 'Brazen thieves steal one-tonne sculpture'. *Westmeath Independent,* 23 March, p. 4.

Heaney, S. (1990) *The Cure at Troy: A Version of Sophocles' Philoctetes.* London: Faber and Faber.

Irish Daily Star (2010) 'Useless gobshites'. *Irish Daily Star,* 23 November, p. 1.

Kerry County Council (2010) *N21 Castleisland Bypass Public Art Work Artistic Embellishment Scheme.* Tralee, Kerry: Kerry County Council.

Kilkenny People (2011) 'A bridge too far; Suir crossing is a rip-off – NRA'. *Kilkenny People,* 9 February, www.kilkennypeople.ie/news/a_bridge_too_far_suir_crossing_is_a_rip_off_nra_1_2395649, accessed 10 June 2011.

Lane, A. (2010) *By the Way: A Selection of Public Art in Ireland.* Dublin: Wordwell.

National Roads Authority (2009) *Archaeology,* www.nra.ie/Archaeology/, accessed 1 June 2011.

Nye, D. (1996) *American Technological Sublime.* Cambridge, MA: MIT Press.

Rollins, W. H. (1995) 'Whose landscape? Technology, fascism, and environmentalism on the National Socialist *Autobahn*', *Annals of the Association of American Geographers* 85, 3: 494–520.

Ronayne, M. (2008) 'The state we're in on the eve of World Archaeological Congress (WAC) 6: archaeology in Ireland vs corporate takeover', *Public Archaeology* 7, 2: 114–29.

Sheller, M. and Urry, J. (2000) 'The city and the car', *International Journal of Urban and Regional Research* 24, 4: 737–57.

Sheridan, B. (2011) 'Making sense of our motorway sculptures'. *Kildare Nationalist,* 31 May, www.kildare-nationalist.ie/tabId/201/itemId/10291/Making-sense-of-our-motorway-sculptures.aspx, accessed 1 June 2011.

Sontag, S. (1970) 'Posters: advertisement, art, political artefact, commodity', in D. Stermer (ed.), *The Art of Revolution: 96 Posters from Cuba, 1959–1970.* London: Pall Mall Press, vii–xxiii.

Tar at Tara (2008) BBC Radio Ulster, 1 March 2008, 11:30.

Tóibín, C. (2005) 'Will Ireland slice up its most mythical site?', *The New York Times,* 26 April, www.nytimes.com/2005/04/25/opinion/25iht-edtoibin.html, accessed 10 June 2011.

Waterford City Council (2010) *N25 Waterford Bypass. Structures: River Suir Bridge*, www.waterfordcity.ie/n25bypass/bridge.htm, accessed 29 June, 2011.

6

Lone parents, leisure mobilities and the everyday

Bernadette Quinn

Recent social and economic commentary on Ireland has tended to accentuate the extreme changes associated with the Celtic Tiger era. Stories of ostentatious consumption patterns dominated discursive narratives in popular, academic and policy forums. This was for good reason as trend data of all descriptions attested to startling transformations in people's lifestyles and mobilities. To take just one example, data from the Census Statistics Office (CSO) (2007; 2008) show that foreign overnight trips taken by Irish residents increased by a staggering 114 per cent over the period 2000 to 2008, rising from 3.76 to 8.04 million trips. In the aftermath of the boom, the rate of Irish trip-taking overseas has begun to decrease: by over 10 per cent between 2008 and 2009, and just under 7 per cent between 2009 and 2010. Everywhere, there is a contraction of activities and mobilities, and a sense of a return to basics as businesses, households and individuals alike variously re-adjust priorities, reduce discretionary consumption or struggle to survive. Social and economic commentary remains equally striking in its highlighting of extremes; now it is mind-boggling debt problems, sharp rises in unemployment and emigration, and the dramatic downturn in consumer confidence that predominate. Omnipresent in these very recent commentaries and debates is the gritty and often harsh lived realities of daily life in everyday places. Irish society is being re-grounded, as the ordinary and the everyday come back into focus.

This chapter picks up on this return to basics. It highlights the importance of the ordinary as a site for enquiring into how people make sense of their world through the routine trajectories that they make and re-make in everyday spaces, and through the jumble of cultural forms and practices that comprise their everyday life (Katz, 2004). The focus is on leisure practices and mobilities. To date, the conceptualisation of leisure in the social sciences has tended to be framed by notions of time rather than space (Henderson and Hickerson, 2007; Kay, 1998) and while interest in spatial issues has increased since the late 1990s (Aitchison, 1999), the spatiality of leisure continues to offer much scope for further theorisation. 'Of all the leisure spaces available to the majority of the population, it is the home that has become increasingly significant in everyday lives' (Dart, 2006: 314). Despite this, the paradox noted by Glyptis, McInnes and Patmore (1987) still holds largely true: while home is the place where most leisure time is spent, it remains under-researched. The research reported here builds on Quinn (2010), where the spatiality of leisure in the ordinary, everyday spaces in and around the home was explored in an Irish urban context. The primary intention here is to highlight the spatiality of everyday leisure practices and to unravel some of the connections that link these to the occasional leisure practice of holidaying. Empirically, the study seeks to develop insights into the lived realities of a particular group of women: lone parents of dependent children living on low incomes in Dublin. To frame the study, the chapter draws on theoretical ideas about leisure and the everyday.

Leisure and the everyday

As Larsen (2008) points out, much theorising about the occasional leisure practice of holidaying has been historically premised on opposing dualisms, the most fundamental of which is the understanding that tourism's *raison d'être* lies in its opposition to practices of the everyday. To go away on holiday was to escape from the mundane realities of the everyday. Cohen (1979: 181), for example, in a seminal contribution to the literature referred to holidays as 'a no-work, no-care, no-thrift situation'. Consequently, the activities and practices of the everyday have tended to be studied in isolation from those of the extra-ordinary. This has even been the case within the specific domain of leisure activities, where as Brey and Lehto (2007: 161) point out, 'few empirical evidences as to the relationship between an individual's daily recreation activities and what he or she, as a tourist, chooses to do at a destination' exist. For a variety of reasons, the shortcomings of this dichotomous way of thinking are becoming more apparent. Most obviously, alertness to 'time–space compression' (Harvey, 1989: 240), to the globalised nature of contemporary society, and to the 'stretching out' of social networks that this entails (Urry, 2000) has been pivotal. Increasingly, it is understood that tourism can 'involve connections with, rather than escape from, social relations and the multiple obligations of everyday social life' (Larsen, Urry and Axhausen, 2007: 245). The relevance of researching the leisure domain has increased, and researchers like Larsen (2008) have drawn on Lefebvre's (1991) belief that no practice escapes everydayness to argue that the social practice of holidaying is strongly conditioned by routine. Advocates of what is referred to as the 'performance turn' in tourism theory have begun to explore these interconnections, proposing that 'although suffused with notions of escape from normativity, tourists carry quotidian habits and responses with them: they are part of their baggage' (Edensor, 2001: 61). Larsen (2008: 22), for example, considers that occasional leisure, in the form of holidaying, is informed by 'everyday performances, social obligations and significant others'. Such researchers argue that it is through understanding the everyday, ordinary practices that tourists undertake in the process of 'doing' tourism, that we can come to a fuller awareness of how tourism is implicated in reproducing social relations.

The need to re-think the link between the ordinary and the extra-ordinary in the leisure domain has also been prompted by developments in feminist contributions to both geography and leisure research. Here can be seen a reminder not to overlook the significance of the apparently mundane spatialities of ordinary places in the rush to investigate the exciting new mobilities and practices that make manifest the stretching out of social relations. Within geography, feminist researchers have paid most heed to the everyday. As Dyck (2005: 234) wrote, 'we need close attention to the spaces of the everyday to keep women visible in rapidly changing world conditions, where their activities tend to slip into the shadows of dominant models in the literature'. Feminist geographers have also made it clear that enquiries into 'the routine, taken-for-granted activity of everyday life in homes, neighbourhoods and communities' can 'help us see how the "local" is structured by wider processes and relations of power' (Dyck, 2005: 234). Specifically, within leisure studies, the problem with separating out the ordinary from the extra-ordinary mirrors the problematic dichotomy that historically characterised thinking about the work–leisure relationship. Traditional definitions of leisure as 'non-work' failed to consider the fact that many people are not engaged in paid work outside the home and that for many women, especially mothers, the notion of describing the private domestic zone as a non-work environment is seriously misguided (Allen, 1993). It is now well-established that notions of home as 'natural' havens of recreation are partial, gendered interpretations that fail to consider how space is socially constructed.

Lone parents in Ireland

In 1990, Winchester asserted that one-parent families constituted one of the most rapidly growing types of household in the developed world. The case of Ireland bears out this assertion. The number of lone-parent families rose sharply in the 1980s and 1990s (Fahey and Russell, 2002) and more than doubled in the twenty-year period from 1986 to 2006 (Lunn, Fahey and Hannan, 2010). Research has consistently found that lone parents are more likely to be from lower social classes than other parents (Lunn, Fahey and Hannan, 2010). According to European Union Statistics on Income and Living Conditions (EU SILC) data (CSO, 2009), they experience the highest at risk of poverty (35.5 per cent), deprivation (63 per cent), and consistent poverty (17 per cent) rates of any household type. These EU SILC trend data suggest that the fortunes of lone-parent families in Ireland improved over the boom years: in 2004, 31 per cent were living in consistent poverty compared to 17 per cent in 2009. Nevertheless, lone-parent families continue to stand out as a societal group clearly exposed to poverty. Their prospects in the face of current economic difficulties are unclear.

In 2006, 91 per cent of the approximately 120,000 lone parents in Ireland were female (Lunn, Fahey and Hannan, 2010). A predominance of females as lone parents is also found elsewhere in Europe (European Commission, 2007; Solomon and Titheridge, 2008) and thus female lone parents formed the group of focus for this research. The research reported here is based on data gathered in 2006 and 2009 and relates to fifteen female lone parents living on low incomes in inner and suburban Dublin city. All of them are Caucasian Irish from Dublin, except for one who is black African. Aged from late twenties to mid-fifties, they parented between one and four dependent children. Small-scale focus groups and in-depth individual structured conversations were used because they offer 'a perspective on women's experiences in a way that more structured methods of research cannot' (Miller and Brown 2005: 408). The study examined how leisure 'fits' into the everyday and occasional lifestyles of these women.

Daily mobilities and practising leisure at home

In spatial terms, the routine mobilities of the women studied had a lot in common, with most being both limited and highly routinised. Three of the women lived with their parent(s), and for them, the main trips were home–work–school–shops/services. For the others (with the exception of the Nigerian woman), these trips were supplemented by very frequent, in many cases daily, trips to the homes of extended family members and to other places significant in the wider family context (e.g. a family grave, a grandmother's nursing home). All of the women lived relatively close to where they worked and, indeed, most lived in or close to the area where they had grown up. None of this is at all surprising. Feminist geography has shown that the space–time fixity constraints that bind women to specific places are stronger than those associated with men (Kwan, 2000; Schwanen, Kwan and Ren, 2008) and that 'care-giving and housework punctuates and fragments [women's] time-space paths' (Schwanen, Kwan and Ren, 2008: 2111). It seemed that most of the daily trip-taking was associated with caring obligations, e.g. helping out an elderly parent or taking a nephew to school. While Solomon and Titheridge (2008) suggest that lone parents in the UK are the least likely of any household type to have private transport, somewhat surprisingly here, several of the women, even those within the inner city, owned and regularly used cars. This perhaps points both to the limitations of Dublin city's public transport system and to gains made by this low-income group during the Celtic Tiger years.

The scale of obligation combined with the nature of the home environment meant that there was little time for women to self-determine ways of being at home. Particularly for those women who did not live with their parents, relaxation was rare. Typical responses when asked about 'time to themselves' were: 'no time'; 'no never'; 'nothing, only when I go to work'. Furthermore, indicating the strong ethic of care that prevailed, this was widely accepted as 'how things were'. As Susan said: 'not to have much time to yourself as a mother is natural. You have to step up to the mark; have to make sure you do your best for your child'.

If these women lacked time, space was also an issue. While some were happy with the quality of their living environs, this was not the case for all. For Hilary, the lack of time was strongly compounded by the quality of the spatial capital available to her. As she explained: 'my child is permanently with me; don't even get five minutes away from her. We don't even lock the bathroom door. We live on the sixth floor of an apartment block and every door in the house is permanently left open because I'm terrified she'd fall out the window'. Hilary articulated how she felt that her difficult spatial environs impacted upon her: 'I've had desperate trouble at home because I'm living on my own. To live in big blocks of flats, you have to be tough. I am quite soft but I have no problem knocking somebody's f**king block off. It's the environment I'm in; it's like adapting to your environment, it's the way you have to survive'. The problematic quality of the private and public space in the home environs was a recurring theme, especially with respect to the surrounding public space, when the women expressed concerns about their children's welfare. For women like Gráinne, it was a constant constraint on the ability to relax: 'it's terrible; there's nothing for them [the children], they're always getting themselves into trouble … if they're out there playing ball, if the ball goes on the [train] tracks, the danger … if they go too far then you're worried where are they, what are they up to? So you've constantly the worry'.

For the three women who lived with a parent(s), things seemed calmer. However, in general, lives were characterised by multi-tasking, juggling, rushing around, and thinking for and about several people simultaneously. Thus, relaxation and a focus on the self only happened in certain times and spaces. Most obviously, albeit very modestly, self-determined relaxation happened at home, sometimes in the early morning before the daily household obligations began and while the communal spaces of the home were calm, quiet and relatively empty. Mostly, however, relaxation happened in the evening, when tasks were complete and communal spaces had emptied out. Listening to the radio and watching television were the dominant forms of recreation. Several of the women regularly watched TV soap operas. Others smoked a cigarette on the balcony, had a beer on the sofa, or read the newspaper after the children had gone to bed.

Leisure outside of the home

Activities that required movement outside of the home specifically for leisure-oriented reasons were rare. Only Laura had a weekly formal leisure engagement: she played bingo in the local pub. Regular, informal leisure activity was almost as rare. Susan explained how she walked her dog on the beach twice a week while her daughter attended a dance class. Patricia described how she walked alone to the shop every Saturday morning to get the newspaper, and this for her was leisure. Pamela regularly dropped into her neighbour for tea, while Adele explained that the only physical activity she took was running to catch the bus on her way to and from work. For the three women who lived with a parent, there seemed to be more opportunities to focus on the self. The one woman who went out regularly in the evening (to play bingo in the local pub) was in this category. Another, Kate, lived with her parents during the week but spent every weekend at a friend's house.

Most of the women, however, did not go out regularly. Sarah explained that she had not had a night out in five months because she could not afford it. This was a common theme; a lack of finances meant that socialising was a rarity. Space was another factor. As James, Jenks and Prout (1998: 39) remind us, social space is never a merely neutral location. In the discussions about where and how the women relaxed, it was evident that they clearly understood both time and space to be socially constructed. While certain places like the workplace or a neighbour's kitchen provided comfortable and positive spaces for the women to be in, other spaces were alienating. The limited socialising that characterised these women's lives was undoubtedly linked to their understandings of how society perceived them. Patricia expressed this very clearly:

'I feel that if you are not married, when you come back [from living abroad] and you're on your own, people don't want to know you. They don't invite you for drinks, are afraid that you'll take their husband or afraid of this/that.' Hilary too spoke about feeling 'easy f**king prey for other people's partners [if you go to parties], because you're on your own'. Adele could also relate to this: 'But you can't go somewhere on your own, what would you be doing? You're not having fun, people are looking at you'. These findings empirically support Bavinton's (2007) contention that leisure spaces are contested political arenas where power is negotiated, won and lost.

For the women who worked outside of the home (in part-time positions, or in community employment schemes), the workplace was a key site for recreation. It constituted an escape from the stresses and burdens of the domestic zone and, in line with other research (Dart, 2006), it was a crucial link into sustaining social networks. The blurring of distinctions between work and leisure evident here was replicated to an extent in the practicing of everyday obligations. The women's social worlds were rooted in their extended family networks. Usually, there was obligation involved, but this was often simultaneously dutiful and fun. For example, while a woman might have been baby-sitting her sister's children, she also may have had a coffee and a chat with her. Similarly, while someone may have had to cook a meal for a parent, she may have also stayed to watch a DVD. This practicing of obligation in conjunction with simple, informal recreation was a very sustaining endeavour.

Holidaying – away from or into the ordinary?

Out of step with the highly mobile lifestyles that apparently characterised the Celtic Tiger years, most of these women did not holiday regularly. Those who did tended to do so for particular reasons. Patricia, for example, travelled to visit her grown-up children who live abroad. She is divorced from a non-Irish partner and travelled regularly to visit family and friends. For her, holidays were replete with mixed emotions, as she engaged with her tension-filled, stretched-out familial network. Adele also travelled regularly but, again, travelling and holidaying were embedded both in obligation and ordinariness. She regularly travelled to Nigeria to visit family but this was a difficult process: she had to leave her children behind because of cost, and arrange for them to be cared for in her absence. Due to her immigrant status, she had to apply for a visa each time she left the State, a costly and burdensome constraint. In both of these cases, holidaying was not so much an escape from the routine of home but rather a way of reaching into the ordinariness of family lives being lived elsewhere. For other women like Angela and Valerie, an annual family holiday was made possible only because of the intervention of a non-governmental organisation. While this break was welcome, and enjoyable to an extent, everyday obligations such as child-care, cooking and cleaning dissipated only modestly, while routine concerns about matters like child safety and finances became increasingly fraught because of the new risks posed by unfamiliar seaside environments and the commercialised nature of holiday resorts with their gambling arcades and fairgrounds. Laura also holidayed regularly. She went away on the annual weekend domestic breaks organised by the pub where she played bingo. In Laura's availing of this social network can be seen a very obvious continuity between the leisure practices of the everyday and those of the occasional.

Access to disposable income is a prerequisite for formal, structured leisure activities like holidaying. For some of the women, like Linda and Kate, holidaying was virtually an unknown social practice for this reason. They were completely excluded from the marked rise in overseas trip-taking that came to characterise Irish lifestyles in recent decades. Some of the others were determined to holiday and made supreme efforts to do so. Gráinne, for example, saved ten euros every week for two years in order to travel on a group pilgrimage to Lourdes. The occasion was her fortieth birthday, and this was her second ever holiday as an adult. As she explained: 'Yeah, the parish, my friend's mother runs it … she'd have to come down because if she didn't come down for me to give the ten euro I wouldn't, you know, you'd spend it on something, so she'd be down the day you got paid to make sure you paid it'. In a similar vein, Hilary was planning to spend two days in Galway for a friend's wedding. This was to be her first trip away in two years and she had been saving for the previous eight months. Meanwhile, Susan determinedly saved regularly to pay for her annual week away. For women like these, a holiday is something that must be budgeted for months or years in advance. It comes only at the expense of other items and is a very considered investment. The 2009 research data showed signs that these holiday savings were coming under increasing pressure from other more essential demands as Ireland's recession deepened.

Yet for several women, it was clear that holidaying is perceived to offer a highly prized and much-desired escape. Holidays seem to restore what the routines, experiences and spaces of these women's everyday lives take away: the ability just to 'be' oneself. As Gráinne said of her holiday: 'you're just totally at peace; it was fantastic', while Linda, who rarely went on holidays, explained: 'well, I actually got away for an overnight … I got away for one night and it was great. Just not worrying about the kids and just time to myself … that was, that I could just relax and do what whatever I wanted'. Susan too, 'loves the build up to the holiday'. For her, it meant a break from obligation: 'no hanging out a wash, no sweeping floors' and complete ease. She claimed that it is only while away on holidays that she can sleep through the night undisturbed. Even though she acts as primary care-giver to four family members while on holidays, once away from home, such duties seem less onerous. Away from the strictures of her home space she finds it easier to self-determine her workload (e.g. she insists on going out for dinner every evening) and to be at ease. This ability to control her experience is vital in how she performs being on holiday.

Routine and occasional leisure mobilities – common constraints

The data showed routine mobilities and holidaying mobilities to be similarly constrained. The constraints at issue relate not only to finances but also to a variety of other factors including the obligations associated with a strong care ethic, the lack of practice in self-determining choices, and the contested nature of social spaces. Hilary, for example, was only going to the wedding in Galway because her daughter had also been invited. She knew that her lone-parent status limited her holidaying mobility, just as it did her social practices more generally. For others, the ability to holiday was constrained by an inability to shake off their sense of family obligation. Ellen, for example, talked about her fear of going on holiday because of having to leave her children in the care of others. Sometimes in the holiday environment, the sense of obligation transposed into guilt, as in Gráinne's case where her struggle to abstract herself from her routine care-giving role was clear: 'Fantastic, absolutely fantastic, it was just a break away. I even said to my family, I said, "I'm not being bad, you didn't even enter my head there was so much holy things going on." Don't get me wrong, at night time I'd say "oh God, I hope my ma was alright today" and things like that'.

The value that many of the women placed on holidaying was accentuated by a general understanding that they were being marginalised and excluded from what had become, during the boom years of the 1990s and 2000s, a widespread social practice in Ireland. In not being able to afford a holiday, they and their children were missing out. The awareness of being marginalised acted to compound the actual marginalisation itself. Women like Rose, Angela and others who could not afford to take a holiday felt this to be a failure on their part as parents, and experienced a sense of guilt. Comments like: '[the children] should be on the beach, they should be doing happy things, so you're not feeling as bad'; 'To be honest with you, it's like: "can I have twenty euro to go to the pictures?"; "can I have ten euro to go swimming?"; "can I have five euro to do whatever?"; everything is just … money, money. I'm like a bleedin' bank machine when they are on holidays … and then you feel lousy if you haven't got it, you know that way'; 'I couldn't go on a Spanish holiday, I have five of them, you know, here on me own with them, you know what I mean, so I couldn't afford to bring them on a holiday'.

Conclusions

Lone-parent families constitute a very sizeable, growing but marginal societal group. They are also a very heterogeneous group. The women studied here differed in numerous ways including age, number and age of children, reason for lone-parent status, living arrangements, employment status, skill levels and income. Race was another differentiating factor. The pattern of immigration that characterised the Celtic Tiger period has been a force of dynamism within this societal group and while this study included just one immigrant parent, it offers the briefest glimpse into the changing landscape of lone parents and of how the inclusion of immigrant parents introduces new complexities that merit much further enquiry. While the recent economic boom period may have generated some improvements for this group (car ownership and evidence of overseas holiday-taking are two indicators noted here), statistics show that lone-parent families remain particularly vulnerable to poverty. This study found indications that the current economic downturn is likely to increase the financial pressures and stressful living conditions constantly negotiated by lone parents. In such a scenario, leisure engagement is likely to become even less feasible than it already is, and thus its quality-of-life enhancing potential will also be diminished.

Overall, the findings presented here concur with research pointing to the holistic nature of women's lives (Gregory, 1982). For the women studied here, leisure constituted informal, unstructured and modest activities that were stitched into daily routines and mobilities in a variety of unremarkable ways. Of note is the extent to which distinctions between work and leisure, between obligation and recreation were blurred. Overwhelmingly clear was the fact that even the most modest engagement in leisure activities facilitated social engagement and served as very important sustaining and coping mechanisms. Undoubtedly, the study group faced numerous constraints on their ability to practise leisure activities. Time and financial limitations were clearly at play; so too were other factors including the quality of everyday spaces, a prevalent ethic of care, social perceptions of lone parents, and the social constructedness of public and certain private spaces. Several of these are well-acknowledged in the leisure literature but the critical and varied roles that space plays in shaping leisure outcomes remains under-researched. Here, empirical evidence of such roles appeared in the poor quality of home spaces; the absence of recreational spaces for these women and their children; the difficulties in negotiating the highly contested nature of certain public spaces; and the vitally sustaining role that safe, comfortable spaces can play in affording leisure engagement. Further enquiries into the complex nature of these roles and outcomes constitute important avenues for future geographical research.

More broadly, the study offers insights into some of the ways in which routine leisure experiences shape the extra-ordinary practice of holidaying, and vice versa. These micro-investigations illustrate the argument that posits the local (ordinary) and the global (extra-ordinary) not in terms of particularity and universality, but rather as mutually constituting sets of practices (Holloway and Valentine, 2000). There is much in the data to suggest that the myriad cultural practices, habits, mobilities and ways of being that make up our everyday existence are far more connected into, and mutually constitutive of, our extra-ordinary endeavours than might be popularly thought. In consequence, a key theme running through this chapter is that dichotomous, bounded ways of thinking about place and the ordinary on the one hand and about space and the extra-ordinary on the other cannot fully capture the complexities of how and why we make sense of our worlds as we do.

Finally, while in this instance data analysis did not specifically emphasise the emotional insights generated, the data clearly communicated how emphatically the women 'felt' their worlds. Anger, frustration and fear, exhaustion, worry and anxiety, joy, ease and pleasure were all articulated in abundance, attesting to the variety of ways that people come to know and understand place. An important challenge for geographers is to correspondingly conceive of place as multi-dimensional and multi-sensorial so as to make room both for the emotions and for the kinds of knowledges that they uncover.

References

Aitchison, C. (1999) 'New cultural geographies: the spatiality of leisure, gender and sexuality', *Leisure Studies* 18, 1: 19–39.

Allen, J. (1993) 'Motherhood, the annihilation of women', in A. M. Jaggar and P. S. Rothenberg (eds), *Feminist Frameworks*. Third edition. New York: McGraw-Hill, pp. 380–5.

Bavinton, N. (2007) 'From obstacle to opportunity: leisure and the reinterpretation of constraints', *Annals of Leisure Research* 10, 3/4: 391–412.

Brey, E. T. and Lehto, X. Y. (2007) 'The relationship between daily and vacation activities', *Annals of Tourism Research* 34, 1: 160–80.

Central Statistics Office (CSO) (2007) *Tourism Trends*. Dublin: Stationery Office.

Central Statistics Office (CSO) (2008) *Tourism Trends*. Dublin: Stationery Office.

Central Statistics Office (CSO) (2009) *Survey on Income and Living Conditions (SILC)*. Dublin: Stationery Office.

Cohen, E. (1979) 'A phenomenology of tourist experience', *Sociology* 13: 179–202.

Dart, J. (2006) 'Home-based work and leisure spaces: settee or work-station?', *Leisure Studies* 25, 3: 313–28.

Dyck, I. (2005) 'Feminist geography, the "everyday", and local-global relations: hidden spaces of place-making', *The Canadian Geographer* 49, 3: 233–43.

Edensor, T. (2001) 'Performing tourism, staging tourism – (re)producing tourist space and practice', *Tourist Studies* 1: 59–81.

European Commission (2007) *Study on Poverty and Social Exclusion among Lone Parent Households*. Brussels: European Commission.

Fahey T. and Russell, H. (2002) *Family Formation in Ireland. Trends, Data Needs and Implications*. Dublin: ESRI.

Glyptis, S., McInnes H. and Patmore, A. (1987) *Leisure and the Home*. London: The Sports Council.

Gregory, S. (1982) 'Women among others: another view', *Leisure Studies* 1, 1: 47–52.

Harvey, D. (1989) *The Condition of Postmodernity*. Oxford: Blackwell.

Henderson, K. A. and Hickerson, B. (2007) 'Women and leisure. Premises and performances uncovered in an integrative review', *Journal of Leisure Research* 39, 4: 591–610.

Holloway, S. L. and Valentine, G. (2000) 'Spatiality and the new social studies of childhood', *Sociology* 34, 4: 763–83.

James, A., Jenks, C. and Prout, A. (1998) *Theorising Childhood*. Cambridge: Polity Press.

Katz, C. (2004) *Growing up Global: Economic Restructuring and Children's Everyday Lives*. Minneapolis, MN: University of Minnesota Press.

Kay, T. (1998) 'Having it all or doing it all? The construction of women's lifestyles in time-crunched households', *Leisure and Society* 21, 2: 438–54.

Kwan, M. P. (2000) 'Gender difference in space-time constraints', *Area* 32, 2: 145–56.

Larsen, J. (2008) 'De-exoticising tourist travel: everyday life and sociality on the move', *Leisure Studies* 27, 1: 21–34.

Larsen, J., Urry, J. and Axhausen, K. W. (2007) 'Networks and tourism: mobile social life', *Annals of Tourism Research* 34, 1: 244–62.

Lefebvre, H. (1991) *Critique of Everyday Life*. London: Verso.

Lunn, P., Fahey, T. and Hannan, C. (2010) *Family Figures: Family Dynamics and Family Types in Ireland, 1986–2006*. ESRI Survey & Statistical Report Series 29. Dublin: Family Support Agency and ESRI.

Miller Y. D. and Brown, W. J. (2005) 'Determinants of active leisure for women with young children – an "ethic of care" prevails', *Leisure Sciences* 27, 5: 405–20.

Quinn, B. (2010) 'Care-givers, leisure and meanings of home: a case study of low income women in Dublin', *Gender, Place and Culture* 17, 6: 759–74.

Schwanen, T., Kwan, M. P. and Ren, F. (2008) 'How fixed is fixed? Gendered rigidity of space-time constraints and geographies of everyday activities', *Geoforum* 39: 2109–21.

Solomon, J. and Titheridge, H. (2008) 'Social exclusion, accessibility and lone parents.' Presented at the UK-Ireland Planning Research Conference, 18–20 March, Belfast.

Winchester, H. P. M. (1990) 'Women and children last: the poverty and marginalisation of one-parent families', *Transactions of the Institute of British Geographers* 15: 70–86.

Urry, J. (2000) *Sociology Beyond Societies*. London: Routledge.

7

Rethinking the liveable city in a post boom-time Ireland

Philip Lawton

> If land is simply given away to the highest bidder, the future of the city will be controlled by the bidders and not by the people who live and work there and must live with the consequences. (Angotti, 2008: 223)

The predominant portrayal of the built environment in Ireland since the economic downturn of 2008 has been that of half-empty housing estates, flooded apartment blocks, and main streets covered in 'to let' and 'for sale' signs. It is a painful reality far removed from the utopian image of the liveable city or suburban dream of the previous two decades. Such imagery, whether it be experienced first-hand or through the media, starkly illustrates the need to rethink ideas of liveability and to recover some form of balance between the needs of society and that of the property sector in Irish cities, suburbs and towns. Although the recent past was dominated by notions of place-making (Montgomery, 1998) and sustainability, these were often little more than the visual gloss on a system that was dominated by unfettered and unregulated urban and suburban growth.

Broadly speaking, the period of the economic boom was marked by two contrasting visions of urban society in Ireland. The official vision was often presented as the desire for an urban village atmosphere based around walkable and sustainable communities, which in reality was largely driven by an entrepreneurial planning agenda dominated by real estate interests (MacLaran and Williams, 2003). The other vision was that of the continued suburban expansion of cities such as Cork and Dublin (Corcoran, Gray and Peillon, 2010; Fagan, Kelly and Lysaght, 2006). Each was presented as an imagined future of prosperity and comfort. The reality has, however, turned out to be significantly different. The current moment allows us to challenge the very basis of the relationship between processes of urbanisation and liveability in cities, suburbs and towns in Ireland. Such a challenge, as will be argued throughout this chapter, necessitates a fundamental change in the approach taken to the connection between the society that exists, or is desired, and the role of processes associated with urbanisation in producing such a society. Drawing on the concept of the geographical imaginary (McCann, 2008), it is argued here that the type of urban society promoted by policy formation must focus in a critical manner upon the impact of different structures and policies – particularly in relation to the role of property – on urban society. This will be examined through three moments; that of the recent past, the current period, and the future.

The 'future that was' sets out to examine the processes and outcomes associated with the economic boom in Ireland. This section predominantly focuses on the impact of what MacLaran and Williams (2003) call entrepreneurial forms of urban planning within Irish cities. The chapter then analyses current approaches to urban planning practice, with a critical focus on the continuity of threads from the economic boom of the past into the present. In calling for a repositioning of notions of community and the common good as central elements of urban planning practice, the final part of the chapter draws on a number of broader urban theories, including concepts of 'the right to the city' (Harvey, 2008; Lefebvre, 1968), 'the just city' (Fainstein, 2010), and Marcuse's (2009) 'commons planning'. Here, the chapter points to the practical means of developing the basis to a more balanced and socially orientated urban and surburban future. It is argued that the existence of vacant property and land, which in the case of the National Asset Management Agency (NAMA) is, by default at least, in state ownership, provides a platform for a shift in the approach taken towards urban liveability in Ireland.

The liveable city

Throughout the last number of decades, the topics of urban liveability and place-making (Montgomery, 1998) have been dominated by two interrelated strands. On the one hand, through the implementation of entrepreneurial forms of planning policies (Hall and Hubbard, 1998), significant attention has been given to the appearance of city centres. This has included the remodelling of public space and the development of high-profile venues, coupled with an intensification of city branding strategies orientated towards boosting the profile of cities in order to attract visitors and investment (Hall and Hubbard, 1998; Lawton, 2009). Running concurrently, there has also been a focus amongst both planning practitioners and theorists on the urban village as an ideal manifestation of urban society (Zukin, 2009). A key factor in each of these strands is the manner in which they draw heavily on a particular image of urban life revolving around a geographical imaginary, whereby the projected future of society can be imagined based on a highly visualised connection between the spaces of everyday life and the form of social life that is promoted in such spaces (McCann, 2008). Thus, the image of the city centre as both a safe entertainment venue and a place for middle-class living has formed the key element in the way the futures of cities have been officially imagined and promoted.

The enhancement of city centres in Europe in recent decades has been directly influenced by what can be summarised as a European city model (McNeill, 1999). The European city model extols a geographic imaginary of the virtues of a relaxed, safe or urbane form of social interaction within a finely grained urban fabric associated with historic European cities. The virtues of the European city are emphasised by its mix of uses, walkability, and focus on public transportation. Furthermore, with increased levels of competition, cities have sought to develop high-profile iconic buildings designed by star architects, such as the Guggenheim Museum in Bilbao by Frank Gehry, or the Imperial War Museum in Manchester by Daniel Libeskind. The development of such buildings acts both as a feature of differentiation, in that through a unique design they stand out from their surroundings and help the city develop a unique identity, and of standardisation, in that they can be experienced in a similar manner to high-profile developments in other cities vying to attract the same tourists and industries (Griffiths, 1998; Lawton, 2009).

The second element of the liveable city revolves around the desire to promote the ideal of the urban village. Although the urban village, which also extols the virtues of density and walkability, can be traced to the work of Jacobs (1961), its form has morphed throughout the last few decades, gradually transforming into a vision of urban society associated with middle-class consumption patterns and gentrification (Lees, Slater and Wyly, 2008; Zukin, 2009). The urban village is more often than not attributed to established urban neighbourhoods, such as East Village in New York, or Bermondsey in London (Lees, Slater and Wyly, 2008). For Zukin (2009), drawing upon notions of authenticity, the urban village has its origins in a view that is counterposed with the forward march of the corporate city of the mid-twentieth century. The dominance of soulless suburbia and the perceived blandness of chain-stores is rejected in favour of an authentic way of life within rejuvenated historic urban areas with various amenities, such as independently owned food stores, cafés and bars, all focused upon the tastes of the new urban middle class.

In recent years, the urban village has received a further boost through the emergence of the creative city (Landry, 2000) and the creative class (Florida, 2002) as focal points of policy formation. For Florida, the attraction and retention of creative people is the key driver of the urban economy. Furthermore, these workers are perceived to be attracted to diverse and tolerant urban areas, predominantly located in established authentic neighbourhoods, akin to those described by Zukin (2010). Thus, Florida's thesis has served as a basis for bringing together the various strands of policy focused on place-making. This has included the continuance of already existing urban strategies at both the level of the city and the neighbourhood (Peck, 2005).

The future that was

The Celtic Tiger boom years were dominated by two images of new Ireland. One was of the continued expansion of suburbs and their associated landscape of motorways, big box retailers, and out-of-town shopping centres located in an ever-expanding commuter-belt along with the accompanying lifescapes of car dependency and semi-detatched houses (Corcoran, Gray and Peillon, 2010; Fagan, Kelly and Lysaght, 2006). However, such imagery was rarely, if ever, utilised as a means of officially imagining the urban, or indeed suburban, future. Instead, notions of liveability were dominated by the second image of new Ireland – the transformation of city centre areas through various interventions.

While the projects varied in scale, the intent was similar throughout different towns and cities – image enhancement for the purpose of attracting tourists, new employees and long-term investment, underpinned by entrepreneurial planning mechanisms (MacLaran and Williams, 2003). Although not officially presented in a cohesive manner at the level of national policy, the rhetoric took on a familiar image in different places. From Dublin's Smithfield Square (Lawton, 2009) to Cork Docklands (O'Callaghan and Linehan, 2007), broad notions of sustainability akin to that associated with the European city were presented in a manner that was underpinned by an increasing focus on both national and international urban competitiveness. Cork Docklands, to draw upon one of many examples, were presented as a new urban quarter that would ' … revitalise the city through high quality, contemporary design and a vibrant mix of uses. Building on the unique character of Cork and the dramatic setting of the Docklands, the vision for the area identifies the need for a development strategy to compete with other Irish and European waterfronts' (Cork Corporation, 2001: 2).

The desire for a more compact European-style city had gained considerable traction through the development of Temple Bar in Dublin city centre in the early 1990s (Lawton, 2009; Montgomery, 1998). Indeed, to a large extent, the approach taken in Temple Bar was laudable in that, by aiming to counteract the negative impact of urban sprawl, it promoted a more liveable city centre and ensured the long-term viability of galleries and artists' studios. Moreover, the Temple Bar model, through the design of Group '91 Architects, sought to reject the destructive tendencies of the modernist city in favour of a more respectful intervention within the existing urban fabric (Temple Bar Properties, 1991).

In the years that followed the original development of Temple Bar, many towns and cities throughout the country were transformed in a manner that picked up on a European ideal of public space. Here, public space became representative of the new ambitions of town and city councils, as they competed both with other cities and with suburban shopping centres. For example, in the mid-2000s, Eyre Square in Galway underwent an almost complete physical transformation (Strohmayer, 2007). With particular reference to the northern part of the square, planes of granite paving interspersed with stone benches and sleek landscaping, in a manner reflecting spaces anywhere from Barcelona to Oslo, symbolised a new image for the city centre. Indeed, polished stone, such as limestone and granite, became the standardised material of choice and a representation of the new meanings of city centres as destination points for tourism, shopping and other forms of leisure. The differentiation of each space took a number of forms, such as unique lamp standards on St Patrick Street in Cork by Catalan architect Beth Gali or, indeed, the Spire as a new landmark for Dublin (Lawton, 2009) (Figure 7.1).

To the extent that public space was opened up to a greater level of usage, these endeavours had a positive impact upon urban space. In reality, however, the virtues of a more compact form of urban living around renewed public spaces became more of a side-show, or gloss, with property and profit dictating the nature of urban development. While one aspect of the European model of city centre living might involve a mix of social classes living in close proximity to affordable shopping districts, the model that predominated in Ireland focused on exclusive upmarket living, primarily orientated towards the attraction of young middle-class workers. The notion of higher densities was itself usurped by an obsessive desire for taller buildings, often proposed in historically sensitive areas such as the Liberties in Dublin. Those that were built stand as reminders of a time now all but vanished. The monumental but almost vacant Elysian Tower in Cork, to take just one example, gives the appearance of being airlifted from London's Docklands and left accidently stranded in the centre of Cork city.

Figure 7.1 Lamp standards on St Patrick Street in Cork city

Urban policies throughout the boom, which sought the true virtues of compact and balanced urban living, were perhaps limited by broader forces largely outside the control of individual city and county councils. Despite the vision for compact city centres, the lack of ability to control urban sprawl, particularly around the cities of Cork, Dublin, Galway and Limerick, became all too visible within the landscape. Opposing the sought-after geographical imaginary of medium and high-density city centres was the reality of low-density, car-oriented suburban sprawl.[1] This real 'imaginary' is probably best captured by Ireland's entry to the Venice Bienniale architecture exhibition in 2006, entitled *Sub-Urban to Super-Rural:*

> Suburban sprawl has become the enemy of both town and country … It expands relentlessly at very low-density, squandering formerly productive agricultural land, stretching services and infrastructure to uneconomic levels and eroding the social fabric of rural life. The line between urban and rural is blurring, robbing both of their essential

character. Urban-generated populations live in suburban enclaves stitched on to towns and villages, generating a new cash crop – sites for houses – as manicured lawns fast replace farmed land. (Fagan, Kelly and Lysaght, 2006: 15)

Here, the curators capture a moment in time in Ireland: a moment where it seemed such growth could and would not stop. Taking a realist vision of what had been developed in the preceding decade, *Sub-Urban to Super-Rural*, perhaps slightly unwittingly, put forward a crucial question for the future of Ireland's built environment of the present: how to accommodate that which exists so as to create a more balanced and sustainable future.

The shock of the present

With the burst of Ireland's property bubble between 2007 and 2008, the nascent visions of suburban and urban ways of life came to a sudden halt. At first, the suburban discourse came centre-stage with the realisation that the estates under construction in the centre of a field were to remain just that: half-built. Then, the discourse began to pick up on similar themes: dead town centres, empty apartment buildings, over-supply of hotels. At the same time, the vocabulary of the built environment shifted from *The Spirit of Gracious Living*[2] to 'firesales' and 'distressed properties'.

With the emergence of a new economic reality, one might have expected a shift in how towns and cities were officially imagined. Yet, in the example of Dublin, and in keeping with the entrepreneurial mould of thinking (Peck, 2005), policy advisers, planners, and other urban practitioners remained focused on a similar vision of urban society as throughout the boom years. Although it gained traction in the years leading up to the economic downturn, it is only since the bust that the creative class thesis has become dominant (Dublin Regional Authority (DRA), 2009; National Competitiveness Council, 2009). Florida's (2002) vision of the city became a central element of the *Economic Development Action Plan for the Dublin Region* (DRA, 2009; see also Lawton, Murphy and Redmond, 2010), where the primary aim is focused on the attraction and retention of creative people. With direct reference to Florida, the focus in attracting these creative people was placed on factors such as vibrancy, café culture, along with tolerance and diversity (DRA, 2009). Moreover, the development of higher-density forms of urban settlements was perceived here as a primary means of promoting growth: 'There is considerable potential for Dublin to have a larger population and a higher quality of life if the benefits of higher density are brought on stream to replace the costs of urban sprawl. A larger and more compact population will in turn make it easier to develop knowledge intensive services, manufacturing and a greener regional economy' (DRA, 2009: 18).

Again, there is much to admire about the desire for higher densities put forward, yet the lifestyles with which they are associated are narrowed to one specific social group. Furthermore, instead of attempting to assess and deal with the reality of the current moment, the DRA's vision overemphasises an imagined reality of city centre living as the natural home of this incumbent group,[3] while at the same time largely ignoring the reality of suburban expansion of both industry and housing within the region in the preceding decades.

At a lesser scale, ideas related to the role of creativity have also had an influence on a number of other bodies throughout the country. For example, Limerick City Council's *Art in Slack Spaces* programme, an outcome of the Creative Limerick initiative (Moloney, 2010), was established as a means of utilising vacant commercial space within Limerick city centre. Here, the City Council approached landlords and agreed short-term use at a low rent in return for a reduction in rates (O'Connell, 2010). This initiative presented recent art graduates with the opportunity to pursue and present their work, with the City Council acting as facilitators and mediators. Such initiatives, which also took place in Cork and Dun Laoghaire, are indicative of the centrality of arts-related strategies within the context of urban change. In periods of economic downturn, short-term uses are applauded, with those once seen as outside, such as artistic spaces, and other temporary ventures, such as pop-up restaurants, perceived as potential saviours of the city. While successful in filling a void and, to a certain extent, challenging official meanings of place, the temporariness of such measures highlights the degree to which they are at the mercy of property market fluctuations. There is a very real danger that without the proper structures in place, the positive role of such initiatives will be sidelined at the first sign of a return to a 'normal' property market.

Re-imagining the future

Creating a more liveable city as an integral part of the development of a better urban society will take a reassessment of the connections between existing social and political structures and the social relationships that they help to produce. Given the scale of impact of the economic downturn and its connection to the built environment, any rethinking of urban life must have at its centre a belief in achieving a more equitable society. Picking up on ideas such as the 'just city' (Fainstein, 2010) or the 'right to the city' (Harvey, 2008; Lefebvre, 1968), it is feasible to question the very structures of society and how they both impact on, and are in turn influenced by, the social and physical form of cities and towns. In short, as commented by Harvey (2008: 2), the right to the city is the 'right to change ourselves by changing the city'. Building a new and better urban future in Ireland therefore requires a commitment to re-examining the connections between the type of society that exists and the everyday reality of urban space, both in terms of the way society influences space and how such space influences society.

One key factor to achieving a shift in the approach to urban space lies in re-establishing the common good as the central tenet of planning policy and practice in Ireland. There is a need for policy makers to look beyond the rhetoric of tolerance and diversity as espoused by creative city literature and focus on how best to achieve a fairer city by incorporating factors related to broader society and community in a holistic sense. This might begin with confronting some of the core issues highlighted by the present moment. Following from authors such as Marcuse (2009) and the focus on commons planning, questions might hone in on the manner in which private ownership of land conflicts with the delivery of the common good.

Picking up on one aspect of the common good, a specific way in which planning policy can directly influence the creation of more liveable towns and cities is in the ownership and control of land for the purposes of promoting public life. If nothing else, the current fallout from the collapse of the property market opens up the potential for the retention of land through government interests in Irish banks and through structures such as NAMA. This was highlighted by the former Minister for Finance, Brian Lenihan, as follows:

> Within the legal boundaries that NAMA must operate, and notwithstanding its commercial remit, NAMA could have a role in creating balanced and desirable places to live with obvious benefits for sustainable social values. NAMA could seek to facilitate the Department of Education and Science and the Department of Environment, Heritage and Local Government where these bodies have requirements, for example, such as schools, parks and so on, which facilitate the creation of desirable development which encourage vibrant sustainable communities. (Quoted in Irish Planning Institute, 2009)

This highlights the potential to recognise the benefits of placing an emphasis on forms of development that are orientated towards society and communities rather than individual benefit (as per Marcuse, 2009). Thus, the control of public land becomes a central feature of social and community structures and must be utilised as a core element in the promotion of public life. In the example of NAMA, there is potential for a shift away from the focus on the commercial role of land as an end in and of itself towards a broader view of land use which has social gain as its focus.[4] The public's stake in NAMA is therefore, in some manner at least, balanced by public gain.

In attempting to address questions of liveability, publicly owned lands could be open to a wide variety of uses as decided at the local and national level in conjunction with both local authorities and central government, such as affordable housing, new business ventures, community farming, and, indeed, a wide variety of cultural uses (Angotti, 2008). The control and ownership of land for the benefit of the broader common good therefore holds the potential to greatly strengthen many of the initiatives that are already taking place and would be a significant step towards promoting a better quality of life within Irish society, particularly in cities, suburbs and towns.

One example of the potential for public land ownership, which has recently attracted attention, is that the current government may seek to repossess the Bank of Ireland building on College Green in Dublin city centre. The repossession and possible transformation of the former Parliament building into a new use has the potential to illustrate the importance of public land ownership at a number of scales. At a macro-scale, it would be a hugely symbolic step for the State to make in declaring a new way of looking at the role of the built environment beyond that of property investment. At the level of the city, that such a building is located on College Green, a historically important location in the heart of Dublin, places it at the centre of commerce, culture and learning, both literally and figuratively (Figure 7.2). The transformed Parliament building could become a focal point for a public square at the centre of the capital city, and a focal point of civic engagement at the national level. It would be a symbol of the importance of the common good in Irish society and a model for similar interventions at different scales throughout Irish towns and cities.

Conclusions

The current moment offers the opportunity to radically rethink the relationships between the structures of society and the built environment. Drawing again upon the notion of the geographical imaginary, it is necessary that processes focused on creating better living conditions within towns and cities have at their centre an in-depth understanding of the factors which produce a more open and balanced urban society. Whereas this necessitates being critical of current notions of place-making, the core elements to which they relate, such as place-attachment, permanence and change, remain of central importance to the future of Irish cities and towns. While planning for a more sustainable

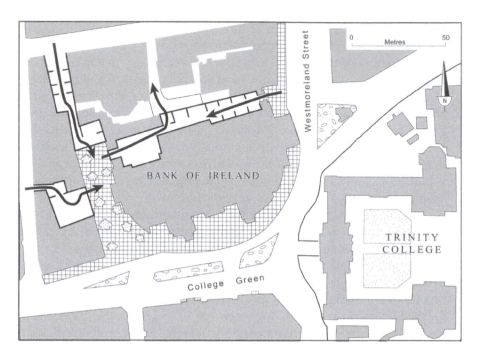

Figure 7.2 Proposed new public space and links through Bank of Ireland, College Green

future must still form a central feature of policy formation, the focus of trans-formation must work within the context of the recent pattern of development and the social structures that have developed therein. This requires a greater recognition of the existence of the suburbs as a significant element in how the urban is defined.

The geographical imaginary presented here encompasses an understand-ing that the reality of urban liveability is related to the real conditions that are created within our society. Creating a society which is more open to truly democratic interaction requires spaces in which such processes are allowed to grow. Through a re-think on the relationship between land ownership and society, individuals and groups can imagine and implement strategies where they can make a direct connection between their own lives and the future of their neighbourhood, town or city. Thus, instead of the imaginary of the city being the preserve of elite structures of power, it would be opened up to more dem-ocratic decision-making processes and, indeed, the conflicts that go with them.

Notes

1   The everyday experience of urban sprawl and personal travel journeys in Dublin is evocatively captured by Anne Cleary and Denis Connolly's *Moving Dublin* project. See www.connolly-cleary.com/Dublin/moving_dublin.html.

2   *The Spirit of Gracious Living* was an advertising slogan placed on a hoarding for The Grange, a residential development in Dublin during the height of the property boom in the mid-2000s. Such slogans became a ubiquitous feature of urban and suburban landscapes throughout the Celtic Tiger period.

3   There is also significant evidence to suggest that those working within the creative and knowledge industries are spread reasonably evenly throughout the Dublin region and are not confined to the hip or up-and-coming parts of Dublin city centre (Lawton, Redmond and Murphy, 2009).

4   At the time of writing in mid-2011, a group of architecture students from Dublin Institute of Technology were proposing alternative uses for NAMA properties in Dublin, under the title of NAMAlab: see http://namalab.tumblr.com/, accessed 23 June 2011. Similarly, architect Paschal Mahony was proposing to convert the half-built Anglo Irish Bank headquarters in Dublin's docklands into a public park: see http://treesonthequays.com/, accessed 29 June 2011.

References

Angotti, T. (2008) *New York for Sale: Community Planning Confronts Global Real Estate*. Cambridge, MA: MIT Press.

Corcoran, M., Gray, J. and Peillon, M. (2010) *Suburban Affiliations: Social Relations in the Greater Dublin Area*. Syracuse, NY: Syracuse University Press.

Cork Corporation (2001) *Cork Docklands Development Strategy: the Vision*. Cork: Cork Corporation.

Dublin Regional Authority (DRA) (2009) *Economic Development Action Plan for the Dublin City Region*. Dublin: Dublin Regional Authority.

Fagan, M., Kelly, P. and Lysaght, G. (2006) 'SubUrban to SuperRural', in S. O'Toole (ed.), *SubUrban to SuperRural: Ireland at the Venice Biennale 10th International Architecture Exhibition*. Kinsale, Cork: Gandon Editions, pp. 12–17.

Fainstein, S. (2010) *The Just City*. Ithaca, NY: Cornell University Press.

Florida R. (2002) *The Rise of the Creative Class and how it's Transforming Work, Leisure, Community and Everyday Life*. New York: Basic Books.

Griffiths, R. (1998) 'Making sameness: place marketing and the new urban entrepreneurialism', in N. Oatley (ed.), *Cities, Economic Competition and Urban Policy*. London: Paul Chapman Publishing, pp. 41–57.

Hall. T. and Hubbard, P. (1998) *The Entrepreneurial City: Geographies of Politics, Regime and Representation*. Chichester: Wiley.

Harvey, D. (2008) 'The right to the city', *New Left Review* 53: 23–40.

Irish Planning Institute (2009) IPI submission on amendments to the NAMA Act – May

2010, 25 May, www.irishplanninginstitute.ie/ipi/news-article/ipi-submission-amendments-to-the-nama-act-may–2010/, accessed 1 March 2010.

Jacobs, J. (1961) *The Death and Life of Great American Cities*. New York: Random House.

Landry C. (2000) *The Creative City: A Toolkit for Urban Innovators*. London: Earthscan.

Lawton, P. (2009) 'An analysis of urban public space in three European cities: London, Dublin and Amsterdam'. Ph.D. thesis, University of Dublin and Trinity College Dublin.

Lawton, P., Redmond, D. and Murphy E. (2009) *Transnational Creative Knowledge Migrants in the Dublin Region. The View of Transnational Migrants*, ACRE report WP7.13. Amsterdam: AMIDSt.

Lawton, P., Murphy, E. and Redmond, D. (2010) 'The role of "creative class" ideas in urban and economic policy formation: the case of Dublin, Ireland', *International Journal of Knowledge-Based Development* 1, 4: 267–86.

Lees, L., Slater, T. and Wyly, E. (2008) *Gentrification*. New York: Routledge.

Lefebvre, H. (1968) 'The right to the city', in E. Kofman and E. Lebas (eds and translators) (1996). *Writings on Cities*. Oxford: Blackwell, pp. 63–181.

MacLaran, A. and Williams, B. (2003) 'Dublin: property development and planning in an entrepreneurial city', in A. MacLaran (ed.), *Making Space: Property Development and Urban Planning*. London: Arnold, pp.148–71.

Marcuse, P. (2009) 'From justice planning to commons planning', in P. Marcuse, J. Connolly, J. Novy, and I. Olivio (eds), *Searching for the Just City: Debates in Urban Theory and Practice*. New York: Routledge, pp. 91–102.

McCann, E. (2008) 'Liveable city/unequal city: the politics of policy making in a "creative" boomtown', *Interventions Economiques*, 37, http://interventionseconomiques.revues.org/489, accessed 13 March 2009.

McNeill, D. (1999) *Urban Change and the European Left: Tales from the New Barcelona*. London: Routledge.

Moloney, A. (2010) *Art in Slack Spaces*. Boyle, Roscommon: Pure Designs.

Montgomery, J. (1998) 'Making a city: urbanity, vitality and urban design', *Journal of Urban Design* 3, 1: 93–116.

National Competitiveness Council (2009) *Our Cities: Drivers of National Competitiveness*. Dublin: National Competitiveness Council.

O'Callaghan C. and Linehan, D. (2007) 'Identity, politics and conflict in dockland development in Cork, Ireland: European Capital of Culture 2005', *Cities* 24, 4: 311–23.

O'Connell, B. (2010) 'Shop 'til the artistic penny drops'. *Irish Times*, 10 March, www.irishtimes.com/newspaper/features/2010/0312/1224266101681.html, accessed 25 February 2011.

Peck, J. (2005) 'Struggling with the creative class', *International Journal of Urban and Regional Research* 29, 4: 740–70.

Strohmayer, U. (2007) 'Ireland as a civil society: public space, the common good and private desires in Galway', in T. McDonough, A. Ní Léime and L. Pilkington (eds), *Re-thinking Irish Democracy*. Galway: Arlen House, pp. 17–58.

Temple Bar Properties (1991) *Temple Bar Lives! Winning Architectural Framework Plan*. Dublin: Gandon Editions.

Zukin, S. (2009) 'Changing landscapes of power: opulence and the urge for authenticity', *International Journal of Urban and Regional Research* 33, 2: 543–53.

Zukin, S. (2010) *Naked City: The Death and Life of Authentic Urban Places*. New York: Oxford University Press.

8

Flocking north: renegotiating the Irish border

Sara McDowell

According to Beck and Sznaider (2010: 390), capital 'tears down all national boundaries and jumbles together the "native" with the "foreign"' producing new patterns of consumption and mobility. But, where the national boundary is one of contention, and the identities of those on either side even more so, the influence of economics on a political divide is more difficult to determine. The changing economic fortunes of both the Republic of Ireland (the South) and Northern Ireland (the North) since 2007 have had a significant effect on the everyday geographies of people living on both sides of the Irish border and have dictated and impacted their negotiation and understanding of it. Borders are dichotomously, as O'Dowd and McCall (2007: 129) note, both 'regulators of movement' and 'make movement possible'; the ability to pass through them varies greatly across time and is dependent on a variety of social, political and economic factors. With the collapse of the Celtic Tiger and the onset of the recession in both jurisdictions in 2008, the dynamics and parameters of the Irish border were altered significantly.

The depreciation of sterling against the euro during the autumn of 2008, together with the high differential in prices between the North and the South, resulted in more and more people flocking north to avail of cheaper goods thus transcending the political border. The volume of shoppers making this journey breathed new life into the border cities, towns and villages. While cross-border shopping is not a new phenomenon, the hysteria surrounding this particular surge of 'Euro shoppers' during a time of economic hardship was accompanied by calls for a return to economic protectionism by some Irish ministers in the

Dáil, the Republic's parliament, unleashing a political storm. Aggrieved at its political connotations, Republican politicians in Northern Ireland denounced the protectionist argument as partitionist. While the trend in cross-border shopping was defended by the then Taoiseach Brian Cowen (2010) as nothing more than a product of functionalism emanating from a volatile exchange rate and the demand for value, the fracas raised significant questions about the permeability and meaning of the border.

This chapter explores the ways in which socio-economic change can influence how people conceptualise and negotiate a political border that, as Creamer and O'Keeffe outline in Chapter 4, has become increasingly permeable. In particular, it questions whether functionalism occasioned by a rapidly changing economic climate can truly override the political and symbolic salience of a border. As well as exploring the cross-border shopping debacle, it examines the controversies surrounding the provision of United Kingdom services to people from the North who moved across the border into the South during the economic and housing boom of the Celtic Tiger period, further complicating and blurring the divide between the two jurisdictions. The chapter begins with a brief discussion of the meaning and significance of national boundaries before moving on to document the ebb and flow of movement across the Irish border since its creation in 1920. The economic tipping point and its impact on cross-border mobility are reviewed in the second part of the chapter while the third part charts the political wrangling that ensued. After a discussion of some of the issues surrounding the everyday geographies of trans-border communities, the chapter concludes with a discussion of the permeability of the border and its ramifications for the relationship between the two parts of the island of Ireland.

Borders and boundaries: ebbs and flows

As our world appears to be increasingly influenced by the forces of globalisation, debates surrounding the meaning, significance and negotiation of national boundaries have intensified. At the crux of these debates are questions concerning the melting of borders, the loss of national identity and the end of the nation-state. Yet, the idea of an interconnected world without borders has been questioned. O'Dowd and McCall (2007: 128), for example, argue for a more subtle appraisal of the erosion of boundaries suggesting that they are not disappearing rather they are being 'reconfigured in other ways' through a simultaneous process of 'de-bordering and new forms of demarcation'. They believe that border creation and negotiation is 'increasingly arbitrary'. Paasi (1995: 42) suggests that boundaries may be simultaneously historical, cultural, political, economic or symbolic phenomena and each of these dimensions may be 'exploited in diverging ways in the construction of territoriality' (also see Sack, 1986). While boundaries demarcate the territorial limits of a state's sovereignty, they are nearly always contested, and the nature and intensity of movements through and across them ebb and flow.

The creation and construction of the Irish border in 1920 had important ramifications for the political, economic and cultural geographies of both parts of the island and its inhabitants. Partition, as Nash and Reid (2010: 281) note:

> effectively superimposed a political boundary on a social geography differentiated by gender, generation, class, denomination and political affiliation but indistinguishable on either side of the border. It ran across networks of agricultural, social and familial interconnection that spanned the old provincial boundaries ... and was misaligned to the distinctive regional boundaries that spanned county and provincial boundaries.

The rupturing of relationships, communities and landscapes produced new spatial patterns and forms of engagement, and had important economic implications for the borderlands. The creation of the border was accompanied by a series of custom posts demarcating an invisible but divisive line between two new jurisdictions, which would become more and more entrenched as the Irish Free State inched ever further from Britain. Like many other national boundaries, however, the Irish border, susceptible to the forces of change, has evolved through time. Its function and significance altered in 'tandem with the decline in imperial power, the growth in institutional power and infrastructure of states within a globalised interstate system and new forms of political, economic and cultural globalisation over the past four decades' (O'Dowd and McCall, 2007: 128).

The relationship between the North and the South was uneasy and often hostile in the decades after partition in 1920. The distance between the two was compounded by the outbreak of a period of acute and sustained violence in 1969, colloquially known as the Troubles, which only served to reify the salience of the political boundary (Howard, 2007). Protracted efforts were made by both the Irish and UK governments to fortify and demarcate the physical divide. The government in the Republic further disengaged from Northern Ireland in order to protect its people from what was perceived to be its destabilising relationship with the North (see Howard, 2007) and the British army constructed a series of checkpoints and watchtowers across the length and breadth of the border, making once easy passage fraught with difficulty.

The possibility of fostering cross-border economic cooperation stood very little chance of success during the worst years of the Troubles. Cross-border trade and cooperation was discussed for the first time during the 1985 Anglo-Irish Agreement but did not materialise. Talk of an all-island economy once again surfaced during the peace process in the early 1990s when Sir George Quigley claimed that an all-island economy was something that everyone 'could enjoy without threat to anyone' (in Gough and Magennis, 2009: 18) but it did not come to fruition until the 1998 Belfast (Good Friday) Agreement. The agreement made the provision for the creation of a series of North–South bodies to foster closer economic and political relationships between both parts of the island while effectively shelving any possibility of the dismantling of the political boundary through the constitutional question (see O'Leary, 2007). Tonge (2005: 7) suggests, however, that while the concept of an all-island economy was useful during the Celtic Tiger period as a marketing tool, it was 'hardly substantive and could only make a small contribution towards economic competiveness'.

The barriers to any fruitful cross-border cooperation, Bradley and Birnie wrote (2001: 8) as the Celtic Tiger period gained momentum, could be attributed to the 'partial market competition and the policy mismatch' borne out of the Irish border's unique features that makes it 'intrinsically different from many other nation states with international land borders'. They pointed to the chequered and difficult history between the two states. In the North, the Unionist population had been historically reticent towards North–South cooperation, 'fearing a process of creeping unification' (Anderson, 2008: 97). This reticence was often shared by the Irish Government fearing the Troubles could spill across the border (which they did at times). Bradley and Birnie (2001: 66) also pointed to both jurisdictions' peripheral geographical location on the edge of Europe and the 'asymmetries in the roles and power of policy-making institutions' which have hampered North-South cooperation.

Despite these barriers, EU support for the borderlands (support that has grown steadily since the peace process) and the reconfiguration of the meaning of the border itself actively encouraged and financed considerable cross-border interaction, redefining the Irish border as another internal and flexible boundary within the EU (Nash and Reid, 2010). The flow of people, ideas and trade across the border improved markedly before the onset of the recession in 2008. In real terms, cross-border trade rose by 20 per cent between 2004 and 2007, harnessed by improved infrastructure between the two jurisdictions with the Republic emerging as the North's most important export market (see InterTradeIreland, 2008). Traffic across the border also increased with an estimated 900,000 people travelling through it annually for a variety of reasons (Tonge, 2005).

Economic prosperity during this time generated a rise in the population living along the boundary and this had further important implications for urban space, planning and politics (see Shuttleworth, 2007). The Derry–Donegal commuter belt offers one example of the increasingly fluid nature of the political boundary and its economic salience. Derry city's population has steadily spilled over from the North into its natural hinterland in Donegal in the South since the demilitarisation of the heavily fortified border that had initially constrained it (Paris, 2005). The housing boom in the UK and the Republic of Ireland, together with the lack of space for development on the almost wholly Nationalist west bank of the city, resulted in the construction of more and more housing developments south of the border. The provision of cheaper housing stock in the South (bolstered by the then relatively strong sterling) altered the dynamics of the border and forged new border identities and spatial patterns. For the thousands of people effectively living in one country and working in another, the border and its functions began to assume new meaning. Underpinning the patterns of mobility and consumption implicit in these new cross-border relationships and movements were, as Tonge (2005) suggests, functionalist ideas that anticipated the demise of the political and emotive power of the border (also see Tannam, 1996; 1999). By the end of 2008, however, the impact of the changing economic climate on the border would see functionalism, protectionism and partitionism collide.

Boom to bust: the tipping point and the invisible border

By October 2008, the economic landscape in both parts of the island had changed considerably with the onset of a global recession and the demise of the Celtic Tiger economy. The appreciation of sterling set against a background of three consecutive quarters of negative growth in the South would transform the economic fortunes of towns and villages north of the border for the better. With a dramatic differential in prices between the two jurisdictions – the Republic being significantly more expensive with prices driven upwards by the Celtic Tiger boom years – the position of retailers just south of the border became as Gorecki (2009: 462) notes 'untenable'. Almost overnight, border municipalities in the North like Enniskillen, Newry, Strabane and Derry became inundated with what the media described as a staggering influx of shoppers from the Republic. This influx was further encouraged by a decision by the UK Government to cut value-added tax (VAT) by 2.5 per cent to 15 per cent in an effort to stimulate the UK economy. The relative strength of the euro against the depreciating British pound presented an opportunity for border retailers and southern shoppers alike and by Christmas 2008 the story of the euro shoppers transcending an invisible yet economically important border had become the source of a media frenzy.

Northern towns and villages that had long watched the Celtic Tiger stop at the border were now sites of significant consumer spending, somewhat sheltering them from the throes of recession in the UK. The primary beneficiaries were the supermarket giants Asda and Sainsburys who did not have a presence in the market in the South. Between them, they are thought to have captured 2.5 per cent of the Republic's grocery market at this time (Collins and Burt, 2011). The re-sited Asda store in Enniskillen reported that almost 60 per cent of its trade in the run-up to Christmas 2008 had come from the Republic making it the sixth most profitable store in the multinational Walmart chain worldwide (Palmer, 2008). The sheer volume of pre-Christmas trade resulted in the supermarket recruiting a further 120 staff and opening another ten checkouts (see Palmer 2008). Asda in Strabane also reported similar success with cross-border trade bolstering their takings, while multinationals in Derry estimated cross-border trade was up 40 per cent on the previous year (Palmer, 2008). Newry's proximity to Dublin, facilitated by improvements in the interconnecting road infrastructure that were completed in 2007, ensured that it received a considerable share of cross-border trade. While the influx of cross-border shoppers was welcomed by retailers (for instance, Sainsburys in the Quays Shopping Centre in Newry offered free breakfasts to southern shoppers who camped out overnight in the run-up to Christmas 2008 and 2009), concerns were raised over sustainability issues and the pressure on infrastructure with increased traffic and the absence of car parking spaces.

The media hype surrounding this trend was relentless. But the phenomenon of cross-border shopping is not unique to Ireland. Timothy and Butler (1995) suggest that cross-border shopping and tourism are two aspects of the movement of people and goods across international borders. Shopping has become a major motivation in cross-border trips all over the world with the flow of people constantly changing in intensity and in direction according to price fluctuations in neighbouring countries (Jansen-Verbeke, 1991). The flow of cross-border shopping between two countries is dependent on which country has the higher exchange rate and lower prices. In the case of the Irish border, cross-border traffic for the purchase of goods has ebbed and flowed in different directions as economic trends develop. Fuel tourism has been particularly susceptible to fluctuating exchange rates. Lower excise tax on fuel in the Republic led to the closure of many petrol stations in border towns and villages north of the border during the early 2000s as motorists crossed south to avail of cheaper prices. The cyclical nature of cross-border shopping is of little relief to businesses on the wrong side of the border.

Debating patriotism and defending protectionism: reconfiguring the border

Despite one journalist's comments that the surge of cross-border shopping was not about politics, simply business (Simpson 2008), the furore surrounding it was certainly political. In December 2008, the then Irish Finance Minister, Brian Lenihan, warned shoppers that when they shopped in Northern Ireland they were 'paying Her Majesty's taxes' instead of those of the state in which they lived (see Simpson, 2008). Social and Family Affairs Minister, Mary Hanafin, joined Lenihan in berating shoppers, asking those who chose to shop north of the border to reflect on the damage they were doing to the economy. These essentially protectionist comments fuelled an already highly charged debate on the ramifications of cross-border shopping not just for the Republic's economy but for the relationship between North and South, and the fluid nature of the border itself. Such was the general hysteria surrounding media reports of shoppers flocking north and the worries of economists (see Millar, 2009) that the Office of the Revenue Commissioners and the Central Statistics Office agreed to attempt to quantify how much was being lost in tax to the Irish exchequer. It devised a series of questions that were incorporated into the Quarterly National Household Survey in 2009 and 2010. The findings, although extremely difficult to quantify in any real sense, estimated that in the first quarter of 2009, southern shoppers had spent approximately €435 million in the North, with groceries the most commonly bought item, followed closely by alcohol and clothing (Office of the Revenue Commission and the Central Statistics Office, 2009). This translated into almost €81 million in lost tax to the Republic.

While the controversy was related primarily to the economic ramifications of crossing the border in a time of considerable financial pressure, the debates raised questions about the political relationship between the two parts of the island and of the nature of the border itself. Lenihan's comments were read by some as underlining the differences and distance between the two jurisdictions. Attempting to defuse the political connotations of members of the Irish parliament reproaching Irish citizens for spending their money in what was presented effectively as a different country, Deputy First Minister of Northern Ireland and member of Sinn Féin (the left-wing Irish Republican Political Party), Martin McGuinness (2009), called the comments 'nonsensical … like racism and sectarianism, partitionism is one of the evils in our society'. Emphasising his interpretation of the border as invisible and fluid, he noted that it was important 'to recognise that there are people working in one jurisdiction and living in the other and that there are people travelling to different parts of the island' (McGuinness, 2009). The then Taoiseach, Brian Cowen (2010), also made light of the ramifications of cross-border shopping, asserting that it was simply an apolitical trend (essentially functionalist) dictated by the exchange rate and value for money.

The malleability of the boundary between the North and the South in this particular instance arguably exposed the delicate nature of the island's political geography and underlined dichotomous interpretations of border. For those travelling to avail of goods, the political border was in many ways irrelevant (confirming functionalist ideology), striking a chord with Bradley and Birnie's assertion that the word integration when discussing greater cross-border co-operation 'should not be challenging from a political or identity point of view' as the 'forces of economic activity ... are too powerful to be resisted' (2001: 67). However, for many businesses and policymakers, market forces were rooted in politics, with the issue of cross-border shopping igniting fierce protectionist instincts.

(Re)flocking north? New trans-border communities

Anderson suggests that where state borders are crossed or contested 'conventional democracy has crucial weaknesses' (2008: 96). The fracas over the meaning of the Irish border and its limitations was not confined to shopping. In the summer of 2007, the beginning of a political storm surrounding border rights was beginning to brew across the Derry–Donegal commuter belt. The increasingly blurred political line between Derry and Donegal, occasioned by the opening-up of the border and the economic boom, meant that hundreds of children whose families had relocated south of the border and were now living in a different jurisdiction with a different education system were travelling north to attend school. However, with pressure over school places, a number of secondary and grammar schools in Northern Ireland decided to reserve admission for children from their own jurisdiction. Parents began using false addresses from family members still residing in Derry city to secure a place for their child. This practice came to light in August 2007 when a legal case was taken to the High Court in Belfast against a secondary school by families whose children's places had been withdrawn following an admissions cap on student numbers by the Department of Education. The families claimed that a number of children from Donegal had received places in the same school through using false addresses registered in Northern Ireland. The Western Education and Library Board came under attack for advising schools to accept applications at face value although Lord Chief Justice Weatherup, who presided over the case, countered that 'it was impossible for them to police the system' and referred to the extremely difficult set of circumstances surrounding the row over border rules (Weir and McDaid, 2007).

Concerns over the rights of cross-border residents were also raised in 2008 by general practitioners (GPs) in the Western Health Board in Northern Ireland who claimed that some 45,000 people living south of the border were falsely registered to northern addresses in order to access the UK health service (Clarke, 2007). While many of these people worked in the North, paid tax to the UK and were consequently permitted to avail of these services, their partners and children were not. Clarke (2007) points to countries in Europe that have managed border relationships much more successfully with regards to healthcare provision. The French and Catalan governments, for example, have pooled resources for a cross-border hospital to service the eastern Pyrenees region while bilateral agreements across the French–Swiss and French–Belgian borders provide services for cross-border workers and their families.

These latest everyday geographies occasioned by economic and social change present new challenges for the political relationship between both parts of the island of Ireland and the management of the border as its permeability evolves through time. Clarke (2007) suggests that the two jurisdictions need to do more to adapt services to fulfil the needs of the increasing number of people who cross the border to work, live, study or retire. Such trans-border communities face a host of challenges, not least in relation to healthcare provision and education. They must also navigate taxation, social welfare and security, pensions and retirement, banking (with a fluctuating exchange rate) and telecommunication issues. In 2007, an online resource was commissioned to provide information and clarity about cross-border legalities yet problems remain. Anderson (2008: 98) argues that the creation of trans-border communities requires practical mobilisation around social, cultural and economic issues that are 'not the preserve of any one ethnicity', which can lead to 'positive sum games' that benefit all. However, he warns that ethno-nationalists will continue to try and drag issues back into their own zero-sum moulds.

Conclusions

The hysteria surrounding southern shoppers and new cross-border residents flocking north raises important questions about the ubiquity of political borders and the salience of functionalist ideas concerning the erosion of the political and emotive power of boundaries. It would appear, at least in the examples discussed here, that it may well be, as Paris (2005) notes, easier for market forces and households to transcend national boundaries than it is for nation states and their protagonists to overcome them. In some ways, this strikes a chord with John Whyte's (1983) analysis of border life during the early 1980s. Whyte argued, somewhat controversially, that the everyday geographies for people living in the Irish borderlands remained largely normal. The connections and networks thought to be ruptured by the imposition of an invisible line and the subsequent construction of two completely distinct jurisdictions, he suggested, were not as pervasive and altering as people perceived. He found that politics and associational life were two completely separate issues. A later survey conducted by Howard in 2007 also found that the boundary had little impact on civil society. While the boundary between Northern Ireland and the Republic remains overtly important, at least politically and symbolically, it does not appear to restrict the movement of those who negotiate it for socio-economic gain. However, the political realities and limitations of living and moving within and across what is effectively two different countries with an invisible yet very real border is not without its problems as the new trans-border communities have been discovering. It is difficult to conceive a possible solution to the complex issues facing such communities in a post-boom era; the socio-economic and political practicalities of border life are an integral part of any border. As Creamer and O'Keeffe conclude in Chapter 4, the role of well-resourced, joint development strategies and closer policy alignment between the two jurisdictions will be key. With the end of the Celtic Tiger economy and the dawn of a very different phase of the economic cycle, new patterns of consumption and mobility are set to influence border living and relationships into the future.

References

Anderson, J. (2008) 'Partition, consociation, border-crossing: some lessons from the national conflict in Ireland/Northern Ireland', *Nations and Nationalism* 14, 1: 85–104.

Beck, U. and Sznaider, N. (2010) 'Unpacking cosmopolitanism for the social sciences: a research agenda', *The British Journal of Sociology* 61: 381–403.

Bradley, J. and Birnie, E. (2001) *Can the Celtic Tiger Cross the Irish Border?* Cork: Cork University Press.

Central Statistics Office (CSO) (2009) *Quarterly National Household Survey: Cross Border Shopping.* Cork and Dublin: Central Statistics Office.

Central Statistics Office (CSO) (2010) *Quarterly National Household Survey: Cross Border Shopping.* Cork and Dublin: Central Statistics Office.

Clarke, P., 2007. 'A cross-border kerfuffle in the north-west', *The Centre for Cross-Border Studies*, www.crossborder.ie/notes-from-the-next-door-neighbours/a-cross-border-kerfuffle-in-the-north-west/, accessed 14 November 2010.

Coakley, J. and O'Dowd, L. (2007) 'The transformation of the Irish border', *Political Geography* 28, 8: 877–95.

Collins, A. and Burt, S. (2011) 'Below cost legislation: lessons from the Republic of Ireland', *International Review of Retail Distribution and Consumer Research* 21, 1: 33–49.

Cowen, B. (2010) 'Making here and now a better place', *The Journal of Cross Border Studies in Ireland* 5, spring: 11–20.

Daly, D. (2007) 'The Irish Free State/Éire/Republic of Ireland/Ireland: "a country by any other name"?', *Journal of British Studies* 46, 1: 72–90.

Gorecki, P. (2009) 'A code of practice for grocery goods and an ombudsman: how to do a lot of harm by trying to do a little good', *Economic and Social Review* 40, 4: 461–84.

Gough, A. and Magennis, E. (2009) *The Impact of Devolution on Everyday Life, 1999–2009: the Case of Cross-border Commerce.* IBIS Working Papers 85. Dublin: Institute for British-Irish Studies, University College Dublin.

Howard, K. (2007) 'Civil society: the permeability of the North–South border', in J. Coakley and L. O'Dowd (eds), *Crossing the Border: New Relationships between Northern Ireland and the Republic of Ireland.* Dublin: Irish Academic Press, pp. 87–103.

InterTradeIreland (2008) *All-island Trade Statistics*, www.intertradeireland.com/trade-statistics, accessed 11 February 2011.

Jansen-Verbeke, M. (1991) 'Leisure shopping: a magic concept for the tourism industry?', *Tourism Management* 12, 1: 9-14.

Jansen-Verbeke, M. (2007) 'Cultural resources and the tourismification of territories', *Acta Turistica Nova* 1, 1: 21–41.

McGuinness, M. (2009) 'McGuinness defends border trade'. *BBC News,* 23 January, http://news.bbc.co.uk/1/hi/northern_ireland/7846175.stm, accessed 14 January 2011.

Millar. S. (2009) 'Claim 11,000 jobs at risk due to North shopping', *Irish Examiner,* 5 December, www.irishexaminer.com/ireland/kfauqlcwcwmh/rss2/, accessed 15 November 2010.

Nash, C. and Reid, B. (2010) 'Border crossings: new approaches to the Irish border', *Irish Studies Review* 18, 3: 265–84.

O'Dowd, L. and McCall, C. (2007) 'The voluntary sector: promoting peace and cooperation', in J. Coakley and L. O'Dowd (eds), *Crossing the Border: New Relationships between Northern Ireland and the Republic of Ireland.* Dublin: Irish Academic Press, pp. 125–51.

O'Leary, B. (2007) 'Analysing partition: definition, classification and explanation', *Political Geography* 26, 8: 886–908.

Office of the Revenue Commission and the Central Statistics Office (2009) *The Implications of Cross-border Shopping for the Irish Exchequer.* Dublin: Office of the Revenue Commission and the Central Statistics Office, www.finance.gov.ie/documents/publications/reports/2009/crossborderefb09.pdf, accessed 10 October 2010.

Paasi, A. (1995) 'Constructing territories, boundaries and regional identities', in T. Forsberg (ed.), *Contested Territory, Border Disputes at the Edge of the Former Soviet Empire.* Aldershot: Edward Elgar, pp. 42–61.

Palmer, A. (2008) 'Tills ring out in Enniskillen as cross-border trade soars', *Fermanagh Today,* 16 December, www.fermanaghtoday.co.uk/fermanaghnews/Tills-ring-out-in-Enniskillen.4796388.jp, accessed 15 February 2011.

Paris, C. (2005) 'From barricades to back gardens: cross-border expansion from the city of Derry to Co. Donegal', in N. Moore and M. Scott (eds), *Renewing Urban Communities: Environment, Citizenship and Sustainability in Ireland*. Aldershot: Ashgate, pp. 113–32.

Sack, R. (1986) *Human Territoriality: Its History and Theory*. Cambridge: Cambridge University Press.

Shuttleworth, I. (2007) 'Reconceptualising local labour markets in the context of cross-border and transnational labour flows: the Irish example', *Political Geography* 26, 8: 968–81.

Simpson, M. (2008) '"Euro tourists" cross the border'. *BBC News*, 22 December, http://news.bbc.co.uk/1/hi/7794882.stm, accessed 16 January 2011.

Tannam, E. (1996) 'The European Union and business cross-border cooperation. The case of Northern Ireland and the Republic of Ireland', *Irish Political Studies* 11; 103–29.

Tannam, E. (1999) *Cross-border Cooperation in the Republic of Ireland and Northern Ireland*. London: Macmillan.

Timothy, D. J. and Butler, R. W. (1995) 'Cross-border shopping: a North American perspective', *Annals of Tourism Research* 22: 6–34.

Tonge, J. (2005) *The EU and the Irish Border: Shaping Aid and Attitudes?* CIBR Electronic Working Papers Series WP05-1. Belfast: Centre for International Borders Research (CIBR), Queens University Belfast, www.qub.ac.uk/research-centres/CentreforInternationalBordersResearch/Publications/WorkingPapers/CIBRWorkingPapers/Filetoupload,174405,en.pdf, accessed 23 March 2011.

Weir, C. and McDaid, B. (2007) 'Girls at heart of "grannying" row attend school', *Belfast Telegraph*, 22 September, p. 5.

Whyte, J. (1983) 'The permeability of the United Kingdom–Irish border: a preliminary reconnaissance', *Administration* 31, 1: 300–15.

9

Growth amidst decline: Ireland's grassroots food growing movement

Aisling Murtagh

A rise in food growing outside the farm has occurred in tandem with Ireland's economic decline as ordinary citizens seek to grow food in alternative spaces such as allotments and community, school and home gardens. This change in Irish society appears to be more than just a reaction to the collapse of the Celtic Tiger. During the Celtic Tiger's reign, such production was dominated by an oppositional minority who sought alternative ways to source their food. As socio-economic circumstances changed, these pioneers supported a new wave of grassroots food growers. In this chapter, the rise of Ireland's grassroots food growing movement is described and a typology of food growing projects is outlined. The broader dynamics of these initiatives is finally considered in order to explore if they are simply the reactionary space of a minority or whether they might become a more sustained resistance.

Resistance to mainstream food

Much discussion related to growing your own food has focused on its potential positive impact on household budgets. However, when the UK consumer watchdog magazine *Which?* uncovered poor value in seedlings, the result was a backlash from gardeners pointing out that: 'growing your own would scarcely be an economic proposition even if every crop turned out prolific and perfect … we do it because we think that by toiling at our winter digging, by meticulously pruning the soft fruit, earthing up the potatoes, hoeing between the rows of cauliflowers, boasting of our rare triumphs and concealing the disasters, we are living a version of *The Good Life*, the rural idyll' (Leapman, 2010). Growing your own food has become a practice by those seeking something better and different from their food, environment and society. Grassroots food initiatives, such as community gardens and allotments, have long been recognised as spaces outside of, and challenging to, conventional political and economic structures. Rather than relying on conventional economic exchange, local resources are mobilised, labour is communal and materials are shared. In the US and UK, increases in demand for urban food growing spaces have been linked with social, economic and political changes that created inequalities, poverty and social unrest (Crouch, 1989; Pudup, 2008; Saldivar-Tanaka and Krasny, 2004; Schmelzkopf, 1995).

Descriptions of the UK allotment culture, traditionally the preserve of the working classes, indicate that allotments were originally established to alleviate poverty and provide social amenity. This allotment culture was restructured during the 1970s with the cultivation of vacant green spaces by environmentalists, signalling the beginnings of community gardening in the UK (Crouch, 1989). Pudup (2008) describes how the US community gardening movement emerged from the grassroots level in the 1970s and was seen as part of urban social movements. In the 1980s, the movement in the US saw greater institutional involvement by state and semi-state bodies who initiated gardens for specific purposes, such as alleviating social marginalisation. As will be shown next, alternative economic and social theories of change and resistance can offer a way to understand what lies beneath these movements and their associated projects, why they occur and how they change.

Alternative changes

Critics of productivism and neoliberal capitalist development argue that external socio-economic circumstances affect a citizen's level of connection with alternatives and their likelihood of entering the mainstream, with greater potential for engagement during crisis periods (Halfacree, 2007; Harvey, 2000). However, Harvey (2000; 2001) is not optimistic about the transformative power of alternative projects, given the strength of the free market that alternatives attempt to oppose. The outcome 'is that any challenge to the glories of the free market ... is to be mercilessly put down or mocked out of existence' (Harvey, 2001: 97–8). This creates an overwhelming sense of powerlessness, with citizens having little to no hope that they can change the system. Not all are overwhelmed, however, and small spaces of hope emerge. For example, Seyfang (2007: 117) describes an organic food co-operative as a 'meeting place for like-minded individuals seeking to carve out a niche in which to act' and thus a space in which to reclaim power and retain hope, attempting to work towards different futures (Lee and Leyshon, 2003). Crucial to the success of such initiatives is how government and society in general respond to them.

For a real challenge, and a more sustained resistance, Harvey (2000; 2001) argues that instead of just small spaces of hope, a clearly defined utopian alternative is needed, creating an aspirational vision, in addition to collective political organisation that is not merely reactionary. The key social and cultural shift is constructing a universal politics out of militant particularisms, described by Harvey (2001: 114) as 'particular struggles at particular places at particular times'. However, this transition is not smooth in practice. While there may be a desire for systemic change, alternative movements face serious challenges: 'the possibility of alternatives does not necessarily lead to the construction of materially effective and socially widespread "spaces of hope" as they may be diminished by material inadequacy, reform of mainstream principles or incorporation into the mainstream' (Lee and Leyshon, 2003: 193). Goodman (2000) drew on Harvey to assess changes in organic and sustainable agriculture movements in the USA, arguing that global ambition emerged from particularistic struggles. However, Goodman found that this occurred within a context of neoliberal market forces and regulation and as Guthman (2004) showed, Californian organic agriculture's vision for sustainable agriculture not only transitioned from a niche market to a large industry but in the process became fragmented as original goals were diluted and compromised. Thus, if the market does not mock and push alternatives out of existence, it may see their economic potential and gradually absorb them into conventional structures, changing them fundamentally (Harvey, 2000; Lee and Leyshon, 2003; Polanyi, 1957). This fits with an appraisal of change in the organic sector and its experience of conventionalisation (Guthman, 2004).

Perhaps a less ambitious and more realistic understanding is the importance of mobilised struggles existing at all, showing that we are 'not entirely helpless puppets of the social process that flows around us' (Harvey, 2001: 113). Many argue that being involved in alternative food initiatives may just be the beginning and inspires an alternative vision, which spreads and motivates others to take part (Allen, Fitzsimons, Goodman et al., 2003; McMahon, 2005). A reading of the practice of grassroots food growing in Ireland through this theoretical lens is a suitable starting point in understanding the overall dynamics of its initiatives. Firstly, some general context for Irish grassroots food growing is given.

Ireland's grassroots food growing

The practice of growing a variety of produce in walled vegetable gardens emerged in Ireland in the 1600s (Sexton, 1998). Over time, rural agricultural households have produced food for their own use as have a minority of urban dwellers in back gardens or allotments (Fox, 2006; Sexton, 1998). Established in 1946, the Irish Country Markets model still demonstrates the importance of home-produced goods, such as eggs and vegetables, as well as their sale, to the domestic rural economy (Sage, 2003). In the 1960s, a small movement of people worked towards self-sufficiency and marked the beginnings of artisan and organic food production in Ireland (Sage, 2003; Tovey, 1997).

Goodman (2000) differentiates alternative food movements suggesting that there are two strands: a sustainable agriculture, producer-led movement in rural space and a community food security, consumer- or citizen-led movement in urban space. In Celtic Tiger Ireland, seemingly unrelenting economic growth was questioned by some, driving a food movement in rural areas, led by local food actors such as farmers, growers and small food producers (Tovey, 2006). One key outcome was the establishment of Ireland's first farmers' markets in the 1990s, which continued to increase in number for around a decade (Moore, 2006). While less is known about the consumer-led food movement in Ireland, there has been a well-documented surge in demand for food growing spaces since the economic downturn (Fallon, 2009; Monaghan, 2008; Ryan, 2009), a demand that actually began during the preceding years of economic growth (Hayes, 2006; Powers, 2004; Viney, 2006). However, when categorising Ireland's grassroots food growing movement, Goodman's (2000) neat classification is not an ideal fit. Describing an urban consumer food movement in Ireland is problematic as initiatives cannot be labelled as strictly urban-based or citizen-driven; nor can the development of farmers' markets be categorised as solely producer-led. Hence, there is a need to begin to understand the dynamics of the consumer- and citizen-driven alternative food movement in Ireland.

This section focuses on a collection of activities and spaces – allotments, community gardens, school gardens and growers' groups – broadly understood as the grassroots food growing movement. This movement, which is both urban and rural, is driven by individual leaders, groups of citizens, or individuals with involvement in food and non-food activities, such as food producers, community activists and other professionals. The chapter draws from interviews with ten grassroots food activists across Ireland in late 2009 and early 2010, as well as informal discussion with numerous others, from participant observation carried out through involvement in garden projects and attendance at related events, and from written narratives such as project newsletters, blogs, e-bulletins, meeting minutes and reports.[1]

Two dominant types of initiative in both urban and rural spaces are allotments and community gardens. Allotments are spaces in urban landscapes specifically designated for growing food and have traditionally been provided by local authorities. However, Irish local authorities do not have a strong track record in allotment provision when compared with the UK. For example, Dublin had four allotment sites in 2004 compared to forty-one in Manchester (Fox, 2006) even though Dublin city's population was some 100,000 greater than Manchester's around that time (Central Statistics Office, 2003; Manchester City Council, 2001). This history of comparatively lower provision of allotments existed in pre-independence Ireland also. In 1916, there were eighty plots in Dublin, compared to 1,200 in Belfast (Hennessy, 2004), even though both cities had comparable populations (see National Archives of Ireland, 2011). Through the 1990s, most of Ireland's few allotment sites were on public land in the Dublin area. With the formation of local allotment associations, campaigns calling for both the preservation of existing allotment sites and the provision of new ones were begun. The South Dublin Allotments Association, representing allotment holders at four public sites, was established in 2004. Subsequently, a number of other allotment associations emerged, in Dublin and beyond (e.g. Sligo and Tipperary). But access to land is a key issue. During the Celtic Tiger period, development pressure on land due to the residential and commercial building boom, combined with a lack of demand for public allotments, resulted in allotment sites being turned over to development. In the post-boom recession, rising interest in allotment growing has resulted in waiting lists with local authorities unable to meet the demand for allotments. If public land is not already available for allotments, local authority budgetary constraints may preclude buying land for this purpose (Murtagh, 2011). The shortfall in public provision has created a market for private landowners to provide allotments for rent with the result that Irish allotments are now diverse spaces provided by both the public and private sectors.

Coinciding with the increase in demand for allotments, Ireland's community gardens emerged around 2005, with the first in Dublin city at Dolphin's Barn and Sitric Road. The other main presence in community gardening at this time was the Cork Mandala of Community Gardens in Cork city. The community garden space is utilised not just to grow food but to meet various aims, such as community building, social inclusion and waste management. The Celtic Tiger building boom made it difficult to secure land for community gardens also, with many initiators reporting that their efforts took as long as a year or more. Other sites came with restrictions. For example, gardeners in one community garden could only secure temporary permission to use the space because of the development potential of the site. Such development threats have waned in line with Ireland's economic decline. Consequently, the number of community gardens has risen alongside the establishment of both national and local groups helping to build connections and provide supports, such as Irish Community Food Growing, the National Network of Community Gardens, Dublin Food Growing and Wicklow Community Gardening Group. Most Irish community gardens emerged at the grassroots level, fuelled by human energy, donations and benevolence, and with little direct support from the State or its institutions. While institutions are not generally associated with community gardens, schools are a notable exception. Increasing interest in the value of gardens as an educational resource is highlighted by projects such as *Organic Gardening for Primary Schools*, a programme run by Bord Bia, Ireland's National Food Promotion Board. Nevertheless, these gardens are still most often driven by the activism of the school's community of parents and teachers.

A change in the nature of action has also been seen with home growers organising to share knowledge, skills and resources through growers' groups, whereby members garden externally to the group's primary activities. While isolated groups existed in the past, a burst of activity occurred in 2009 with the launch of a national non-profit organisation called Grow it Yourself (GIY) Ireland to promote and support the development of growers' groups nationally. Whereas Ireland has lagged behind the UK in the provision of allotments and behind the USA in terms of the development of community gardens, it has led the way with the GIY model, which has now been adopted overseas with the establishment of GIY Australia's first growing group in 2010. A close look at the grassroots food growing movement in Irish society reveals that it can be classified broadly into four types of dynamics in terms of how grassroots food projects emerge, change and are driven, and these are considered next.

Organised food growing

Pudup's (2008) term 'organised garden project' is useful in beginning to classify projects promoting the knowledge and providing the physical space for people to grow their own food. The term is used to capture a range of projects, from those in institutional settings (such as jails and schools) to community gardens. One of its central principles is that 'an organized group of people is involved in cultivation, even if gardening is individualized in its spatial arrangement and practice' (Pudup, 2008: 1231). However, Pudup's term excludes allotments and growers' groups. Therefore, the term is adapted and expanded here as 'organised food growing project' to capture the diversity of grassroots food growing activities in Ireland. An organised food growing project refers to any kind of organised group whose members grow food for their own consumption and promote this approach, regardless of where the growing takes place. In Ireland at least four types of organised food growing projects can be discerned (Table 9.1).

Table 9.1 Organised food growing projects in Ireland

Led by	Initiation/coordination	Example
Institution or organisation	School, local authority, community organisation or charity.	GIY Ireland is a charity that promotes the development of autonomous growers' groups. Local groups are managed independently while linked to the parent organisation.
Group	A number of people come together to establish the project. The group may emerge from the existing community or the group may exist because of the project, i.e. over and beyond an extant community.	South Dublin Allotments Association formed when a group of allotment holders got together to help preserve the allotments originally provided by the City Council that were falling into disrepair and under threat of development.
Private landowner	Farmer or landowner establishes allotments and rents them out.	Hydro Farm Allotments in County Cork was established by a landowner who opened up farmland to the public.
Pioneer	Primarily one individual sets up and coordinates the project, at least initially.	Dunhill Ecopark Community Garden in County Waterford was initiated by a pioneer who worked in a community organisation and held a vision for a garden to eventually be managed by the community.

The categorisations are dynamic; one form may morph into another and there are also cross-over, hybrid categories. For example, institution-initiated allotments can become increasingly community- or individual-driven as institutional engagement lessens, necessitating a community or individual to strive to preserve them. Initiatives are also liable to grow in ways that initiators may not have envisaged. When Hydro Farm Allotments was established in the late 1990s, demand was low and allotments were left vacant: 'nobody knew what an allotment was … it used to take me weeks of encouraging people, nearly begging them to take allotments'. By 2010, the situation had reversed and demand exceeded supply: 'now I have people ringing me and emailing me [looking for allotments]' (Interview 9). From the beginning of GIY in 2008, local meetings were well attended and by autumn 2011, GIY Ireland numbered over 5,000 registered members (GIY Ireland, 2011). These trends illustrate how interest in organised food growing not only increases during periods of crisis but how initiatives can spread from local to national (and international in the case of GIY).

Wider dynamics and change

Having considered the types of organised food growing projects, it is informative to assess the values that underpin them. In general, the projects lie in contrast to the practice of personal gratification through consumption that came to characterise the Celtic Tiger years and demonstrate how food consumption can reflect a vision for a politics of change towards a better society. This follows the logic of alternative economic theorists such as Harvey (2000), who argues that when the dominant economic paradigm fails, this is the time when more people look to alternatives. There is a sense of populism about the food growing movement's development in that as both it and Ireland's economic decline gained momentum, the movement transitioned from being the preserve of just a niche group. As one activist commented: 'It's not just the usual suspects … the people who came out here would have called you a tree hugger a year before … it's phenomenal … a switch has happened' (Interview 4). While only time will tell if wider support for the movement will be sustained, an assessment of the range of values communicated by grassroots food growers offers a complex picture and also suggests more than a superficial or reactionary response.

Food consumption becomes a thoughtful act as grassroots food growers attempt to reclaim some control over how their food is produced, with an emphasis on sustainability, the use of traditional methods and a closer affinity and respect for the processes of nature, all of which seem to contradict the Celtic Tiger culture of unsustainable consumption. Participants are also rewarded with more nutritious, quality produce. As one grassroots grower explained it: 'Traditional thinking is useful … there are ways of [growing] that are sustainable and many of them are based on traditional skills … the soil is alive … the plant when you take it out of the ground, be it a carrot, a parsnip, a cabbage, a potato, is full of vitality and it is only full of vitality if the ground is full of life' (Interview 2). While a desire to re-connect with the land is also evident from the growers' narratives, the movement does not appear to be a quest for the rural idyll but rather a call for the reintroduction of elements of the traditional and the rural into everyday life, whether in urban or rural space: 'Maybe if I can't go out and live in the country, well, maybe I can go out and bring some of the country back here … [to] this allotment site … it just felt to me like a real haven without having to uproot' (Interview 2).

Organised food growing projects provide spaces of hope and possibility within a world, as epitomised by Celtic Tiger Ireland, that does not meet these needs. They are dynamic spaces created with limited inputs and most depend on mobilising a local social economy. Money is secondary to local giving, human labour, skills and knowledge sharing, which again runs counter to the individualistic, throwaway society that characterised the Celtic Tiger era. For example, the bulk of resources for community gardens are not bought in garden centres. Old carpets are recycled into mulch, wooden pallets are re-used as frames for compost bins, and the practices of seed sharing and swopping are also strong. There is even a sense of impermanence and recycling about community gardens themselves as the lands on which they are established are often borrowed spaces with allotment holders as merely temporary tenants. Projects with some funding may use it to buy new materials; however, reusing and sourcing locally are still central tenets with self-reliance highly valued: 'If a thing can't stand on its own two feet, it's not worth anything' (Interview 9).

Different layers of meaning can also be identified. Some see organised food growing spaces as an arena for influencing the attitudes of others. Mobilising participation is seen to have a multiplier effect, with people's initial interest becoming deeper and strengthened by their involvement. As one grassroots grower stated, 'I knew that when you brought connection to the soil … it had an effect on how you cared about it' (Interview 6). This approach is fundamental to the movement's activism. Participants acknowledged that mobilising such food activism can change people's views while also empowering them, as exemplified by the act of seed saving: 'When you think of all that Monsanto stuff, you know, I could be out protesting or writing emails but I think I'm doing much more, being subversive and gaining power, by teaching [others] how to save their own seeds' (Interview 8). Participation in organised food growing projects can also have more straightforward meanings with some growers citing a return to ways that were once the norm, driven by economic reasons or by nostalgia for a simpler way of life in opposition to the Celtic Tiger's fast-paced, high-consumption lifestyle: 'I grew up with the stories … the farm, having a cow, collecting the eggs, eating the peas, you know, and I thought: "I want that"' (Interview 1). The presence of such layers of meaning among participants reveals differing levels of engagement with the food movement as some identify with a broader ideology of societal change while others are simply making a personal lifestyle choice. This diversity may weaken the potential of the food movement to bring about widespread societal change.

The very existence of the movement and its organised food growing projects signal that some retain hope and continue to work towards spreading the seeds of the change that they seek. Activists recognise that to effect broader social change, organised food growing projects need to progress from a state of particularism to a wider movement for change. One activist summarised the need in this way: 'The cry of someone at an individual basis, who is saying something is terribly wrong, may not have the same effect' (Interview 3). However, along with the diversity of values held by proponents of the movement, the nature of resistance, such as its position outside of the formal economy and its dependence primarily on voluntary resources, poses limitations. Referring to an attempt to organise growers, one activist explained that: 'it has, kind of, just limped along … it needs support … it needs one full-time person to, kind of, be there … and to hold the vision for it' (Interview 3). This highlights the struggle involved in attempting to operate outside of the conventional marketplace but an even greater challenge may be that the demands of a movement's own principles can hinder its development. While the Celtic Tiger's collapse increased interest in grassroots food growing and thereby helped to mainstream the movement, such mainstreaming leaves it vulnerable to co-option as 'soft' social values may be compromised by the 'hard' market logic of supply and demand. For example, one development that signals a departure from the grassroots, community-based approach was described as follows:

> I would get … [landowners] asking 'how much are you charging for an allotment?' … then they'd work out how many square feet that was and then make it into an acre and then they'd say … 'can you imagine how much money I'll make out of that?', and I'd say, 'no no no, it doesn't work like that' … you have to do it slowly and actually get people in who are going to establish themselves and become part of a community. (Interview 9)

Local authority allotments have increased in price since the downturn. Many local authorities in the Dublin area have moved to charging per square metre for their allotment sites (Murtagh 2011). One private allotment provider interviewed also commented that their insurance costs have increased, forcing them in turn to increase rents for plotholders. With public bodies not keeping pace with demand, this research found that the private market stepped in with the result that the number of private allotment sites increased in post-boom Ireland. While mobilising local free resources helps to maintain projects, gaining access to land, the prime commodity for growing, can be the biggest issue for organised food growing projects. They often depend on land provided by a local authority, community group or even the philanthropic act of a local business. Thus, a key challenge for the movement's capacity to sustain its purism as it develops into the future is whether it has the support of local government institutions or whether it needs to look to the private market to allow for its continued expansion.

Conclusions

The emergence of grassroots and organised food growing projects in periods of economic growth and their surge during periods of decline is an established phenomenon since the mid-twentieth century. While the food movement discussed here does not offer a utopian vision for systematic change, it does represent spaces of hope in which alternatives are possible. Aligned with the Celtic Tiger's demise, the boom in demand for alternative food growing spaces does seem somewhat populist but there is simultaneously a wave of oppositional thought and organisation that may succeed in driving this trend beyond the reactionary moment created by economic recession. The typology of organised food growing projects outlined here shows that initiatives could tend towards more institutional or community management models, or that a market-driven logic may take hold. There are already some signs of co-option and absorption by dominant conventional market structures, which suggests that any sustained resistance may be a paler imitation of the initial vision of grassroots food activists. Nevertheless, stronger reactionary spaces of hope may persist amongst mainstreamed initiatives. Like other food movements, offshoots and iterations will change its shape through time; how they will exactly in the case of post-boom Ireland remains to be seen.

Notes

1   Supported by the Irish Research Council for Humanities and Social Sciences Postgraduate Scholarship Scheme 2009–10.

References

Allen, P., Fitzsimons, M., Goodman, M. and Warner, K. (2003) 'Shifting plates in the agrifood landscape: the tectonics of alternative agrifood initiatives in California', *Journal of Rural Studies* 19: 61–75.

Central Statistics Office (CSO) (2003) *Census 2002: Principal Demographic Results.* Dublin: The Stationery Office.

Crouch, D. (1989) 'The allotment, landscape and locality: ways of seeing landscape and culture', *Area* 21, 3: 261–7.

Fallon, F. (2009) 'New gardeners need to dig up the basics first', Irish Times, 9 April, p. 27.

Fox, M. (2006) 'Good news from the allotment campaign', *Local Planet,* 28 March, http://localplanet.ie/content/view/193/56/, accessed 20 January 2010.

GIY Ireland (2011) www.giyireland.com, accessed 29 September 2011.

Goodman, D. (2000) 'Organic and conventional agriculture: materialising discourse and agro-ecological managerialism', *Agriculture and Human Values* 17: 215–19.

Guthman, J. (2004) *Agrarian Dreams: The Paradox of Organic Farming in California.* Berkeley, CA: University of California Press.

Halfacree, K. (2007) 'Trial by space for a "radical rural": introducing alternative localities, representations and lives', *Journal of Rural Studies* 23: 125–41.

Harvey, D. (2000) *Spaces of Hope.* Edinburgh: Edinburgh University Press.

Harvey, D. (2001) 'The spaces of utopia', in L. Bower, D. Goldberg and M. Musheno (eds), *Between Law and Culture: Relocating Legal Studies.* Minneapolis, MN: University of Minnesota Press, pp. 95–121.

Hayes, I. (2006) 'Dubliners plot return to the land as demand for city allotments surges', *Sunday Tribune,* 23 April, www.tribune.ie/archive/article/2006/apr/23/dubliners-plot-return-to-the-land-as-demand-for-ci/, accessed 20 January 2010.

Hennessy, D. (2004) 'Ireland's forgotten allotment scheme – 1. The allotment movement', *Waterford County Museum – Historical Articles,* 3 December, www. waterfordcountymuseum.org/exhibit/web/WAIVersion/article/191/1/, accessed 20 January 2010.

Leapman, M. (2010) 'Growing carrots can make you lose the plot', *Daily Telegraph,* 2 March, www.telegraph.co.uk/gardening/7350124/Growing-carrots-can-make-you-lose-the-plot.html, accessed 2 March 2010.

Lee, R. and Leyshon, A. (2003) 'Conclusion: re-making geographies and the construction of spaces of hope', in A. Leyshon, R. Lee and C. Williams (eds), *Alternative Economic Spaces.* London: Sage, pp. 193–8.

McMahon, N. (2005) 'Biodynamic farmers in Ireland. Transforming society through purity, solitude and bearing witness', *Sociologia Ruralis* 45, 1–2: 98–114.

Monaghan, G. (2008) 'Scramble for allotment plots as veg growing booms', *Sunday Times,* 12 October, www.timesonline.co.uk/tol/news/world/ireland/article4926762.ece, accessed 3 December 2009.

Moore, O. (2006) 'Farmers' markets', in M. P. Corcoran and M. Peillon (eds), *Uncertain Ireland: A Sociological Chronicle 2003–4.* Dublin: Institute of Public Administration, pp. 129–40.

Murtagh, A. (2011) 'Losing the plot', *Consumer Choice,* April: 88–91.

National Archives of Ireland (2011) *Ireland in the early 20th century,* www.census. nationalarchives.ie/exhibition/index.html, accessed 20 September 2011.

Polanyi, K. (1957) *The Great Transformation: The Political and Economic Origins of our Time.* Boston, MA: Beacon Press.

Powers, J. (2004) 'Dig deep for a greener city', *Irish Times*, 28 January, p. 17.

Pudup, M. B. (2008) 'It takes a garden: cultivating citizen-subjects in organized garden projects', *Geoforum* 39: 1228–40.

Ryan, R. (2009) 'Allotment demand phenomenal, says minister', *Irish Examiner*, 30 May, www.irishexaminer.com/ireland/sncwsnqlql/rss2/, accessed 9 January 2010.

Sage, C. (2003) 'Social embeddedness and relations of regard: "good food" networks in south-west Ireland', *Journal of Rural Studies* 19, 1: 47–60.

Saldivar-Tanaka, L. and Krasny, M. (2004) 'Culturing community development, neighbourhood open space and civic agriculture: the case of Latino community gardens in New York City', *Agriculture and Human Values* 21: 399–412.

Schmelzkopf, K. (1995) 'Urban community gardens as contested space', *Geographical Review* 85, 3: 364–81.

Sexton, R. (1998) *A Little History of Irish Food*. Dublin: Gill and Macmillan.

Seyfang, G. (2007) 'Cultivating carrots and community: local organic food and sustainable consumption', *Environmental Values* 16: 105–23.

Tovey, H. (1997) 'Food, environmentalism and rural sociology: on the organic farming movement in Ireland', *Sociologia Ruralis* 37, 1: 21–37.

Tovey, H. (2006) 'New movements in old places? The alternative food movement in rural Ireland', in L. Connolly and N. Hourigan (eds), *Social Movements in Ireland*. Manchester: Manchester University Press, pp. 168–89.

Viney, M. (2006) 'Don't lose the plot – grow your own veggies', *Irish Times*, 27 May, p. 9.

Part III

Culture and place

10

Ancestors in the field:
Irish farming knowledges

Caroline Crowley

> Seek wisdom, not knowledge, knowledge is of the past, wisdom is of the future.
>
> Native American proverb from the Lumbee tribe.

Ireland's economic realities have undergone a spectacular transition from an apparently booming economy through the early 2000s, to an economy in recession by the end of the decade. While debates rage as to who and what is responsible, there is general agreement that the economic crisis presents an opportunity to re-imagine the future and that any recovery will be driven by innovation underpinned by knowledge. Agri-Food is one of four sectors identified for employment growth by the Irish Government (Department of Finance, 2011). *Food Harvest 2020* is the main strategic policy document for Irish agriculture and proposes smart green growth in the sector that remains one of Ireland's largest indigenous industries accounting for roughly 6 per cent of Gross Value Added and 7 per cent of employment in 2010 (DAFF, 2011). The world's rising demand for food is seen as an opportunity for exploitation by Irish farmers, some 99,500 according to the latest estimate (Hennessey, Moran, Kinsella and Quinlan, 2011). But the Irish sector is economically unsustainable: 2009 figures show an average farm income of €12,000 (approximately 37 per cent of the average industrial wage) with farming subsidies comprising 143 per cent of family farm income (DAFF, 2011). In other words, farm products are sold below cost and the average farm would have a negative income without subsidies. Thus, while promoted as a sector of future economic promise, many farmers have come to expect a low income from their agricultural output and that income is vulnerable to the volatile global food markets and changes in the highly politicised Common Agricultural Policy (CAP). Low farm income is related to a number of factors, in particular the dominance of productivism – an ever more neoliberal and globalised system of capitalist agricultural development. With farms exposed to freer market conditions, the result is a farmscape of inequality where 'winners' in the system operate increasingly larger and technologised farms whereas the 'losers' that comprise the majority are left dependent on either CAP subsidisation or on income from non-farming employment, if they do not exit farming altogether (Ní Laoire, 2004). The CAP's helping hand seems to have impeded the evolution of farm-centred solutions whereby capital and human resources are used in different ways to address the problem of falling farm incomes. For instance, Meredith (2011) estimated that just 4 per cent of Irish farms in 2007 had on-farm diversified activity, that is, were using farmland, buildings or labour resources in new and alternative ways. Neither market forces nor the CAP fully explain such a dearth of alternative farm enterprises. The role of diverse forms of farming knowledge and knowledge cultures must also be considered. This chapter explores the ways in which different forms of farming knowledges are produced, disseminated and influence farmers' willingness or ability to make changes to their farming systems.

The chapter adopts two concepts from Morgan and Murdoch (2000): a simple classification of forms of knowledge, and the idea of networks to help understand relations among possessors of knowledge and the process of disseminating knowledge. They outline a dichotomy of forms of knowledge, whereby codified knowledge is objectively derived from scientific enquiry by experts, and is 'standardised and easily transferable' whereas tacit or lay knowledge is 'often personal and context-dependent' (Morgan and Murdoch, 2000: 160–1) resulting as it does from the subjective interaction of practice, people and place. Thus, codified knowledge is universalisable or global, whereas tacit or lay knowledge is situated or local. These knowledge forms are employed here as Weberian ideal types that help uncover the hidden social structures that influence the production and dissemination of knowledge, and consequently, the evolution (or not) of alternative farming practices and systems. Global knowledge underpins the productivist model of agricultural development, particularly production intensification whereby technological and chemical innovations overcome natural resource limitations. Conversely, local knowledges are associated with traditional agriculture that overcomes resource constraints through less invasive practices cognisant of natural limitations. A key difference between the two sets of knowledge is that local knowledge evolves in a distinctive ecological, socio-cultural and historical context, whereas global knowledge is informed by universalisable scientific and technological information and is not therefore embedded in any particular locale (see Tovey, 2008).

In terms of knowledge possessors and dissemination, Morgan and Murdoch (2000) note that knowledge moves through networks of actors and organisations permeated by power relations where links or relations of trust in the network represent a mix of coercion and cooperation. These networks help to explain why farming knowledges are neither freely available to all nor readily adoptable even by farmers with access to them. Since this chapter considers the knowledges of farmers (directly) and state agricultural agents (indirectly), Riley's (2008: 1279) exploration of knowledge cultures or 'socially negotiated structures of meaning that enable and constrain action' among these two groups is especially informative. Knowledge cultures represent 'an active sediment of past experiences that function in the present to influence perceptions and action' (Riley, 2008: 1280) highlighting both the socio-cultural evolution and the durability of knowledges over time.

The capacity to innovate appropriately, using traditional methods, technological advances or a combination of both, can be seen as essential to adapting to Ireland's new economic realities and the changing agricultural policy and market landscapes of the twenty-first century. Current uncertainties combined with an unknowable future call for an openness in the agri-food sector to engaging with diverse knowledges. This in turn requires a more negotiative approach to knowledge generation and exchange, and thus greater relations of trust within farming knowledge networks together with a breaking down of established power relations. The hegemony of expert and global knowledges over lay and local knowledges in recent decades has drawn criticism. Fonte (2008: 213) argues that: '[s]cientific knowledge … needs to be integrated, adapted and mediated by those with expertise and trained in specific traditional and artisan modes of food production, and by those who know the "place"'. The transfer of power in knowledge creation from lay practitioners to experts through the industrialisation of agriculture has, according to Fonte (2008), interrupted the evolution of Europe's rich stock of lay knowledge in recent decades. Neoliberal, capitalist globalisation has strongly influenced the sector with farm development trajectories focusing on achieving economies of scale to input cheap commodities to food processing and retailing multinationals. As Massey (2005) opines, this logic turns geography into history; places unsuited to the dominant model of development (and, for the purposes of this chapter, their indigenous farming knowledges and knowledge cultures) are not understood as simply different but rather of the past, thereby delegitimising their own particularistic development trajectories. In Ireland, a network comprised of the State's agricultural agents and large farmers, along with the farming media and mainstream farming organisations, has been complicit in this co-option of farming knowledges by the agricultural industry. The network has contributed to the spread and hegemony of the productivist paradigm underpinned by global knowledges to the detriment of local farming knowledges and has contributed to the economic and political marginalisation of the majority of farmers.

Since discursive strategies are key to knowledge cultures, farmer narratives offer a rich insight into how, as Riley (2008: 1280) describes it, farmers 'are able to structure discourse in a way that prioritises their individual and collective understandings and identities'. They reveal how knowledge cultures shape farmer identities and influence their farming practices. This chapter draws from interviews in 2008 with young farmers in two distinct farming regions in Ireland (the South-East broadly characterised by more favourable land resources and farm commercialisation; and the North-West, with comparatively challenging land resources and more traditional pastoral farming (Crowley, Walsh and Meredith, 2008; Lafferty, Commins and Walsh, 1999)). It describes how as children they begin to imbibe knowledge of everyday farming practices as well as to develop understandings of farming ways or philosophies from their families and the local farming community. Later in life, they engage directly with knowledge from state agents through agricultural training and farm inspections. Farming knowledges promoted by the State combined with the way in which its agents disseminate them and/or their reception by farmers are assessed in relation to two alternative farm enterprises – farm forestry and on-farm milk pasteurisation/cheese production. The chapter concludes by introducing a relative newcomer to rural and farming knowledge networks that may already be playing a key role in revalourising local knowledges.

Knowledges and agricultural values from family and community

Farmers learn their craft and business from different sources and in different ways over their life course. The initial source of knowledge about farming is other family members, particularly the father – the family member invariably identified as the farmer. When asked to recall their earliest farming memory, respondents often reminisced that as soon as they could walk they followed their father around the farm. This activity seems to be a form of play through which the child displays an attraction to farming and appears to identify with the father. Experiential lay knowledges based on resource use (Tovey, 2008) are readily picked up in this way, as the following quotes demonstrate: 'Farming was very dominant to me in my life from ... when I was fit to walk nearly' (SE017);[1] 'Yeah, just from, I suppose, being a daft, wee child ... and playing around with animals and tractors and the whole lot. I kind of grew into it more and more, so it's the only thing I was interested in' (NW004); 'I was always out with Dad, even before I'd go to school. I had my few calves and feeding the calves and that, always, just kinda grew up out on the farm around with Dad' (NW023).

Growing up on a farm exposes children to another kind of local and tacit farming knowledge informing everyday practices; an awareness of broader and more abstract farming philosophies or approaches. Such knowledge seems to be instilled in members of the farm family rather than consciously demonstrated and copied; a type of social capital that allows actors to perform as competent members of their community (Tovey, 2008) or as agents conversant in their particular knowledge culture. While concern for the environment is expressed occasionally, the dominant underlying themes are socio-cultural: maintaining family tradition and looking after the land in order to pass it on in good order to the next generation. Caring for and progressing the farm (with discussions centred on the land) seem entwined with notions of sustaining the family lineage on that land: 'I want to continue on from my father and grandfather and before that' (NW004); 'Dad was always of the opinion you should give the land down to the next generation in the same condition you got it, if not better' (NW023).

The wider farming community also influences knowledges related to farming practices and agricultural values as the young farmers described how neighbours identified aptitudes and shaped attitudes with regard to their personal farming performances or the family's farming system. Here, one young man recalls how locals admired his ability to distinguish sheep in a flock when he was still a boy: 'from an early age, I was earmarked as somebody who'd an awful interest in sheep ... it's just something that's there and I think from a very early age that was spotted in me by other farmers. It was kind of encouraged that I was the one for the land' (NW008). However, the attitudes of local farmers can be discouraging and cause distress to those who are seen to do things differently. The following young farmer revealed his frustration with local attitudes (and the agricultural values they imply) to the unconventional crop grown on his family farm:

> I talk to farmers in the area ... and, ah, they tell me that we're not farmers ... because ... we grow [flowers]. 'Wha'? Flower farmers?' Which disappoints me, ya know; like, farming is farming and you should respect somebody who's doing something well and grows good crops ... it's sad in a way, you know, that [sighs], when ... you know that some farmers in the area wouldn't respect you because of what you do, even though you might do it really well. (SE025)

These narratives reveal how the farmers experience a sense of social circumscription, recalling the notion of knowledge cultures. Community admiration for one's talent for being able to recognise hundreds of individual sheep is flattering. Even though the young man admits that there is no money to be made from this particular skill, there is an impression of enjoying others' esteem and from them he learns that he may have a future in farming. Conversely, the lack of respect among locals for another family's financially successful enterprise troubles a well-educated and ambitious young farmer. While believing in the family's farming enterprise and their openness to experimenting with new ventures, the young person is keenly aware of the deprecating views of local farmers who undervalue their entrepreneurial approach to farming. Although it is understood that those unhelpful views signify a conservative mindset that the young person dislikes, nevertheless, the negative psychological effect of such commentary on the young person's perception of their own standing in the community seems keenly felt. One senses the power of the local farming knowledge cultures in shaping farmers' own beliefs and practices, directing them down certain farm development pathways rather than others and not simply for reasons underpinned by economic gain. Some of the narratives suggest an orientation towards the past that constrains present practices and this is most evident in discussions about farm forestry. But as will be seen, the resistance to this form of externally imposed knowledge appears to be related to the value placed on factors other than economic return rather than being indicative of a conservative mindset towards innovation.

Ancestors in the field: farmer identities and the temporal orientation of farming knowledge cultures

Many farmers have exhibited a strong buy-in to the productivist discourse since the 1960s. It concurs with farmers' understandings of their role as producers of food commodities using conventional methods. Specialising in a particular farming system and intensifying production signifies the modernisation of traditional mixed farming systems whereby farmers still retain their accustomed roles of livestock husbandry or crop growing although the characteristics of their farm business is quite different to that of their predecessors. As one farmer summed it up: 'I'm a farmer ... and farming ... for me is a generational thing that I've always seen. It's a farmer goes out and he tends his stock, he tends his crop' (SE017). But 'his stock' and 'his crop' cannot be just any kind, apparently, as another young farmer laments: 'We boxed ourselves into a category. Farming to an Irish person is cows or cattle, sheep, pigs, cereals and maybe potatoes and carrots, nothing else, that's farming, that's it, close the gate. We'll put all them in that room and the other lads: the forestry, the salad growers, the daffodil growers, you know, any of these lads, they're not farmers' (SE025).

Exploration of farm forestry as an alternative farm enterprise (because planting and growing trees as a crop is not a traditional farming activity in Ireland) elicited strong reactions. Although grants to incentivise farmland afforestation have been available since the 1980s, and Teagasc (the Irish Agriculture and Food Development Agency) has long promoted the economic viability of forestry on disadvantaged farmland, various studies reveal a negative cultural bias among farmers towards forestry (e.g. Kearney, 2001). Local knowledge cultures appear to constrain engagement with forestry for a number of reasons. Farmers do not consider forestry as farming, particularly because it does not require the same day-to-day management as other crops: 'That's not farming in my aspect ... If you've a forest, you can go away for fifty weeks of the year, two weeks you can spend fencing it. If you're farming cattle, you have to spend 365 days of the year with them ... . one is farming, the other isn't' (NW011).

There is also recourse to the implications for the wider community of planting forestry in relation to rural decline and in the following quote one can read the broader discouragement of the practice: 'When you plant the land, that land's gone forever ... That's why people leave [rural areas] ... because there's nothing left ... forestry became a kind of a dirty word, particularly when I was comin' up in the early '80s. Like, if you talked about planting your land it was the biggest sin you could commit nearly' (NW008). One young farmer who actually works for Coillte, the private limited company that owns and commercially manages the state's forests, invoked his ancestors when he explained why he would not plant trees on his land:

> If you're reared on a farm along with your family ... when you see people passing on, dying on, and you kind of remember when they were there and the craic [fun] that was on the farm and the things they done, all the effort they put in and all the work, that it's sad, kind of, to put a tree in their work, destroy the fields, like, the fields where they lifted stones and made drains and everything, and to see it all, kind of, ploughed up for the last time. (NW004)

This recourse to the social history of the farm highlights how planting trees is not only seen as a reversal of the former practice of clearing trees from the land to farm it and therefore represents a revolutionary break with the past and with tradition for a farmer, but it also signifies the concealment of a landscape rich in familial and cultural meaning and value: 'There's more to farming than money, you know ... especially for land that has come through the generations; it's the end of a link to the past' (NW008). Riley (2008: 1280) also found this narrative of continuity in farmers' resistance to certain agri-environmental land management prescriptions in the UK, whereby farming knowledges, practices and identities not only become standardised through local knowledge cultures but are intertwined with the past; 'the past serves to act as a moral template for current action'. Here, decisions with regards to farm forestry appear orientated towards the past and draw upon ancestors and cultural values, a highly subjective and personalised orientation that seems to inhibit a break with tradition.

However, the power of this narrative may dissipate over spatial distance. It is revealing that while farmers are very reluctant to plant forestry on their own farmland or in the local area, they may not be against the practice in and of itself. One farmer who disapproves of planting his own farmland, where he recalls the work his father invested in consolidating and improving the farm, would consider planting forestry on land with which he does not have family connections and that lies beyond the local area: 'I could buy land in Longford, Carlow and plant it … but when you plant land that was … in your family name … I can't' (NW011). The farmer appears to make two points: firstly, he cannot plant forestry on family land and, secondly, that if he was to plant forestry, he would only consider it on non-family land beyond the locale. The farmer reveals that his land management choices are limited not only with regard to his ancestors and family, but also with regard to the contemporary local community. It suggests that there is spatiality to the social influence of knowledge cultures so that farmers' actions are enabled or constrained by them *within particular geographical areas*.

While forestry was denigrated as a farming practice in both the commercial and marginal farming case study areas, the invocation of ancestors, and thus an orientation of local knowledge cultures to the past, was only evident in the latter. Ní Laoire (2004) surmised that such valuing of tradition among marginal farmers is a way of coping with their lack of economic success under the productivist paradigm. This lack of success, underpinned by such characteristics as smaller and more fragmented farms, where commercialisation of agriculture is stymied by climate, topography, soil quality and distance to urban markets (Crowley, Walsh and Meredith, 2008), is combined with the tendency for land in marginal farming areas to be transferred primarily via inheritance and thereby remain in the family (Lafferty, Commins and Walsh, 1999).

State agents

Low uptake of alternative farm enterprises that may offer economic viability implies the strength of local knowledge cultures in restricting some forms of innovation among farmers. But the narratives also revealed non-place specific knowledge barriers that originate beyond the local farming community. The main external, expert sources of information used by farmers are Teagasc (a semi-state agency), and the Department of Agriculture, Fisheries and Food (DAFF). Teagasc and the DAFF, along with most of the farming media and national farming organisations, are proponents of the productivist farming paradigm that promotes processes of production intensification, specialisation of farms and the regional concentration of farming systems, all of which characterise the general development of Ireland's farming sector in recent decades (Crowley, Walsh and Meredith, 2008). Despite negative externalities including environmental degradation, food scares and international trade disputes, the hegemony of this productivist paradigm persists through ongoing modifications such as ecological modernisation, escalating industry regulations, and the development of a two-track farm policy system under the CAP. Over time, back-to-the-land social movements have emerged to challenge the productivist paradigm such as organics and food relocalisation, both of which have emerged from activists beyond the core farming sector. In spite of some political concessions to alternative approaches to agriculture, such as organic farming subsidies and CAP modulation to increase funding to broader rural development including artisanal food production, the agricultural and food industry support system at the EU level and at the level of the Irish State remains firmly predicated on a productivist discourse.

In Ireland, this has significant consequences for knowledge production, dissemination and promotion via expert sources of information like Teagasc and the DAFF. These comprise authoritative groups within conventional Irish farming circles who propagate a knowledge culture of state-sanctioned farming ideologies and values that support and promote the productivist paradigm, conceding minimal resources and offering little validation for other approaches to farming to allow them to develop as truly viable alternatives.

The knowledge culture of the state's farm education, research and advisory system and its agents

Teagasc provides advisory, training and research services to farmers, the agriculture and food industry and the wider rural community. It receives 75 per cent of its funding from the Irish exchequer and EU,[2] absorbing much of the public monies available for agricultural research and education in Ireland and leaving little for groups that promulgate alternative farming ideologies such as the National Organic Training Skillnet (NOTS). The concentration of funding in a state-wide organisation that is a proponent of the productivist paradigm and that is the primary training provider to the agricultural sector does not meet the needs of farmers seeking alternative knowledges. In one case, an organic farmer who needed to complete the Teagasc Certificate of Agriculture could only access a course designed for conventional, non-organic farming.

The experience reveals the clash between conventional and organic knowledge cultures as the programme seems designed to inculcate just one form of expert knowledge in the young farmers and to do so in a prescriptive fashion. It reveals a lack of openness to alternative knowledges in the established farm education system, part of what Morgan and Murdoch (2000: 167) call 'the systemic bias against organic farming', including among 'formal organs of the State':

> I was the only [student from an organic farm], I had to do [the course] … I just answered all the questions the way they wanted the questions answered … I had my complete different opinions to some of the things … What they call weeds, what I might call herbs … I would challenge them a bit … but I'd still have to answer the questions in the fashion they wanted them answered in. They have right and wrong and that's it. (NW023)

The knowledge is non-negotiable in the classroom but the organic farmer knows how to play the game: give the conventional answers to acquire the Green Cert and return home to farm organically. Even conventional farmers engaged in productivism provided examples where expert knowledge was un-suitable for their particular local farming conditions. Here, a young farmer describes how his older brother, earmarked to take over the family farm, became disillusioned with the prospects of farming a hill farm after attending a Teagasc agricultural college in a neighbouring county:

> Well, me own brother … , he actually would've been the farmer only he went to [Agricultural College] … and he didn't want to farm at all once he came back … I suppose he thought, maybe, there was no future in farming in hilly areas … That's one of the awful problems with Teagasc. Young fellas went off, such as me brother; he went off to college … and they were talking about a totally different land to back here. So you have to separate the two [land types] if you want to stay farming, if you want to stay sane to start with. (NW008)

These examples highlight the standardised nature of knowledge dissemi-nated by the state agricultural education system and how it appears to best serve a subset of the country's farmers – productivist farmers with superior land resources. The same may be said for Teagasc's research and advisory serv-ices also. Below, the young farmer goes on to describe how he must adjust advice emanating from research conducted in field stations with good land quality before he can apply it to his own farm. This underscores the problem with applying uniform global knowledge to diverse farming locales.

> Ye can't make a silk purse of a sow's ear, ye know. The land is very limited. If you're going to survive farming around here, you're going to

have to accept the limits of the land … like, when I hear Teagasc people, I do have to adjust everything down to me own land because if you think that you're going to do what they're talking about in Meath or in Tipperary or wherever, it's not going to happen. You're going to be out, it's just going to go wrong on you. (NW008)

Contrary to Morgan and Murdoch's (2000) description of tacit knowledge simply giving way to codified knowledge, one can see how the farmer employs local, tacit knowledge to reinterpret and adjust global, standardised knowledge to better suit his particular land resources. However, as the next section shows, other global knowledge derived from state agents is non-negotiable, even on one's own farm.

The knowledge culture of the state's farm inspection infrastructure and its agents

The second dominant state agent in the lives of Irish farmers is the DAFF that serves to promote and develop agriculture, food and rural development, with responsibilities that include farm inspections. In light of constantly changing market conditions and consumer preferences, farmers are encouraged to be entrepreneurial and to diversify into alternative areas (DAFF, 2010). *Food Harvest 2020* emphasises the delivery of high-quality, safe and naturally based produce and urges stakeholders to act smart (encourage innovation, creativity and collaboration across the food supply chain) and to think green (capitalise on natural advantages and resources). However, in spite of official government discourse that encourages farmers to innovate and add value to their output in apparently locally appropriate ways, the examples below show how entrepreneurship can be frustrated by the contestation of knowledge by state agents. The following farm family experienced a power struggle with a state agent's 'hygienist regulatory mind-set' (Sage, 2007: 3) when, in seeking to address the poor profitability of their family dairy farm, they began to produce a value-added milk product: 'Unpasteurised milk was a "no go" area according to our [DAFF] inspector. She didn't want to hear tell of it and she wouldn't let us batch-pasteurise, which is what we're doing at the moment … I think she just didn't want it in her area because it's, kind of, a high risk product' (NW023). Then, one year later: 'we tried a raw milk hard cheese and that was a "no go" area … she was out here every two or three days, stuck into it, doing tests, testing every bit. She didn't like it at all … you can't challenge it. It's like being in school at eight years of age; you can't challenge the teacher or the teacher's going to be right' (NW023).

This dairy farmer's story suggests 'regulatory harassment' (Sage, 2007: 3) by a state agent of farmers trying to innovate by adding value to their milk output via milk pasteurisation and cheese-making. It also reveals the power of state agents to distort the interpretation of regulations because when the family subsequently sought advice from a Teagasc researcher, contrary to the DAFF inspector's advice, the appropriateness of batch-pasteurisation was confirmed. The example highlights not only the persistence of a traditional, paternalistic model of knowledge dissemination as identified by Farrell, McDonagh and Mahon (2008) among Teagasc advisers, but the non-negotiative nature of expert knowledges as well as uneven power relations between farmers and state agents where the former are seen more as receptacles of codified knowledge rather than co-creators. Tovey (2008: 196) highlights the failure of state and policy actors to recognise and valorise 'local social, cultural and cognitive capitals' as a 'serious obstacle' to sustainable rural development. It can also be seen here as a roadblock to sustainable agricultural innovation through alternative farm enterprises.

Conclusions

The chapter reveals the reproduction of inequalities, already in evidence at the farmscape level, in Irish farming knowledges as well and the reproduction of barriers to farming innovation among networks throughout the farmer life course that serve to maintain those inequalities. Focusing on the barrier of institutional inertia to conclude, Morgan and Murdoch (2000) noted that the vacuum it created in the face of changing economic conditions and knowledge requirements is being filled by rural development groups. In Ireland, Local Development Companies (LDCs) have driven rural development initiatives since the 1990s, through the LEADER (Liaison Entre Actions de Développement de l'Economie Rurale) approach in particular, by recognising the value of negotiated knowledges, experimenting with and developing innovative farming and food networks, and supporting alternative farm enterprises. LDCs can be seen as a source of knowledge mediators who bring together diverse stakeholders such as farmers and state agents with their associated knowledge networks and knowledge cultures to agree locally appropriate actions that are integrated with regional and national strategies.

The chapter reveals that there does not appear to be a knowledge deficit in the Irish agricultural sector but rather a deficit in the wisdom required to value different types of knowledge and to understand knowledge generation and exchange as an open, cooperative process. Being both rural development professionals and local residents aware of situated socio-economic relations,

LDC intermediaries seem to offer the managerial knowledge to oversee such a process. Sounds idealistic? A track record for supporting award-winning alternative farm enterprises (together with the results of the EU FP6 CORASON project)[3] suggests not. They may be key to agriculture leading the Irish economic recovery as forecast in *Food Harvest 2020*. Unfortunately, the committee who delivered that strategy document included representatives from the food industry and conventional producer organisations but not LDCs. Their exclusion suggests that the hegemony of the productivist approach to agriculture and its associated knowledges is set to continue.

Notes

1 SE denotes an interviewee from the south-east of the country while NW denotes one from the north-west.
2 See www.teagasc.ie, accessed 19 June 2011.
3 See *Sociologia Ruralis*, 48 (2008).

References

Crowley, C., Walsh, J. and Meredith, D. (2008) *Irish Farming at the Millennium: a Census Atlas*. Maynooth: National Institute for Regional and Spatial Analysis.

Department of Agriculture, Fisheries and Food (DAFF) (2010) *Food harvest 2020: A Vision for Irish Agri-food and Fisheries*. Dublin: Department of Agriculture, Fisheries and Food.

Department of Agriculture, Fisheries and Food (DAFF) (2011) *Annual Review and Outlook for Agriculture, Fisheries and Food 2010/2011*. Dublin: Department of Agriculture, Fisheries and Food.

Department of Finance (2011) *The National Recovery Plan 2011–2014*, www.finance. gov.ie/documents/publications/other/2011/natrecplanlatest.pdf, accessed 8 August 2011.

Farrell, M., McDonagh, J. and Mahon, M. (2008) *Agricultural extension advisory services: the challenge of implementing a multifunctional advisory programme*. The Rural Economy Research Centre Working Paper Series 08-WP-RE-06. Athenry: Teagasc.

Fonte, M. (2008) 'Knowledge, food and place. A way of producing, a way of knowing', *Sociologia Ruralis* 48, 3: 200–22.

Hennessey, T., Moran, B., Kinsella, A. and Quinlan, G. (2011) *National Farm Survey*. Athenry: Teagasc.

Kearney, B. (2001) *A Review of Relevant Studies Concerning Farm Forestry Trends and Farmers' Attitudes to Forestry*. Dublin: Council for Forest Research and Development.

Lafferty, S., Commins, P. and Walsh, J. (1999) *Irish Agriculture in Transition: A Census Atlas of Agriculture in the Republic of Ireland*. Dublin: Teagasc.

Meredith, D. (2011) 'Potential for income generation on farms.' Presented at the National Rural Network, LEADER and Teagasc National Rural Development Conference, 2 February, Tullamore, Offaly.

Massey, D. (2005) *For Space*. London: Sage.

Morgan, K. and Murdoch, J. (2000) 'Organic vs. conventional agriculture: knowledge, power and innovation in the food chain', *Geoforum* 31: 159–73.

Ní Laoire, C. (2004) 'Winners and losers? Rural restructuring, economic status and masculine identities among young farmers in south-west Ireland', in L. Holloway and M. Kneafsey (eds), *Geographies of Rural Cultures and Societies*. Aldershot: Ashgate, pp. 283–301.

Riley, M. (2008) 'Experts in their fields: farmer-expert knowledges and environmentally friendly farming practices', *Environment and Planning A 40*, 6: 1277–93.

Sage, C. (2007) '"Bending science to match their convictions": hygienist conceptions of food safety as a challenge to alternative food enterprises in Ireland', in D. Maye, L. Holloway and M. Kneafsey (eds), *Alternative Food Geographies: Representation and Practice*. London: Elsevier, pp. 205–23.

Tovey, H. (2008) 'Introduction: rural sustainable development in the knowledge society era', *Sociologia Ruralis* 48, 3: 185–99.

11

Health and wellness or conspicuous consumption? The spa in Celtic Tiger Ireland

Ronan Foley

Alongside taking up golf and buying overseas property, attending spas was a signifier of Celtic Tiger Ireland's new affluence. Whether associated with the latest hotel and spa development or as part of a wider wellness practice, the word 'spa' suggests a whole range of contradictory meanings from pampering and luxury to retreat and mindfulness (Smith and Puczko, 2009). This chapter begins with a short discussion of the history and development of the modern spa with a focus on Ireland and how that history in part reflects wider narratives of boom and bust. The chapter then describes the micro-geographies of spa sites alongside wider discussions on classification and regulation to show how wellness and tourism geographies overlap in such spaces. The chapter goes on to look at the modern spa through the lens of therapeutic landscapes and critically discusses the different practices identifiable at the sites, both of health/wellness but also of conspicuous consumption (Gesler, 2003). Finally, the chapter concludes by showing how applying a critical therapeutic landscapes approach can enable us to see spas as sites where complex and contested social relations are acted out in place.

Context

Sites and settings which connect people, health and place can be described as therapeutic landscapes (Gesler, 1993; Kearns and Moon, 2002; Williams, 2007). These are 'places that have achieved lasting reputations for providing physical, mental and spiritual healing' (Kearns and Gesler, 1998: 8). Central to early therapeutic landscapes research was the historic spa town with studies drawn from Britain and France that looked at towns like Bath and Vichy (Gesler, 2003; Mackaman, 1998; Porter, 1990). Ireland too has a spa history between 1700 and the late nineteenth century based on towns such as Lisdoonvarna, Lucan, Mallow and Swanlinbar (Foley, 2010; Kelly, 2009). Several of these towns subsequently developed new identities as hydropathic centres where the earlier natural curative mineral springs were reinvented via more commercial forms of water-based therapies and treatments (Foley, 2010; O'Leary, 2000). In many ways, a mix of these two identities forms the foundations for the modern spa.

Though the use of hot springs is embedded in many global cultures, especially in East Asia, the focus of this work will be on the commercially developed western spa model. Originating on the west coast of the USA in the 1940s, the popularity of the modern spa drew from a range of cultural shifts (Erfurt-Cooper and Cooper, 2009). Firstly, while European spa medicine had been practiced for centuries, the counter-cultural revolution of the 1960s brought with it a more critical take on conventional medicine and an increased interest in alternative and complementary forms. A second element was economic and cultural globalisation, shaped by increased international travel and cross-cultural fertilisations within which health and medicine were relevant components (Doel and Segrott, 2003). Worldwide, the spa business developed markedly from 1990 and by 2008, the Global Spa Summit estimated an annual turnover of €60 billion for spas alone and close to €2 trillion for the wider 'wellness' market (SRI International, 2008).

In Ireland, these trends were reflected in the opening of new health farms and the first purpose-built destination spa at Temple in 1992. Yet, it was not until the beginning of the new millennium that the spa boom took off in Ireland. Annual growth rates in the Irish health and wellness tourism market in the first decade of the century ranged from 40 per cent to over 200 per cent (Euromonitor International, 2010). In 2006 alone, more than thirty new spa facilities were opened and Fáilte Ireland, the national tourism management agency, set about developing a categorisation system to audit spas in Ireland (Fáilte Ireland, 2007). Sites included the comprehensive and expensive destination spa, complete with five-star accommodation, a full range of designed spaces and treatments, and a cachet of luxury and exclusivity. At the opposite end of the scale, opportunist small hotels put a jacuzzi or a sauna in a separate building and labelled themselves a hotel and spa. Even nail salons were reinvented as beauty spas. However, by 2011 some of the more exclusive resorts were in trouble, others had closed down, and the annual growth rate in the Irish health and wellness tourism market had dropped to just 3 per cent (Euromonitor International, 2010). In many ways, the short intense history of spa development as a cultural phenomenon in Ireland reflects the wider boom and bust story of the Celtic Tiger. But there are more interesting stories to be uncovered beneath this bigger picture.

This chapter is based on a study of watering places in Ireland (Foley, 2010) with empirical material and observer participation drawn from modern spas with additional material gathered from key stakeholders in the spa business as well as from wider primary and secondary materials. Semi-structured interviews were carried out with hotel owners, commercial and spa managers as well as with a national spa marketing organisation. In addition, semi-structured interviews were held with seaweed bath owners who adhered to a strong spa identity in their establishments. In choosing the sites, the intention was to draw from as wide a range as possible; from destination spas, where narratives of health are expected to be more central, to commercial and social centres, where the spa is an addition to older hotel facilities. The spas were also chosen to reflect both older sites updated to contemporary practices and new developments with designed spa identities. In classifying the representative spas that inform this chapter, three are destination spas (Monart, Temple and Inchydoney), three are old hotels updated with a new spa (Kelly's, Slieve Donard, Cliff House), while the remaining four are newly constructed hotel and spa establishments (Kingsley, Farnham, Bellinter, and Delphi). Five seaweed baths are also assessed and these are Ballybunion, Kilkee, Enniscrone, Strandhill and Newcastle. The locations of the spas and seaweed baths are shown in Figure 11.1 along with the distribution of spa establishments listed on the Spa-Ireland website.[1] A number of spa and bath managers and owners were also interviewed in 2008 and 2009 on the themes discussed in the chapter.

To more fully understand health practices at spas during the period of the Celtic Tiger, it should be noted that they were also framed by wider public understandings of spa settings. Spas have well-developed social and cultural identities, wherein performances of class, power and social status are always prominent. Those identities have shaped the society of the historic spa and are documented in critical and imaginative literatures (Austen, 1818; Durie, 2003). In assessing various spa-based health practices and social performances here, two core themes are addressed. The first focuses on the material forms and inhabitations of the spa and draws from a broad tourist geography perspective. The second takes a therapeutic landscapes approach to explore how two very different meanings, of healing and wellness and of consumption and pampering, were attached to the modern Irish spa.

The micro-geographies of the spa as wellness and tourist spaces

The classic image of the spa during the Celtic Tiger period was of an expensive country retreat within which silent figures in fluffy white robes and slippers

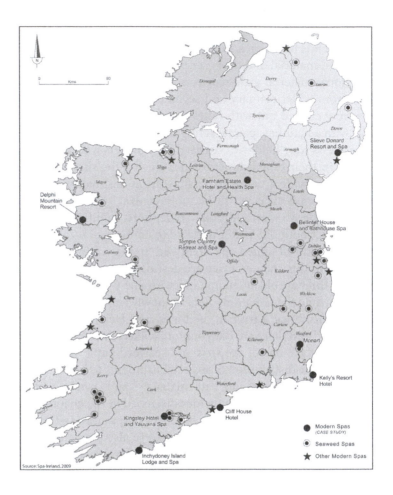

Figure 11.1 Distribution of spas and seaweed baths in Ireland, 2010

glided through contemporary spaces of glass, wood and water. The interior spaces were carefully, even clinically, designed while the extensive grounds were equally shaped by therapeutic walks, streams, ponds and the surrounding land- or sea-scapes. In addition, the spa image was associated with treatment, both in terms of rooms for Reiki (a form of palm healing that originated in Japan) and other exotic bodily therapies as well as expensive spa products for the visitor to take home. This mixture of wellness and tourism was also evident in the facilities in the hotel, through a range of healing spaces (saunas, steam rooms, relaxation rooms, swimming pools) and more conventional tourist facilities (restaurants, shops, gyms). The remainder of this section assesses the micro-geographies of the modern spa by outlining how the development of spas during the Celtic Tiger era was shaped by a number of factors, namely classification, design and facilities, along with location and clientele.

Table 11.1 shows an adapted version of the spa classification drawn up by Fáilte Ireland in conjunction with a representative group of spa owners (Fáilte Ireland, 2011). One can see in this classification scheme a tension between tourist and wellness identities. Indeed, one of the key drivers behind the development of the classification was a concern from high-end spa owners and managers of the debasement of the term 'spa', especially when tacked on to an ever increasing range of cosmetic and other facilities. As one spa owner commented pointedly: 'When is a spa not a spa? When it's a hotel!' (M1).

The table also reveals a strong commercial focus with targeted services and clienteles. The row displaying what guests were buying provides a clearer sense of the tourism and wellness intentions of the different spa types.

During the Celtic Tiger, there was a marked change in the nature and extent of the marketing of the spa concept, with the deliberate design or redesign of the spaces in line with international best practice. Most of the spas considered in this chapter were established between 2000 and 2005 as commercial ventures providing accommodation, food and other leisure facilities alongside the spa treatments and services. While Temple's construction in 1992 pre-dated the Celtic Tiger years, Monart was deliberately designed in 2005 to take advantage of the spa boom, although it still had a strong holistic health focus. Older sites, especially Kelly's (upgraded to SeaSpa in 2004) and Slieve Donard (redesigned in 2006 by the spa design consultancy ESPA) were comfortable with their traditional hotel identities but recognised that health was becoming part of the range of services sought by customers; this awareness was reflected in the development of new spa facilities as they 'didn't want to get left behind' (KY1). For newly established hotels, it became almost compulsory to build the spa as a deliberate development of wellness identity within either new or redesigned settings such as Delphi (relaunched in 2008) and Bellinter, respectively. In fact, Bellinter drew from its history as a country retreat, a point that was emphasised in its brochures upon its launch in 2006. Bellinter House also had a branch of a well-established Dublin restaurant while the restaurant at the Cliff House earned a Michelin star in 2010. These additional features may help to sustain the sites, but more as hotels than spas. The five seaweed baths considered here were also a mix of new and old. The two newer baths, in Kilkee and especially in Newcastle, were contemporary reproductions of the original versions still extant at Enniscrone (founded in 1916) and Ballybunion (built in the 1920s). While the seaweed baths seemed to maintain a largely unglamourised identity, even these underwent change, especially the Voya Baths at

Table 11.1 Classification of modern spas

	Hotel spa with:				Resort spa	Destination spa	Specialised retreats		
	comprehensive spa	extensive spa	selective spa	leisure club spa			Health farm	Thalassotherapy resort	Seaweed baths
Definition	A hotel that offers full-service spa treatments in a comprehensive spa facility as well as other hotel functions and events.	A hotel that offers extensive spa treatments in a substantial spa facility as well as other hotel functions and events.	A hotel that offers selective spa treatments in a modest spa facility as well as other hotel functions and events.	A hotel with a leisure club facility in or adjacent to it within which spa treatments are offered.	A holiday resort that offers a wide range of leisure activities on site, as well spa treatments in a full-service spa facility.	A hotel or a guesthouse where the main purpose of the business is to offer full-service spa treatments in a comprehensive spa facility.	A retreat offering a wide range of health and wellness spa programmes.	A centre that offers therapeutic marine-based treatments using heated seawater, seaweed and mud.	A marine health centre offering seaweed baths.
Facility specifics	Basic hotel with a full-service spa.	Basic hotel where the spa-goer may escape to the extensive spa.	Basic hotel with a moderate-sized spa offering a smaller selection of spa and salon treatments.	Basic hotel leisure facility with treatment rooms or a small spa facility.	The central activity of this property is as a holiday destination and one of the key activities is a spa.	A spa with accommodation. The majority of guests come to partake of spa breaks.	Wellness retreat and spa health farm sanctuary with accommodation. The majority of guests come to partake of spa activities.	Centred on a large thalassotherapy spa. The majority of guests come to enjoy the marine spa.	N/A

	Hotel spa with:				Resort spa	Destination spa	Specialised retreats		
	comprehensive spa	extensive spa	selective spa	leisure club spa			Health farm	Thalassotherapy resort	Seaweed baths
Guests buy	Spa facilities, rituals and treatments.	Spa treatments.	Spa treatments.	Beauty treatments and salon spa treatments.	Spa facilities, rituals and treatments.	Time out for a complete wellness/lifestyle reorientation programme as well as spa treatments.	Time out for a complete wellness programme as well as spa treatments.	Therapeutic marine treatments.	Health-giving seaweed baths.
Example	Kingsley	Kelly's	Slieve Donard	Bellinter	Monart	Delphi	Temple	Inchydoney	Enniscrone

Source: Fáilte Ireland, 2011

Strandhill. These were extensively redesigned in 2006 in parallel with a marketing overhaul and updating that took place in the wake of a reality television programme. As a result, a range of new seaweed-based products from Voya were marketed and sold in other spas including Bellinter House, whose owners were behind the television programme.

Proximity to a therapeutic landscape played a role in the location of all of the destination spas, whether a potassium-rich spring site (Monart), a historic energetic site (Temple) or on the edge of the sea (Inchydoney) to provide a clear thalassotherapeutic identity for seawater-based therapy. The older hotels were already located at traditional seaside settings, several with spectacular views, and these settings were in turn incorporated into their new health spa identities. The manager of the Cliff House Hotel, overlooking Ardmore Bay, called the sea view 'part of our estate' (CH1). In the newly built Kingsley Hotel in Cork, a unique ayurvedic spa (based on traditional Indian medicine) called Yauvana was located on the site of the old public Lee Baths, a bathing and cleansing site for generations of working-class Corkonians. This juxtaposition of local and global health meanings was particularly representative of the ways in which globalised therapeutic landscapes became embedded within an affluent and aspirational Celtic Tiger landscape (Hoyez, 2007). Seaweed baths were also purposefully located, namely for their proximity to good supplies of two core seaweed species, serrated wrack (*Fucus serrata*) and bladder wrack (*Fucus vesiculosus*), and all the owners used sustainable harvesting methods by manually collecting the day's supply at low tide.

In considering the micro-geographies of spas, it is also important to comment on their inhabitation and the nature of typical clienteles. In parallel with the categorisation of the spas, Fáilte Ireland (2007) produced a commercial vision for the booming spa and wellness tourism sector. This included a social classification system for spa users, ranging from 'fun seekers', 'beauty queens' (also called 'Ryder Cup Wives') and 'occasional pamperers' to 'help seekers' and 'serenity seekers'. While all were identifiable from site visits and interviews, the more spiritual and healing-orientated visitors were associated with destination spas like Temple and Inchydoney. Newer hotel spas tended to attract the type of visitor where a more pampered aesthetic was prominent. As a site with mixed wellness/tourism identities, Monart struck a balance between the two main types of user with a leaning towards the destination spa market while still remaining attractive to an aspirational and beauty/pampering-focused clientele. In older hotels, especially at Kelly's and Slieve Donard, there were established clienteles from across generations for whom the hotels had deeper familial and place connections. Indeed, at such sites, the older clienteles were less likely to use the spas. This differentiation of users was not so much the case at destination spas where all ages and genders were evident. While traditional seaweed bath clienteles were older, the baths' rediscovery and re-commodification within the wider spa renaissance had drawn newer and younger patrons, especially at Strandhill and to a lesser extent at Enniscrone.

The spa in Celtic Tiger Ireland – performances of health and pampering

Extending the discussion on the tensions between the wellness and tourism dimensions of the Celtic Tiger spa, it is useful to consider their two seemingly different identities; as places of recovery, rest and wellness and as places of pampering, luxury and excess. Cultural geographers are increasingly interested in the importance of inhabitation and performance in creating and shaping social spaces and this ties in well with recent research in therapeutic landscapes. Conradson's work is central here, given his concern with the extent to which individual experiences in place shape individual outcomes (Conradson, 2005; 2007). In thinking about one's experiential encounters in spas, one must also identify how this is framed by the physical spa spaces and their sounds, smells, sights, tastes and feel. Yet, the extent to which experiences are solely therapeutic is also part of the wider debate and for many users, their presence at a spa may be for a completely different set of meanings and identities than those solely associated with a wellness benefit (Conradson, 2007). The rest of this section will explore some of these ideas around the conflicting wellness and social performances of the spa and how these co-exist in popular perception and actual practice.

As literal performances of health, the range of treatments provided in spas represent a mix of the traditional and contemporary. At Temple, complementary and alternative medicine (CAM) treatments such as kinesiology were contextualised within the design of the site wherein emplaced energies were invoked during the treatment. In the destination and newer spa settings, fluffy dressing-gowned bodies circulated through reproduced hammams and steam rooms in an evocative set of movements reflecting much older practices, both local and global (Figure 11.2). Mindfulness and stillness were identifiable in organised and private performances of health both inside and outside the buildings at Monart, Delphi and Bellinter, reflecting Conradson's (2007) observations on the increased popularity of personal spiritual retreats in contemporary society. In some of the older redeveloped hotels, the treatments were associated with external cosmetic as much as with internal physical or mental health. The Yauvana spa at the Kingsley Hotel offered ayurvedic treatments including a pre-treatment medical consultation with a qualified doctor to identify specific personalised treatments based on the ayurvedic notion of

Figure 11.2 Relaxation room at Monart Destination Spa

dosha or bodily balance. Other globalised treatments included acupuncture at Delphi and Farnham. At the seaweed baths, the performance of health was expressed through simple immersion in a hot bath, with its historic associations with the treatment of asthma, arthritis and skin disorders.

In considering a more contested social identity, there is no doubt that the popularity of spas and their associated affluential meanings were strongly evident during the core years of the Celtic Tiger from 2000 onwards. The visual and narrative imagery of the spa entailed a selling of luxury and pampering alongside the curative and wellness dimension. For a market well-positioned, both economically and socially, to support such developments, there was an undoubted social cachet to the 'weekend away at the spa'. In the busy world of the boom, narratives of luxury and the need to be visibly conspicuous in its consumption, meant that the spas were in many ways emblematic symbols of the era; health and treatments were more by-products than necessities. As most spas also had swimming pools, jacuzzis, saunas and gyms, there was an additional leisure dimension to the spaces. While the spa might have had a strong initial identity as a gendered space, where women were more at ease than men, several spas, especially Monart and Inchydoney, developed active recreational facilities to increase male presence in these traditionally female preserves. The sporty weekend break, wherein the younger male could engage in more active pursuits while his (usually) female partner indulged in the pampering services, became a popular tagline for couples using spas.

How central was health to spa identities? It ranged in importance from being central to the identity of the destination spa to being less significant in the newer hotel spa, where it was described by one manager as an 'added option, it's not central to what we do' (BH1). Inchydoney had a strong medical identity, with the thalassotherapy treatments specifically validated by a French institute of spa medicine and the overall organisation of treatments supervised by a local biomedical professional. Even some of the older hotels such as Kelly's, while seeing their role as that of a general hotel with added spa facilities, also ran a range of health-related courses for residents and guests and provided CAM therapies in their SeaSpa. At the seaweed baths, such as Ballybunion, treatments were used in much more specifically therapeutic ways by patients who came on repeated visits for pragmatic treatment of recurrent and chronic conditions such as eczema, and where a fortnightly stay led to considerable relief, if not a permanent cure, of conditions.

Consideration of the relative positions of spa health and social/pampering identities revealed a number of interesting temporal shifts. The position of the body as a site of healing emerged within some of the narratives, noted at both Inchydoney and Enniscrone Seaweed Baths. Here, suspicion of health treatments such as massage (often given a quite sexualised meaning as a lingering link to a more repressed past) gradually gave way to a greater comfort with the body and touch-based treatments. A return to an emphasis on health was also in evidence. The spa manager at Slieve Donard noted in 2008 that although just five years earlier people rarely used the word 'health' in discussing their reasons for being there, the term had been curiously disinterred as a justification for visits. At Inchydoney, the spa manager noted that when the names of the treatments were changed to simplified forms in the late 2000s, the clients demanded that the older medicalised tags be reinstated. In the rapidly shifting social space of the post-Celtic Tiger recession, where conspicuous consumption was now less celebrated or tolerated, the healing and wellness aspects of spas had come to assume a renewed importance.

Summary: conflicting health and consumer identities

Using a critical therapeutic landscapes approach can enable us to see spas as sites where complex and contested social relations are enacted in place. In looking at the rise and uncertain future of the modern Irish spa, one could consider it a revealing representation of the excesses that characterised the

Celtic Tiger era. During this period of conspicuous consumption, the Irish were arguably losing their longstanding moorings in terms of their identities and becoming hybridised uber-capitalist global citizens, as much at ease in South Africa or California as in an ayurvedic spa in Cork city. Yet, at another level, the rise of the spa was also evidence of a wider awareness of the need for work–life balance and mindfulness in the midst of an over-heated and speeded-up society. In ironic recent commentaries from within the sector, spas are considered to have a future as spaces where people will go to escape the stress of the global economic collapse (Euromonitor International, 2010). There is a sense that the high quality of the Irish destination spa – and Monart's consistent ranking in the Condé-Nast global top ten list is evidence of this – could sustain them through the same market difficulties that their patrons seek to escape. However, not all spas are likely to survive the recession; for instance, in May 2011, the press reported considerable financial difficulties at Temple destination spa (Irish Times, 2011).

Conflicting health and consumer identities were evident in the very design of the modern Irish spa through its curious mix of the local and the global. Inside some of the spas, especially those that were newly built or redesigned, it would be hard to identify one's exact location on the earth's surface. Global spa companies such as ESPA create a standard format in their designs and these were used at several of the sites. Newer hotel spas, such as Farnham, are owned by multinational hotel chains and one can even see the overlaying of such a globalised model as an echo of the imposition of the original spa town model on an unprepared Irish landscape in the early eighteenth century (Kelly, 2009). Yet, at Monart in particular, but also in Kelly's, some resistance to this global template was evident in the deliberate hibernicisation of the design and physical material used, with native Irish species and Celtic patterns a deliberate part of the gardens at the former.

The contestation of health identities against wider social and cultural practices identifies the spa as a place with multiple meanings. These hybrid identities and utilisations are perhaps symbolic of the impact of the Celtic Tiger by re-commodifying simpler health and cultural performances through their re-production within luxurious and pampered spaces. Other issues such as commercial management and regulation were visible in the efforts by Fáilte Ireland to classify the sites into specific categories. This classification was driven primarily by the large-scale spa sub-sector concerned with the misuse of the term 'spa' by sites which were clearly neither healthy nor luxurious. Indeed, they saw tourism agencies themselves as being complicit in this misuse. Yet, in the midst of all this commodification and regulation, the seaweed baths at Enniscrone vigorously defied attempts to bring them under health and safety or tourist schemes, preferring to operate in time-tested ways.

In connecting spaces of healing, which are representative of old and new cultural traditions and that function as contemporary markers of cultural consumption, the story of the modern Irish spa might in part be seen as a signifier of wider hubristic narratives of excess, wealth and living beyond one's means. Characterised in the media as the home of 'ladies who lunch', the imagery of the spa usually involved young, beautiful people who seemed remarkably healthy and vigorous. Yet, the spa experience neither was nor is exclusively confined to the rich, the young or the beautiful and all of the spa owners and managers interviewed noted that around 40 per cent of their business was related to the spa voucher. Here, the caring granting of a healing break from the stresses of everyday life is seen as a gift of health to those, often very ordinary and even unhealthy people, who would traditionally not have been able to afford, financially or temporally, such an experience.

Conclusions

Performances of health at the spa, even historically, have always been a mix of the curative and the social, and modern spas are no different in their adherence to older patterns, spaces and inhabitations (Foley, 2010). In turn, the new internal geographies of the spa shape performances of health and consumption. Health and wellness remain, however, central to the watering-place identity and thus the modern spa and baths draw from older health histories. In the narratives of health at both types of watering-places, hitherto disregarded metaphors of restoration, retreat and stillness can be uncovered that address contemporary understandings of healing and wellness as a mix of personal experience and health product. In taking such a position and using ideas drawn from the reputational power of therapeutic landscapes, it is possible to re-imagine constructions of therapeutic space and society that move beyond a reductive Celtic Tiger narrative.

Notes

1   Available at www.spa-ireland.com, accessed 25 April 2009.

References

Austen, J. (1993 [1818]) *Persuasion*. Ware: Wordsworth Classics..
Conradson, D. (2005) 'Landscape, care and the relational self: therapeutic encounters in rural England', *Health & Place* 11: 337–48.

Conradson, D. (2007) 'The experiential economy of stillness: places of retreat in contemporary Britain', in A. Williams (ed.), *Therapeutic Landscapes*. Aldershot: Ashgate, pp. 33–48.

Doel, M. and Segrott, J. (2003) 'Beyond belief? Consumer culture, complementary medicine, and the dis-ease of everyday life', *Environment and Planning D* 21: 739–59.

Durie, A. (2003) 'Medicine, health and economic development: promoting spa and seaside resorts in Scotland c. 1750–1830', *Medical History* 47: 195–216.

Erfurt-Cooper, P. and Cooper, M. (2009) *Health and Wellness Tourism. Spas and Hot Springs*. Bristol: Channel View.

Euromonitor International (2010) *Country Report: Travel and Tourism in Ireland*. London: Euromonitor International.

Fáilte Ireland (2007) *Health and Wellness. Positioning Strategy for Key Markets*. Dublin: Fáilte Ireland.

Fáilte Ireland (2011) Spa and wellness categorisation criteria. Dublin: Fáilte Ireland, www.failteireland.ie/FailteCorp/media/FailteIreland/documents/Quality%20and%20Standards/Spa%20and%20Wellness/Categorisation_Criteria_.pdf, accessed 14 June 2011.

Foley, R. (2010) *Healing Waters: Therapeutic Landscapes in Historic and Contemporary Ireland*. Farnham: Ashgate.

Gesler, W. M. (1993) 'Therapeutic landscapes: theory and a case study of Epidauros, Greece', *Environment and Planning D* 11, 2: 171–89.

Gesler, W. M. (2003) *Healing Places*. Lanham: Rowman & Littlefield.

Hoyez, A. C. (2007) 'The "world of yoga": the production and reproduction of therapeutic landscapes', *Social Science and Medicine* 65: 112–24.

Irish Times (2011) '€5.8m order against spa owners', *Irish Times*, 10 May, www.irishtimes.com/newspaper/ireland/2011/0510/1224296602806.html, accessed 13 July 2011.

Kearns, R. and Gesler, W. M. (eds) (1998) *Putting Health into Place: Landscape, Identity and Well-Being*. Syracuse, NY: Syracuse University Press.

Kearns, R. and Moon, G. (2002) 'From medical to health geography: novelty, place and theory after a decade of change', *Progress in Human Geography* 26, 5: 605–25.

Kelly, J. (2009) '"Drinking the waters": Balneotherapeutic medicine in Ireland, 1660–1850. Medicine in 17th and 18th century Ireland', *Studia Hibernica* 35: 99–145.

Mackaman, D. P. (1998) *Leisure Settings: Bourgeois Culture, Medicine and the Spa in Modern France*. Chicago: University of Chicago Press.

O'Leary, S. (2000) 'St. Ann's Hydro', *Old Blarney: Journal of the Blarney and District Historical Society* 5: 3–31.

Porter, R. (1990) 'The medical history of waters and spas: introduction', in R. Porter (ed.), *Medical History, Supplement no. 10*. London: Wellcome Institute for the History of Medicine, pp. vii–xii.

Smith, M. and Puczko, L. (eds) (2009) *Health and Wellness Tourism*. Oxford: Butterworth-Heinemann.

SRI International (2008) *The Global Spa Economy 2007*. Arlington: SRI International.

Williams, A. (ed.) (2007) *Therapeutic Landscapes*. Aldershot: Ashgate.

12

'Traditional Irish music here tonight': exploring the session space

Daithí Kearney

It is a Tuesday night, November 2010, approaching half past nine in a bar in east Cork. Two television screens show European Champions League soccer matches featuring teams from the English Premier League. A scattering of people are gathered around watching with varied levels of interest; many are regulars in that they come here when the team they support is playing, or simply for a quiet pint. Séamus, the manager, is behind the bar, greeting many by name and knows their drinks order before they ask. There are fewer faces here now than five years ago. The pub trade has been hit by the economic downturn. It has also been felt by musicians and music lovers as pubs cut back on entertainment or close altogether. In spite of the changes, at this pub tonight, a sign outside still advertises an Irish music session. The setting provides a multi-sensory engagement with life in Ireland at the end of the first decade of the twenty-first century, informed in particular by the soundscape.

I am one of the performers for tonight's Irish traditional music session. A session is often an informal gathering of musicians that usually takes place in a public house. It can appear disorganised and without rules to the observer. Musicians gather in a corner and some turn their backs to the talking crowd. There is a hierarchy and etiquette for the session. Sometimes, one or two musicians are paid to be present and get the session going; others who wish to participate simply join them. Even people at the bar come down at times to sing a song and contribute. For some, the session is an opportunity to earn money; for others, it is a social occasion with their musical talents the key to inclusion.

In this bar, there is an ongoing arrangement that two other musicians and I are paid to play from around 9.30 p.m. until closing time each Tuesday night. I am a teacher, living locally but originally from Kerry where I grew up in a community rich in the traditions of Irish music, song and dance. These days, I listen to a lot of music during my 100km commute to work in Tipperary and while Tuesday is my only regular session, I do teach music as well. John, a truck driver, is another 'blow-in', this time from north-west Cork. He also grew up surrounded by a strong local musical tradition. He listens to a lot of music while driving but participates in more sessions in the area than I. Éamonn, a local farmer, gets here by taxi and does not come from a traditional music background. The three of us are often joined by other musicians or singers, very few from the locality, some even from overseas.

Reflecting on this session, the setting, the audience and the wider world of Irish traditional music evokes questions concerning life in Ireland today, concepts of identity and the importance of tradition in an ever-changing world. The session both incorporates and suggests changes, not only in sound but in the biographical details of the people present, their economic situations and the multitude of cultural references that can be found in the bar. How my fellow musicians and I along with our audience got here provides an insight into changes in contemporary Ireland. The nature of the session throws light on the transition from boom to bust in Ireland in the last decade.

Is it traditional music you play?

When I come in with my instrument case, a few strangers ask what music we play and what time we will start. The start time is fairly flexible – many of the locals are still watching the matches. This can agitate the tourists as they want to hear traditional Irish music before they retire to bed early. They will not stay for the full session; they wait to hear a little, take some photographs or video, and sample the alcoholic offerings associated with Ireland – stout, whiskey, Baileys liqueur. Sometimes they enquire about our instruments – the banjo, accordion, uilleann pipes and bodhrán – which appear strange to them.

I play the Irish tenor banjo, a four-stringed, fretted instrument tuned like the violin and played with a plectrum. Hardly the most traditional of instruments in an Irish context, the banjo probably developed from instruments of African origin. The tuning, frets, and method of playing with a plectrum are all examples of cultural development over the course of about three centuries in both America and Ireland. In the nineteenth century, the popularity of the banjo grew through minstrel shows on both sides of the Atlantic. I was influenced to take up the banjo having heard a neighbour play, learning on an instrument that belonged to my primary school. However, the music of the school band was not Irish traditional music – this I learned from local groups including *Siamsa Tíre*, a folk theatre group based in north Kerry, and the local branch of *Comhaltas Ceoltóirí Éireann* (CCE), an organisation involved in the promotion of Irish traditional music around the world.

As the soccer matches near the final whistles, John comes through the door. Approaching sixty-five, John comes from Sliabh Luachra, a region renowned for Irish traditional music. He relocated in the 1970s and raised his family here. Commenting on the differences in the local economies of Sliabh Luachra and east Cork, he tells me he came in search of work and has not been unemployed since. He learned many tunes as a young boy from his father and neighbours, some of whose names remain attached to tunes in the tradition. He plays an accordion tuned to C#/D in the style of many Sliabh Luachra musicians, in contrast to the more widespread B/C tuning. He readily admits that he did not fully appreciate the cultural world of Sliabh Luachra when he was younger but his link to a region considered rich in Irish music tradition gives him status in this part of the world where a sense of tradition is largely absent.

Often Éamonn is here before me. A semi-retired farmer, he enjoys playing the guitar and singing. The session is a social outlet for him. He often takes a secondary position in the session space although he has rarely missed a night in seven years. He has a few pints during the session and gets a taxi home around midnight. Irish traditional music is often associated with a rural way of life but, while he makes reference to his rural background, Éamonn's first choice in music is the popular songs of the 1960s and 1970s. The session helps Éamonn create an identity in his retirement. For him, leaving his job was a choice and he can still be involved in the farm by providing his experience through advice. Éamonn's repertoire reflects a blurred identity that is in sync with some in the bar who also do not have a job, more by imposition than choice. These individuals are part of the statistics and anonymity of post-boom unemployment figures. For some, their job was an integral part of their identity; an identity now shaped by their joblessness. The bar is shared by people of various national origins and sometimes a tension exists. To sing an Irish song is not just a statement of identity but of coming to terms with identity, location and assimilation. The Irish-born singer provides a rendition of an American song before his Polish-born neighbour sings the Irish/Scottish folk song, 'The Wild Rover'. The boom brought them together on the building sites but they still hum a different tune.

As we take out our instruments, Séamus turns off the sound from the televisions and comes over to offer us a drink. He comments on the scarcity of people in the bar, how things are getting slack and predicts a quiet night. He often wonders how he could get more customers. People do not go out in the middle of the week any more. During the boom, the bar had a steady flow of patrons every day of the week. Reference is made to the smoking ban introduced in 2004, changing attitudes in relation to drinking and driving, and the economic downturn. Access to cheap alcohol in shops and off-licences is another factor but instead we comment on the social benefits of the pub. This pub is one of the more popular in town and behind the bar are numerous posters of events and groups. Music is here every night of the week, of all styles and genres, and it helps to attract customers. Séamus uses catchphrases of the downturn such as 'value for money' and is increasingly selective in his choice of music to best match his customers' preferences. However, he, like many bar managers who support Irish traditional music sessions, has a personal appreciation for this type of music.

It is difficult to see the difference between boom and bust in the session. The winter was always quieter on a Tuesday night but the sharp decline in tourist numbers is also impacting on pubs' summer turnovers. Some of the musicians who join us remark on sessions in bars elsewhere that have stopped because of financial constraints. There is always a suggestion that they will start up again and in the summer many do to attract the passing tourist or add atmosphere and a sense of life. The session, like the Tango in Argentina (Goertzen and Azzi, 1999) or *Fado* in Portugal, is partly dependent on tourism.

On the pub's front door, a large poster proclaims: 'Traditional Irish Music Here Tonight'. Tradition, in this context, may be defined as 'a cultural practice or behaviour with some historic continuity with the past' (Kaul, 2006: 50). John was raised in a musical house, in a musical locale. His father played fiddle, as did his uncle who learned from the famous fiddle player Pádraig O'Keeffe. John remembers that when he was young, people had sessions in each other's houses up to six nights a week in the lead-up to Christmas. Music was part of local gathering and the rambling house, the house where people would gather for a night of social entertainment, was an important part of rural life.

I was born in Listowel in north Kerry. My first experience of Irish traditional music was as a baby when *Fleadh Cheoil na hÉireann*, the largest annual festival of Irish traditional music in Ireland, was held there. The Fleadh, as it is more generally known, is the culmination of a series of local and regional festivals that are primarily competitive events run by CCE. It changes location, usually every two to three years, but from the 1970s to the 1990s it was regularly held in Listowel. As well as my own immediate experiences, my mother told me stories of the wonderful nights of music and dance that she experienced in Sliabh Luachra but my father, who worked in a bar when he was a younger man, associated the music with public disorder.

As an accordion and banjo duet, John and I reflect a particular aspect of the tradition. Whether the banjo and accordion duet, accompanied by guitar, is more or less traditional than other manifestations of Irish traditional music may well be debated but here few question it. To most, it sounds Irish and old and for many from Ireland, evokes memories of the past. For foreign visitors, it equates with the expectations they have developed from the varied forms of promotion of Irish traditional music around the world, all of which increased from the mid-1990s. While the Celtic Tiger boom attracted a new, young, urban-based, cash-rich audience for Irish traditional music to venues such as the Point Theatre in Dublin and Madison Square Garden in New York, the bust has, in a sense, given the music back to the folk. The rigorous standards of *Riverdance*, with its military precision, has been replaced with the untrained voice at the bar singing 'Take Me Home, Country Roads' with passion, albeit in a varying key signature. The notion of authentic tradition is replaced by a concern for context and setting.

As well as the tunes passed down orally – Irish traditional music tunes are learned by ear from other musicians rather than from books or written notation – Irish traditional musicians have adapted to changes in communication technology. John and I listen to radio programmes and recordings to learn tunes and use the internet to view video clips of traditional Irish music. We are part of a global community of traditional Irish musicians that share tunes and stories. John has a wealth of history from his youth and home place but also adapts to changes in a living musical tradition.

Changing spaces and going global

The conflict between notions of tradition/purism and change/innovation has been a central focus of the discourse on Irish traditional music through the 1990s to the present (Vallely, Hamilton, Vallely *et al.*, 1999). One aspect of change has been the performance of Irish traditional music around the world, particularly in America, and the relationship between Irish traditional music and other genres (O'Connor, 2001). As a living tradition, Irish traditional music is constantly undergoing change. These changes have been influenced by social, economic and geographic transformations in Ireland and among the Irish diaspora over the past two centuries at least. Each performance of a tune by a musician may be considered, in itself, a reinterpretation of the tradition. The very existence of a pub session, probably the most common setting for the performance of Irish traditional music today, is itself a reflection of change in the tradition.

Irish traditional music has been performed in private homes, at crossroads, fairs and markets, and in dancehalls at various times in history. While it entered pubs in the 1930s in some parts of the country, the pub session is predominantly a post-Second World War phenomenon (Hamilton, 1999). The development of pub sessions owed much to the perceived revival in Irish traditional music, facilitated by two factors in particular: the formation of CCE in 1951 as a significant cultural organisation that sought to promote Irish culture, and the work of composer Seán Ó Riada, who reshaped the sounds and contexts for Irish traditional music in the 1950s and 1960s. As O'Shea notes:

> The confluence of economic growth with this mid-twentieth-century revival allowed an emerging subculture of musicians simultaneously to embrace these cultivated forms of Irish traditional music and to emulate the informal practices of an older generation of musicians in the session. During this period, publicans began to build 'music lounges' to cater for a young and more prosperous clientele, who now included women. (2008: 51)

O'Shea also notes the growing commodification of the session in the 1970s and the employment of musicians by publicans as session leaders. In a case of history repeating itself, the session tonight has emerged from the popular post-*Riverdance* revival of Irish traditional music that coincided with another period of economic prosperity, during which time the pub itself was also remodelled. For some, the popularisation and globalisation of Irish traditional music is epitomised by the emergence of *Riverdance* as a cultural phenomenon in the 1990s. I was approaching my twelfth birthday in April 1994 when *Riverdance* was first performed as the interval act in the Eurovision Song Contest. It was to have a significant influence on me as a young musician and dancer. A few weeks previously, I had competed at *Oireachtas Rince na Cruinne* (the World Irish Dancing Championships) in Dublin, the stepping stone for many who would go on to perform in *Riverdance* and similar shows. At that stage, Irish dancing was not considered 'cool' for a boy of my age who lacked popular heroes in the arts that could compete with the many great Kerry Gaelic footballers admired by my peers. The commercial success of *Riverdance* and the celebrity status afforded its stars were linked to the evolving social and economic changes in 1990s Ireland. *Riverdance*, for many, represented the new, young, confident Ireland that was taking a prominent place on the world stage (Brennan, 1999; Ó Cinnéide, 2002; Scahill, 2009). It is worth noting, however, that the lead dancers in the first performances of *Riverdance* – Michael Flatley, Jean Butler and, later, Colin Dunne – were not themselves a product of this new Ireland but actually descendants of the Irish diaspora in the USA and England.

Riverdance emerged from, rather than encapsulated, the traditional arts. The apparent sudden unveiling of confident, sexy, scantily-clad, young Irish dancers, led by members of the diaspora dancing to exotic Balkan rhythms performed on bodhrán and uilleann pipes in front of a massive global audience placed Irish musical traditions centre stage in the new Ireland (see also O'Flynn, 2009). Ó Cinnéide explains how, after decades of gradual evolution, Irish dancing developed into 'an exhilarating modern form' in the spring of 1994, 'its traditional rigour being given a new, free expression in keeping with the new spirit of enterprise and natural well-being that is abroad in Ireland today, underpinning "The Celtic Tiger"' (2002: 184). The importance of *Riverdance* lies in the power of musical change to not only reflect but also become a metaphor for cultural change (Bohlman, 1988).

In the 1990s, and particularly in the years following *Riverdance*, Irish traditional music became increasingly popular. It was now considered sophisticated to see an Irish dance show and to send children to Irish dance lessons. Media coverage of Irish music, song and dance increased. Although Irish traditional music was already played in many parts of the world where emigrant Irish communities had settled, by the late 1990s Irish traditional music, song and dance truly went global. Since 1999, I have performed throughout Ireland and internationally. Many of these trips were not only motivated by a desire to perform Irish traditional music, song and dance but were financially supported by people and groups seeking to promote Ireland to an international market. A 2009 performance at the White House for President Barack Obama as part of the St Patrick's Day celebrations highlighted the importance attached to Irish heritage and the arts at an event dominated by political and business interests. Other performances have included musical events organised by Irish embassies in Mexico and China, as well as cultural festivals in countries where Ireland does not maintain close diplomatic ties, such as Venezuela. In all instances, the arts provide a powerful reference point for Ireland.

Home again

The internationalisation of Irish art and cultural identity has led in turn to a desire to rediscover local meaning and a sense of belonging (Gray, 1997; Kearney, 1997). Lovering (1998) notes the importance of spatial proximity for creative musical activity while O'Shea (2008) points to the role of places such as Clare (a western Irish county with a strong musical heritage) in the imagination of authenticity, belonging and pilgrimage in Irish traditional music. The importance of the local session to the development of a sense of place and community is highlighted by Cohen's reflection on musical activity: 'The consumption and production of music also draws people together and symbolises their sense of collectivity and place' (Cohen, 1998: 273).

There has been increased interest in and promotion of local traditions in response to *Riverdance* (Seaver, 2010). Tonight's session is an example of a post-*Riverdance* session that may initially have hoped to cash in on the popularity of Irish traditional music in the 1990s. It is typical of many of the sessions around the country and in Irish pubs around the world. Outlining the development of sessions with a mind towards sponsorship, Vallely states: 'In the past, the bar proprietor merely made the space available, or maybe provided the musicians with some drinks (which in poorer times were not insignificant gestures). At present, the publican hires two or three players to simply be there for speci-fied hours each night, effectively to act as catalysts to encourage and/or bait other players and particularly drink-consumers' (Vallely, 2008: 138). Through this practice, 'the community gains a cultural venue or reputation, while the performer carries on a music tradition, gets the chance to play, the possibility of developing a career and, at least, minor fame' (Vallely, 2008: 136). In some instances, the musicians of the bar may avail of opportunities to play in a pro-fessional manner to international audiences at festivals and venues around the world.

My own musical adventures have brought some brief moments of local attention. For a few weeks after prominent performances, especially at such venues as the White House, there are newspaper reports, radio interviews and acknowledgement on the street before the achievement and related fame fades once more. Despite the apparent popularity of Irish traditional music in a post-*Riverdance* context, there is anecdotal evidence of a lack of value placed on the session by an Irish audience. The proprietor of a bar in Cork pointed to the paradox that while musicians who have played all over the world play in the bar there is little interest amongst local customers. O'Flynn notes a pub customer in his study stating he would not pay to attend a pub session (2009). Similarly, a music teacher in Cork who does not play in his locality explained it as follows: experience has taught him that regular pub customers in the area are not interested, to the point of leaving when a session takes place.

Despite potential fame and success, anonymity serves us well in the local pub, creating nostalgic images of a musical community that plays for enjoy-ment alone with silent acclaim from those listening. Few realise that the set of polkas we play are named after John's father, the source and possible composer for these tunes. Few know that one of us has played in the White House as part of a celebration of Irish heritage. Even fewer are aware that some of the occasional visiting musicians to the session have themselves achieved fame through albums, television appearances and world tours. Many of the musi-cians who play in this pub have been awarded all-Ireland titles at *Fleadh Cheoil na hÉireann* in various instrumental competitions, amongst the highest acco-lades achievable in the Irish traditional music community.

Is anybody listening?

If *Riverdance* signified the Celtic Tiger and Ireland's potential on the world stage, it might be argued that *The Pirate Queen*, by the same producers – Moya Doherty and John McColgan – epitomised the lavish spending that followed. The most expensive show ever staged on Broadway when it opened in March 2007, it combined the story of Gráinne O'Malley, an Irish clan leader and pirate who fought to resist colonisation by the English during the reign of Queen Elizabeth I. The producers adopted a money-no-object approach but, having suffered from scathing reviews, the show's run ended in June 2007 (McKeone, 2007: 1), around the same time that the curtain was coming down on Ireland's economic fortunes.

It is worth considering who is in attendance at the session tonight. As the matches finish, a number of the men finish their drinks and head for home. They are replaced by other customers, some of whom have an interest in the music. A few girls from Eastern Europe are sitting on a couch to one side. They are disinterested in the soccer and spend time chatting and slowly consuming their drinks. They wait with anticipation for the music to start and acknowledge us when we approach our reserved corner. They may request a song such as 'The Galway Girl' or 'The Wild Rover' but they will not stay late and they will not spend much money. They are the new Irish who are enjoying the culture of their migrant home and want to become more familiar with it. Their song choices raise questions regarding the nature of tradition. 'The Galway Girl' is actually by American singer-songwriter Steve Earle, although it was first recorded in 2000 on an album featuring Irish accordion player Sharon Shannon. Songs such as these have become popular through modern mass media, the ready accessibility of recordings and the affordability of live music performances.

The session in this bar continues despite the economic downturn. Photos on the wall recall some of the musicians who have contributed to it over the years. Séamus always wanted to create a traditional Irish pub complete with Irish traditional music sessions and on a quiet night like this, with many punters leaving soon after the soccer ends, it is his desire for a particular pub identity that keeps this session going. The concept of an Irish pub is attractive to many and the music adds to the atmosphere, albeit in the background whereby conversations can continue and applause is optional. The concept of tradition employed is loose enough to include songs that have entered the local folk repertoire, including 'The Galway Girl' and 'Hotel California'.

Summertime is different. Groups of tourists arrive early, having visited the nearby attractions and dined in local restaurants. Many of the visitors have some Irish heritage but increasingly there is interest from others with little connection to Ireland. The tourists are anxious when the music does not start on time. They wonder at the informality and apparent chaos as the session grows from three musicians to eight or more. They try a glass of Guinness, often sharing it. Like the girls from Eastern Europe, many of the tourists will also retire early, in readiness for the following morning's bus to their next holiday destination. The session remains part of what tourists to Ireland expect, along with Guinness and the Ring of Kerry.

Conclusions

Although this is an autobiographical account of a regular session in one public house, it echoes the stories of other traditional Irish musicians throughout the country. It is, in some ways, a hidden Ireland yet the character (and characters) of the session is central to the construction and promotion of Irish identity around the world. The session links the local and the global, making links between the West Wing and the West of Ireland. The waves of Irish economic activity have always shaped the landscape of the traditional arts, and the links across the Atlantic are hardly new. From the early recordings of Irish traditional music by emigrants to America at the start of the twentieth century to the increased availability of funding for musicians and organisations at the start of the twenty-first century, Irish traditional music has evolved and remained a significant marker of Irish identity. The traditional arts are not the property of a single community or organisation. Rather, they comprise a multi-layered, multi-regional and even multi-national culture that contributes to the Irish economy and the social life of many.

The representation of Ireland and Irish culture on the global stage is an integral part of the politics and economics of the nation, exemplified by the prominent role of the arts in discussions at the 2009 Global Irish Economic Forum (White, 2010). Irish traditional music is integrally connected to Irish identity but the identity represented by Irish traditional music has changed greatly, as have the spaces for its performance and consumption. The image of the musician has changed from bearded, old men in caps carrying fiddles under large coats to sexually attractive, young men and women in trendy outfits (Brennan, 1999). While Irish traditional music developed in the homesteads of rural Ireland, having entered public spaces in the twentieth century, it has become a globally and commercially successful genre. In a post-Celtic Tiger era, the significance of tourism to Ireland's economic recovery, and the continuing attachment to place in Irish traditional music, are two keys to understanding the way forward for the traditional arts. As part of the 2009 Global Irish Economic Forum, Irish businessman and financier Dermot Desmond invited a wide range of well-known Irish performers including U2, Enya, The Corrs and Van Morrison to engage in what he called a cultural odyssey. Signalling the end of the cultural odyssey represented by *Riverdance*, this marked the changing perceptions towards the relationship between the arts and the economy. The arts are not a luxury for the entertainment of the wealthy but a fundamental part of our economy and self-belief as a nation. While discussions on economic policies and strategies are ongoing, *Riverdance* continues to sell out shows around the world, and John and I carry on playing a few tunes in the local pub as part of our cultural odyssey. The session may be a local portal to a global industry of Irish culture but it also remains a space for all those present to realise and to negotiate their own identities.

References

Bohlman, P. V. (1988) *The Study of Folk Music in the Modern World.* Bloomington, IN: Indiana University Press.

Brennan, H. (1999) *The Story of Irish Dance.* Dingle: Brandon.

Cohen, S. (1998) 'Sounding out the city: music and the sensuous production of place', in A. Leyshon, D. Matless and G. Revill (eds), *The Place of Music.* New York: Guilford Press, pp. 269–90.

Goertzen, C. and Azzi, M. S. (1999) 'Globalization and the Tango', *Yearbook for Traditional Music* 31: 67–76.

Gray, B. (1997) 'Unmasking Irishness: Irish women, the Irish nation and the Irish diaspora', in J. McLaughlin (ed.), *Location and Dislocation in Contemporary Irish Society.* Cork: Cork University Press, pp. 209–35.

Hamilton, C. (1999) 'Session', in F. Vallely (ed.), *The Companion to Irish Traditional Music.* Cork: Cork University Press, pp. 345–6.

Kaul, A. R. (2006) 'On "tradition": between the local and the global in a traditional Irish music scene', *Folklife* 45: 49–59.

Kearney, R. (1997) *Postnationalist Ireland.* London: Routledge.

Lovering, J. (1998) 'The global music industry: contradictions in the commodification of the sublime', in A. Leyshon, D. Matless and G. Revill (eds), *The Place of Music.* New York: Guilford Press, pp. 31–56.

McKeone, M. (2007) 'Brickbats over Broadway', *Irish Times Weekend Review*, 4 April, p. 1.

Ó Cinnéide, B. (2002) *Riverdance: The Phenomenon.* Dublin: Blackhall.

O'Connor, N. (2001) *Bringing it All Back Home: The Influence of Irish Music at Home and Overseas.* Dublin: Merlin.

O'Flynn, J. (2009) *The Irishness of Irish Music.* Farnham: Ashgate.

O'Shea, H. (2008) *The Making of Irish Traditional Music.* Cork: Cork University Press.

Scahill, A. (2009) 'Riverdance: representing Irish traditional music', *New Hibernia Review* 13, 2: 70–6.

Seaver, M. (2010) 'Between the jigs and the reels, did something get lost?', *Irish Times*, 13 November, p. 9.

Vallely, F. (2008) *Tuned Out: Traditional Music and Identity in Northern Ireland*. Cork: Cork University Press.

Vallely, F., Hamilton, H., Vallely, E. and Doherty, L. (1999) *Crossbhealach an Cheoil – The Crossroads Conference 1996*. Dublin: Whinstone Music.

White, W. (2010) 'Arts Council bogged down in procedure', *Irish Times*, 12 February, p. 16.

13

'Through American eyes': 100 years of Ireland in *National Geographic* magazine

Patrick J. Duffy

For more than a century, *National Geographic* magazine (NG) has been an American window on the world. It has had significant influence on the ways Americans have viewed other peoples and places. Its approach has been marked by a combination of text and photograph, in an imperial narrative of linear progress from tradition to modernity. Articles on Ireland have featured many times since 1915 and the purpose of this chapter is to examine the representation of Ireland as an exotic other on the edge of Europe. For much of the twentieth century, Ireland was perceived as a comparatively poor, quaintly nostalgic location for the American imagination. Even during the brash economic boom in the late twentieth century, NG's representations of Irish landscape and society frequently reached back to earlier lyrical imagery of a laid-back, misty isle. While critically evaluating its depictions of Ireland, our own self-image in the first half of the twentieth century in many ways mirrored what NG was doing – a discourse of rural social harmony situated in the West of Ireland, which was often repeated in art and literature. However, the transformation of the country in the early twenty-first century did not mesh well with the NG discourse, which may well account for its silence since then.

The *National Geographic* perspective

Established in 1888, the magazine has a monthly circulation of some 8.5 million copies, with more than fifty million readers worldwide.[1] Most critical assessments of the NG have seen it as an early manifestation of US imperialism in the ways it represented and exoticised third-world peoples especially (Lutz and Collins, 1993). Its photojournalistic style has been enormously influential in promulgating popular geography (McCarry, 1989) in what some see as an American eye on the world: up until the 1970s, it had all the hallmarks of an older nineteenth-century imperial perspective – focusing on otherness and difference in places and peoples – the exotic, the strange, the wild, and the onward march of modernity. A 1988 review celebrated the magazine's early role in the heroic exploration and conquest of 'disease, paganism and ignorance' with colonialism framed as part of a gigantic good-works project (Steet, 1996: 195).

For most of the twentieth century, NG's depiction of Ireland fits into this scenario as a remote, exotic, different place on the western ends of the Old World. There were some sixteen issues with articles on Ireland through the twentieth century (see Appendix)[2]. While the sometimes stunning photography focused on an often misty, romantic rural landscape, most often located in the west of the country, the writing was characterised by lyrical rhapsody, which for much of the twentieth century emphasised the tranquil timeless nature of this backwater of Europe. The title of the Howell Walker 1940 article captured this sometimes mawkish sentimentality: 'Old Ireland, mother of new Éire' was subtitled 'By whatever name, 'tis the same fair land with the grass growing green on the hills of her and the peat smoke hanging low.' Cape Clear Island, off the west Cork coast, was seen through a primitive, exotic lens: 'About Clear Island folk there's a wistful strangeness. They climb to horizons where they stand like statues or crouch like fakirs seemingly staring at nothing. Cows and horses, sheep and asses follow the example. No matter what time of day … if I look up toward the land horizon, I see a man or woman or child or animal against the sky' (Walker, May 1940: 662).

Recurring images in these romantic renditions of Ireland were red hair, red petticoats (following the introduction of limited colour photo printing in the 1930s), black shawls, thatched houses, the Irish language (on signposts for instance), donkeys, talk and music, pubs and drink. Superbly photographed landscapes were regularly bathed in mist or soft rain. From the 1920s, newly independent Ireland was attractive for visitors. Harold Speakman's and H. V. Morton's tours in the late 1920s addressed a popular curiosity about this new state (Morton, 1930; Speakman, 1931) and their accounts and others were echoed in much of the NG reportage. Following almost a century of Irish immigration to the USA, there was a wellspring of sentimental memory of Irish landscapes and music in Irish America and *National Geographic* reporters in Ireland had regular encounters with Irish people who had lived in the USA, or had numerous relatives there. By the end of the twentieth century, however, the gap between the magazine's sentimental representations of Ireland, the diasporic memory in America, and the emerging landscapes and lifestyles in Ireland had widened considerably.

Beguiling unreality

In the last quarter of the twentieth century, two NG reporters were intoxicated with the Irish scene. In Dingle, 'we watch the slow peregrinations of the tides and see the dawn's light turn mist to mystery while pony carts clatter past towards the creamery' (Hodgson, April 1976: 576). Another spoke of the:

> heartbreaking beauty in the Irish landscape: dark cliffs against the sea, fingers of green land pushing out against the sea, meadows of yellow gorse and slate blue rock, brown boglands, sometimes a house and two figures in the distance. More often the landscapes are empty, and so we can populate them with our dreams, the ideal of man, uncorrupted, living in harmony and touch with the earth and the sea.' (Putnam, April 1981: 442)

For more than fifty years, Ireland appears as a sort of magic roundabout for NG writers, caught in a kind of mystic spell. This manner of approaching Ireland had been epitomised in Speakman's early account of his trip round Ireland in 1927, which is based on an 'aisling' device where he meets a beautiful girl along the boreen to whom he tells the story of his tour of Ireland, and finishes with the disclosure that she is Ireland!

In 1931, on the first of many visits to the Aran islands at the mouth of Galway Bay, the NG considered that their history and distinctive way of life enhanced 'the charm, the strangeness, the beguiling sense of unreality ... [there is] simplicity, harmony and a feeling of remoteness' (Cushman Murphy, June 1931: 747) (Figure 13.1). Like other NG writers, Morton was bewitched too: 'A breeze off the land brought the scent of Ireland, indescribably earthy, sweet, and nostalgic – the scent of rain-wet fields and peat smoke and flowers' (Morton, March 1961: 293). His itinerary and images followed a well-travelled tourist trail: O'Connell Street, the Book of Kells in Trinity College Dublin, hunting in Kildare, Waterford Glass, Irish dancing in Cork, the Blarney Stone, jaunting in Killarney, gannets round the Skelligs, red-skirted girl with turf creel in Inishere, fair day in Galway, donkey and creel on Achill Island.

Talk and conversation – the 'incessant spate of talk ... out to please and beguile the stranger' (Morton, March 1961: 296); 'a flood tide of talk ... as warm and reassuring as a peat fire on a winter's day' (Putnam, April 1981: 446) – seemed to entrance the visitors. In the 1981 issue, which noted the beginnings of the biggest building boom in Dublin since the eighteenth century,

Figure 13.1 A funeral cortège, Inishmaan, 1931

the photo captions of Dublin and other historic sites in Ireland continued the dreamscape theme – composed of lines from Irish poets and writers: Fallon, Synge, Clarke, O'Casey and Heaney, 'Who dreamt that we might dwell among ourselves/In rain and scoured light and wind-dried stones' (in Judge, April 1981: 436).

Timeless landscapes

'Time is not a tyrant in Ireland; indeed, hurry and hustle only rouse mild amusement' (Morton, March 1961: 296). Donn Byrne in March 1927 was the only Irish contributor to *National Geographic*, though he had lived in the USA for many years. Byrne was a romantic nationalist whose essay celebrated an Ireland resolutely opposed to change and modernity. Ireland was represented as an old country, and poor, 'but we have purple heather and mountain golden with gorse, and rivers, great-bosomed and friendly, where men may dream' (Byrne, March 1927: 296). In Ireland 'you will have to be content with kindliness and understanding … and a wind that may sweep you from your feet, but will sweep life into you' (Byrne, March 1927: 298). Byrne's return to Ireland, after almost two decades in the USA, solidified his opposition to change: tourism – 'the most horrible word in any language' – would change it, he said (Byrne, March 1927: 298). His influential article probably set the tone for many of the subsequent essays on Ireland by NG staff writers throughout the twentieth century.

Robert Cushman Murphy came in 1931 and headed for the Aran Islands, which along with other islands and Connemara were to become iconic destinations for subsequent NG visits. His essay, *The Timeless Arans*, depicted a land beyond the horizon of time and space where 'the soul of ancient Ireland now has its ephemeral resting place' (Cushman Murphy, June 1931: 748). For another reporter a decade later, 'out of the mist loomed [Cape] Clear Island like a mountain top floating on clouds … islanders came down to watch the boat dock, there being no more exciting pastime. White-bearded men wearing peaked black hats, and women wrapped in heavy woollen shawls showed as much curiosity as the barefoot children' (Howell Walker, May 1940: 660).

Coming ashore in Cobh in 1951, the initial impression was of timelessness – 'clocks stop ticking here. Nobody hurries. … Sure, we're easygoing, praise be to God' (Sheats, May 1951: 653). Indeed, looking at Walker's account and photographs in 1940 returns us to an Ireland as distant from us today as it was from America then – as one Corkman told him, 'returning to Ireland from America is like stepping from the 20th century back into the 18th' (Howell Walker, May 1940: 691). Even urban landscapes in the West of Ireland seem part of a land beyond time:

> In black or brown shawls above red flannel skirts, women of the west move through Galway. Their Old World reflections in modern shop windows make time's hour-glass turn turtle. Men wearing baggy home-spun tweed tilt back broad brimmed hats to ring out a laugh that echoes down the narrow streets. … donkey carts delay auto traffic. Horses and wagons impede cyclists balancing baskets and buckets. (Howell Walker, May 1940: 675)

By the 1981 issue, Ireland is 'a small island on the edge of Europe, where time has stood still', with even Dublin giving an impression of having escaped the twentieth century, as if 'the clouds … merely passed over, leaving a soft, magical city, evoking childhoods, familiar nooks, a human scale, gardens and black iron fences, where anonymity remains both suspect and transient' (Putnam, April 1981: 442). By 1994, following acknowledgement of the social and economic transformation under way in the country, the NG climbed Croagh Patrick in Mayo and reached for a vaguely orientalist metaphor to represent changeless time and place: 'in the dark clouds at the top, we passed back into a former age. Voices muttering their prayers rose above the wind. The faithful paced around a cairn in a tight circle, each as keen and focused as a tooth on a gear, many also ticking off the smaller gear of the rosary in one hand, a fierce clockwork of prayer' (Conniff, September 1994: 20).

Material worlds

Throughout the NG until the 1970s the juxtaposition of advertisements of American life and lifestyles with images of the poverty of other worlds especially in Africa and Asia was a notable feature, in what has been called a voyeuristic strategy of innocence (Rothenberg, 2007). Pre-electric Ireland was a world away from urban America, and its backwardness and poverty had charm for affluent visitors. Bucolic images of Ireland ironically contrasted, and yet romantically accorded, with the consumerism of American life at the time (featured in advertisements for cars, refrigerators, washing machines, cruises and sun holidays). The poverty of the West of Ireland in black and white images before 1920 echoed similar representations from colonial Africa (see Cutler, December 1915; Neville, 1991). But Northern Ireland in 1935 was closer to the industrialised world of the USA. The scale and enormity of Belfast's 'Linenopolis' contrasted with the more pastoral scenes from the rest of Ireland. Belfast displayed enormous steel cranes and colossal gantries erected before the depression for construction of huge ships.

Beyond Belfast, however, Ulster's landscape was significantly uncluttered for American visitors: 'No ugly billboards mar the landscape ... Sign-covered filling stations and ramshackle refreshment huts are still conspicuously absent' (Rogers, November 1935: 603). Traffic-free driving was a measure of Ireland's backwardness. As Morton had observed in Kerry – 'nothing ever comes over the road but little vermilion carts drawn by donkeys and loaded with turf like bricks of dark chocolate. Old men, or old women with their heads in black shawls, crouch above the shafts' (Morton, 1930: 119). Thirty years later he 're-joiced in the emptiness of the Irish roads. ... pleasure in driving mile and mile without meeting another car' (Morton, March 1961: 314). In 1978, in west Clare 'you can drive miles with only the wind for companion, past hedgerows and stone fences, the Atlantic on one side, the Shannon on the other' (Fisher Jr., November 1978: 679).

Morton was a good observer of economic conditions in Ireland, noting that its 611-page telephone directory in 1961 served the whole country, half of it referring to Dublin: he calculated that only one in thirty people had a phone (Morton, March 1961: 296). The pre-electric Irish kitchens with open fires, crucifixes and kerosene lamps (sites of rollicking music and dancing in many issues) were a source of fascination for American visitors. On the Great Blasket Island, off the Kerry coast, inhabited by ninety-nine people, the kitchen dressers proudly displayed the family china alongside collections of electric light bulbs tossed from passing ships, exotic curios of the outside world. The reporter's photographic flash bulbs were fondled lovingly by his hostess who found them 'round and smooth like a gull's egg' (Howell Walker, May 1940: 675).

By 1951, Dorothea Sheats noted a number of important markers of change: listening to football matches on the wireless on Sundays – though 'one warm summer evening, eight of us sat around the Healy kitchen, enjoying a gathering for storytelling' (Sheats, May 1951: 666). The rural electrification scheme was under way – marking the beginnings of a convergence between Irish and American lifestyles and living standards. The house had recently been 'measured' for the electricity but there was some reluctance in take-up: 'only 40 per cent had accepted, the remainder declining because of high rates, or because they had always managed without it' (Sheats, May 1951: 666). On Achill Island in Mayo in 1961, Morton was struck by the changes which had followed electricity – 'electric poles and new roads cross the peat bogs. Many thatched cottages have been replaced by prim little suburban houses which look about uneasily, as if startled by the gaunt mountains and the sea' (Morton, March 1961: 328).

A 1964 essay on Northern Ireland, however, highlighted its continuing distinctiveness from the rest of Ireland. Its more modern progressive economy was reflected in crowded bars, bustling restaurants and buses 'bulging with humanity' (Conly, August 1964: 238). Its industrial heritage still marked it off from the rest of Ireland with clattering looms of linen mills working at near capacity making damask, fine nylon, Dacron and other synthetic fabrics, along with new industrial estates and advance factories primed for a whole range of foreign investment. However, ominously, Harland and Wolff's shipbuilding had laid off half its 20,000 workforce, and the unbalanced political representation in the province was a cause for concern: nationalists 'remain aloof. Most go to their own parochial schools; most favor [*sic*] reunification with southern Ireland, which the British Protestant community in Ulster vehemently opposes' (Conly, August 1964: 267).

The Aran Islands in 1971 continued as an Edenic destination for visitors – symbols of timeless tradition and nostalgia, enduring in the words of another commentator, as a 'captive indigenous spectacle throughout the twentieth century' (Solnit, 1998: 113). There were photos of red-haired, freckled-faced children still going to bed by candle or gaslight on Inishmore. The islanders 'bake their daily bread. They build their own houses and cut their own hair. They make their curraghs – and their coffins' (Thomas, April 1971: 550).

Seeing ourselves as others see us

One of the recurring questions addressed to visitors to Ireland through much of the last century was 'how do you like Ireland?' either seeking affirmation of its other-worldliness or its advancing modernity. The NG frequently recorded

Irish impressions of themselves: in 1951, one local asserted that 'Ireland is a spiritual country, not materialistic, as is so much of the world. Isn't that what you've found?' (Sheats, May 1951: 662). While critically evaluating the representation of Ireland by the NG, it is also worth considering Ireland's complicity in this discourse and the extent to which our own self-image mirrored what NG was doing. From the 1930s, the official State's rhetoric of a traditional, rural, Gaelic, Catholic Ireland – frequently satirised by Flann O'Brien and *Dublin Opinion* – was mirrored in the pages of the NG. The romantic evocation of the west, for instance, as location for a bucolic geographical imagination, lost in the past for many NG visitors, has been characterised as an example of auto-exoticism, or delighting in seeing ourselves as others see us (Leersen, 1996: 35). This perspective matched an intellectual discourse of harmony between rural society and nature, well represented in the works of artists and writers like Synge, Yeats, Henry and Keating. Movies such as Robert Flaherty's *Man of Aran* (1934) or John Ford's *The Quiet Man* (1952) also promoted and celebrated such an Ireland.

The NG perspective from the 1930s also reflected the preoccupations of the Harvard Irish Survey 1932 to 1936, which was interested in the ethno-racial typology of the Irish, especially in the west. Arensberg and Kimball (1940) documented the enduring social harmony and stability in traditional farming communities in the west. And the tourist gaze from the 1930s helped shape a self-image of an ancient, mystical, magical and musical Ireland, 'always friendly people, living in an "emerald" isle that is lush, green and sparsely populated' (Bell, 1995: 41), and iterated in postcards and early tourism advertising. According to Brett (1996: 125), 'the toured are complicit in their representation' and internalise it as their own. There were contradictions and tensions in these images, however, which accelerated by century's close. Artist Robert Ballagh observed that the Industrial Development Authority was in the USA selling Ireland as a modern progressive capitalist society and 'you have Bord Fáilte eulogising roads where you won't see a car from one end of the day to the other: it's almost as if they're advertising a country nobody lives in' (quoted in Gibbons 1996: 86). These contradictions were apparent up until the 1980s in many of the NG's depictions of empty roads, thatched houses and donkey carts.

'Hurtling into a honky-tonk future'

The 1980s marked a turning point in the NG's commentary on Ireland – with early reports of impending change in the country, which did not accord with the established NG discourse on Ireland and the Irish. Richard Conniff observed later that 'it feels as if the entire nation is hurtling into a honky-tonk future with the rag ends of its discarded peasant culture still fluttering wildly in its wake' (Conniff, September 1994: 12). By 1981, John J. Putnam noted that policies of rapid industrialisation and membership of the European Economic Community (EEC) in the previous decade had resulted in unparalleled growth and prosperity. Ireland had the fastest growing and youngest population in Western Europe, with more Irish returning from abroad than were leaving. He noted overseas investment of $4bn throughout the country by the likes of Black and Decker, Asahi, Liebherr International, etc. Irish farming was in the process of being revolutionised by EEC membership. Money had brought in 'suburbs, automobiles, television sets, charter flights to Miami ... for the wealthy, holiday homes in Spain' (Putnam, April 1981: 469), portents of things to come. In spite of recession in 1980 and rising oil prices, the magazine noted a looming anxiety about the effects of the new prosperity on Ireland. There was apprehension among some political leaders that it would change the character of the Irish. Garret FitzGerald, then leader of opposition in parliament, suggested prophetically that Irish society had become more selfish and competitive. 'They want to take our increased wealth in terms of higher incomes now, rather than to plow it back into savings and investments for the future' (Putnam, April 1981: 463). Taoiseach Charles Haughey considered that people were more confident because 'they have not had to confront the decision of whether to emigrate or not'. Ireland will be changed in twenty years, he said – in technology, living standards and levels of education (Putnam, April 1981: 469).

By 1994, Conniff observed with a tinge of regret that shifting moral values and global economics were driving Ireland towards modernity. A prosperous Ireland was emerging with a new enterprise economy. 'Real Ireland is an urban nation now ... The light of Ireland now is often neon', which represented a sharp break from the earlier Irelands of the *National Geographic* (Conniff, September 1994: 9). He rings the changes in social and cultural life – the 'X case',[3] abortion controversies, the Bishop Eamonn Casey scandal,[4] Northern Ireland fatigue, and the election of Mary Robinson as the first woman President: 'there is a sense that the Irish have come adrift from their old social anchors in the land, the Church, and the family' with De Valera's dreamy rural myth of Catholic Ireland living in frugal comfort well faded by the 1990s (Conniff, September 1994: 12).

In tone, his report reflected the more critical focus of NG in a prophetic assessment of the subsequent boom and bust economy in Ireland, which marked it out from the earlier renditions of Ireland and the Irish. Conniff had an impression that many people thought that 'traditional Irish values have failed or been corrupted' (September 1994: 16). In Dublin, there was a lost sense of neighbourhood in a rush to modernity in new buildings, shopping malls and commuter roadways. The far west, favoured locale of NG sentimental journeys, did not escape the changes. By 1994, the holding of an old farmer on Clare Island (who in the 1970s had quoted Swift to the author – 'the sort of character only the old Ireland could produce' (Conniff, September 1994: 29)) had passed to a young American woman who had lived with him in his last years. Now, with ferry, bottled milk, store-bought butter, agri-tourism and horse-trekking, 'Ireland was to become the playground of the world' (Conniff, September 1994: 29).

NG's final visit to the Aran Islands in 1996 echoed Conniff's sentiments, with islanders ambivalent about the future. Hordes of tourists seeking soli-tude and beauty were threatening these very values. LaRoe's jaunting car driver however condemned the hard life in the old days – 'no work, no light, no sew-erage, no water, no nothing. We'd dip the bucket into the well and take it home for tea and washing. And all we had was paraffin lamps hanging up on the wall …' and 'no tourists, no buses, no bicycles, no restaurants … [now] we've never had it so good' (Moore LaRoe, April 1996: 118–20). New piers were being con-structed on all the islands, new houses with satellite dishes beaming in TV soap operas and sitcoms – changes which the author considered had threat-ened the islands' subtle beauty. And yet she met a young couple from Seattle sitting on a rock ledge on Inishmaan: 'this is as untainted a place as I've ever seen' said the woman (Moore LaRoe, April 1996: 132).

In the end, both reporters were concerned about the direction Ireland was taking with Conniff hopeful that the Irish would construct a new identity, not a hackneyed Ireland branded for heritage tourism. But, as he departed, he feared that the country 'was in danger of making itself look like everyplace else in the world' (Conniff, September 1994: 29) whose difference and distinctiveness would no longer appeal. There was now a convergence between the adver-tisements of American life and the signs and signage of the Irish landscape. Following the 1996 article on Aran, there were no further reports on Ireland, almost as if Celtic Tiger Ireland had lost all attraction for *National Geographic* magazine. A photospread in March 2005, *Beneath Irish Isles*, reported on an underwater diving expedition off the south-west coast, adding to the sense that the land had lost its mystic appeal (Holland, March 2005).

After the Tiger

During the years of silence, the NG's predictions of change in Ireland were more than realised. The Celtic Tiger economy transformed the life and land-scape that had been a core aspect of the magazine's word and picture reportage on Ireland. Fintan O'Toole (1998: xiv) confirmed the NG's impression of the 1990s: 'The fixed points on the compass of life – Church, nation, family – had been unsettled'. As predicted in 1994, Ireland looked like everywhere else, globalising on a Berlin–Boston axis, though more like Boston than Berlin as it transformed into a cultural and political colony of the USA (Kirby, Gibbons and Cronin, 2002). The birth of *Riverdance* in 1994, commemorating Irish-American migration links, might be viewed as a curtain-raiser to the annihilation of traditional Ireland that was ushered in with the Celtic Tiger. There was an escalation in anxiety about loss of cultural identity and of what made us uniquely Irish that was regularly aired by the chattering media elites. The property boom resulted in rapid suburbanisation of a landscape that had so captivated American visitors. Widely dispersed commuter landscapes matched an exploding population in counties throughout the midlands and in the regional hinterlands of Irish cities and towns. An accompanying expansion in what McCarthy (2000) humorously labelled the 'noodle belt', and 'sundried tomato zones', symbolised the cosmopolitan cultural transformation that took place. McWilliams (2005) has characterised the new Ireland and new lifestyles that emerged in inimitable fashion – a homogenised world of BMWs, bustling restaurants, trophy houses, teak decking, slate wet-rooms, patio heaters, lattes, Pilates and Americanised English. A native propensity for self-mocking satire tapped into the Celtic Tiger transformation: Ross O'Carroll-Kelly, a fictional tiger cub, first appeared in the *Sunday Tribune* in 1998 and lampooned all the extravagant symbols of the boom: the accents, clothes, cars, property investors, developers, overseas holiday homes and the mania for celebrity. The landscape changes accompanying the economic boom had the most dramatic consequences for the stock of images illustrating the NG discourse. The sprawl of commuter housing estates arising from the rezoning mania in local authorities, the rash of hotels and shopping malls, the recycling of landlord estates and mansions as spa and golf resorts were prefigured in Conniff's account of the revival of Millstreet town in north Cork in the 1990s by one of its native sons (September 1994: 14–16).

Since the crash, these changes have ground to a halt and there is a preoccupation with what was lost during the boom years. Ghost estates sit as stark reminders of the destructive legacy of the property bubble: tentative discussion of proposals to demolish and reinstate them as greenfield sites symbolise a desire to return to pre-Celtic Tiger Ireland. The tourism industry is especially keen on salvaging as much of our traditional cultural identity as possible. But in the dawn of the post-Celtic Tiger recession, there are signs that some things did not change. The plethora of festivals throughout the country, many relying on or reviving traditional music, crafts and customs, is a vibrant reminder of such continuity. The enduring popularity of local radio with its unselfconscious celebration of local life and community is a relic of an earlier Ireland. The Gaelic Athletic Association (GAA), though its new sports facilities are products of the boom, continues to promote traditional games and values. A 2011 television documentary called *The Home Place* on RTÉ, Ireland's national broadcaster, highlighted the continuing strength and importance of the land and family, and memory and heritage, in the Irish sense of identity – echoing many of the NG's sentiments, but also accommodating the socio-economic changes of the past decade.

Plus ça change, plus c'est la même chose is reflected in two recent references by NG sources that resurrect earlier renditions of Ireland. In 2010, one of NG's leading photographers was still responding to Ireland and the Irish in familiar terms: 'it's a beautiful country. I'll not spend precious words arguing what any fool can see. But Ireland promises more than beauty, and when you go there, it's something more like magic that you're looking for. In the western Irish town of Dingle, I go looking for magic in Dick Mack's Pub. I usually find it' (Richardson, 2010). In a recent report on Ireland, the NG's *Adventure* magazine, which is aimed at activity holidaymakers in wilder parts of the world, managed to find a legendary Ireland underneath the brash residue of the Celtic Tiger (Mone, n.d.). It reveals a rugged landscape of mountain, bog and surf, uncrowded with people, a land full of myth, folklore and fairies where a new motorway through Clare was re-routed to protect a famous fairy thorn bush. Even the Celtic Tiger, according to the author, heeded the warning of *seanchaí*[5] Eddie Lenihan – 'you don't feck with fairies'!

Notes

1   From http://press.nationalgeographic.com/pressroom/index.jsp?pageID=factSheets _detail&siteID=1&cid=1058466231550, accessed 14 January 2011.
2   NG articles cited in this chapter are listed in the Appendix.
3   A 1992 Irish Supreme Court Case involving the right of a fourteen-year-old girl raped by a neighbour to an abortion (illegal in Ireland at the time under any circumstances; subsequently deemed legal if there is a substantial risk to the life of the mother).
4   A popular Roman Catholic bishop who resigned in 1992 after revelations that he fathered a son with an American divorcée.
5   Traditional Irish storyteller.

References

Arensberg, C. M. and Kimball, S. T. (1940) *Family and Community in Ireland.* Cambridge, MA: Harvard University Press.

Bell, D. (1995) 'Picturing the landscape: Die grune insel: tourist images of Ireland', *European Journal of Communication* 10, 1: 41–62.

Brett, D. (1996) *The Construction of Heritage*. Cork: Cork University Press.

Gibbons, L. (1996) *Transformations in Irish Culture*. Cork: Cork University Press.

Kirby, P., Gibbons, L. and Cronin, M. (2002) *Reinventing Ireland: Culture, Society and the Global Economy*. London: Pluto Press.

Leersen, J. (1996) *Remembrance and Imagination*. Cork: Cork University Press.

Lutz, C. and Collins, J. L. (1993) *Reading National Geographic*. Chicago: University of Chicago Press.

McCarry, C. (1989) '"Let the world hear from you": the inventor, the architect, and the spiritual leader', in W. E. Garrett (ed.), *National Geographic Index, 1888–1988*. Washington, DC: National Geographic Society.

McCarthy, P. (2000) *McCarthy's Bar*. London: Hodder and Stoughton.

McWilliams, D. (2005) *The Pope's Children: Ireland's New Elite*. Dublin: Gill and Macmillan.

Mone, G. (n.d.) 'Ireland uncorked', *National Geographic Adventure*, www.nationalgeographic.com/adventure/adventure-travel/europe/ireland.html, accessed 1 November 2010.

Morton, H. V. (1930) *In Search of Ireland*. London: Methuen.

Neville, G. (1991) 'A la recherche de l'Irlande perdue: two French photographers in Ireland in 1913', *Etudes Irlandaises* 16, 2: 75–89.

O'Toole, F. (1998) *The Lie of the Land: Irish Identities*. Dublin: New Island Books.

Richardson, J. (2010) 'Irish moments', *National Geographic*, 22 May, http://photography.nationalgeographic.com/photography/photo-tips/irish-moments-richardson/, accessed 20 July 2010.

Rothenberg, T. Y. (1994) 'Voyeurs of imperialism: the *National Geographic Magazine* before World War II', in A. Godleska and N. Smith (eds), *Geography and Empire*. Oxford: Basil Blackwell, pp. 155–72.

Rothenberg, T. (2007) *Presenting America's World: Strategies of Innocence in National Geographic Magazine, 1888–1945*. Aldershot: Ashgate.

Solnit, R. (1998) *A Book of Migrations: Some Passages in Ireland*. London: Verso.

Speakman, H. (1931) *Here's Ireland*. New York: Robert McBride & Co.

Steet, L. (1996) 'Initial lessons in popular orientalism from *National Geographic Magazine*', in M. Morgan and S. Leggett (eds), *Mainstream(s) and Margins: Cultural Politics in the 90s*. London: Greenwood Press, pp. 194–220.

Appendix

Articles on Ireland in *National Geographic* magazine

1915 December   A. C. Cutler, 'British Isles', 28, 6: 551–66.

1927 March   D. Byrne, 'Ireland: the rock whence I was hewn', 51, 3: 257–316.

1931 June   R. Cushman Murphy, 'The timeless Arans – the workaday world lies beyond the horizon of three rocky islets off the Irish coast', 59, 6: 747–75.

1935 November   B. F. Rogers, 'The mist and sunshine of Ulster', 68, 5: 571–610.

1940 May   H. Howell Walker, 'Old Ireland, mother of new Eire: by whatever name, 'tis the same fair land with grass growing green on the hills of her and the peat smoke hanging low', 77, 5: 649–91.

1943 August   'Yanks in Northern Ireland', 84, 2: 191–204.

1951 May   D. Sheats, 'I walked some Irish miles', 99, 5: 653–78.

1961 March   H. V. Morton, 'The magic road round Ireland', 119, 3: 293–333.

1964 August   R. L. Conly, 'Northern Ireland from Derry to Down', 126, 2: 232–67.

1969 September   J. Scofield, 'The friendly Irish', 136, 3: 354–91.

1971 April   V. Thomas, 'The Arans, Ireland's invincible isles', 139, 4: 545–72.

1976 April   B. Hodgson, 'Irish ways live on in Dingle', 149, 4: 551–76.

1978 November   A. J. Fisher Jr., 'Where the river Shannon flows', 154, 5: 652–79.

1981 April   J. Judge, 'The travail of Ireland', 159, 4: 432–41.

1981 April   J. J. Putnam, 'A new day for Ireland', 159, 4: 442–99.

1994 September   R. Conniff, 'Ireland on fast forward', 186, 3: 2–36.

1996 April   L. Moore LaRoe, 'The Aran Islands: ancient hearts, modern minds', 189, 4: 118–33.

2005 March   J. Holland, 'Beneath Irish Isles', 207, 3: 58–71.

Index

Lightning Source UK Ltd.
Milton Keynes UK
UKOW06f1900180616

276556UK00006B/83/P